OPENING BARS

OPENING BARS

BEGINNING
AN AUTOBIOGRAPHY BY

SPIKE HUGHES

LONDON

PILOT PRESS LTD

1946

First published in March, 1946
by Pilot Press Ltd.,
45 Great Russell Street, London, W.C.1

This book is produced in complete
conformity with the authorized economy
standards

PRINTED AND BOUND IN GREAT BRITAIN BY
W. & J. MACKAY AND CO., LTD., CHATHAM

CONTENTS

TO BARBARA
who is sure to
misunderstand the title

CHAPTER I

DAWN'S EARLY LIGHT

FOR many years now I have been looking forward to this moment : the opening sentence of the book I was always going to write. I was going to think of startling things to say that would make the reader sit up ; I was going to plaster Page 1 with sensational and sordid incidents which would cause the reader to put a brown paper cover round the book at once and forbid his daughters to read it.

Now that it comes to the point all I can remember is some advice James Agate once gave me, and which I shall naturally proceed to ignore. " You ought to write a book, Spike," said Jimmy, " but for heaven's sake don't write about your childhood."

Which is probably sound advice unless you are a celebrity and people are interested in the nature of the Child that was Father to The Man. On the other hand, as I have failed disastrously to fulfil any of the few hopes my parents and teachers may have had of my success in the world and I have never come within miles of realising even my most modest secret ambitions, I am tempted to think that my childhood has been by far the most successful period of my life.

It was eccentric, to say the least. My mother, who has been married three times, was always a woman of enormous vitality, adventurousness and courage ; she has also, to this day, never shown any great interest in physical comfort. If she travels she does so with all her belongings wrapped in paper or bulging from the four corners of a fibre suitcase tied up with rope. In addition to innumerable spirit stoves, bottles of milk, jugs, cups and

7

plates the circus is usually completed by livestock of some kind—a dove to keep her company, a goat in case she needs more milk, or half a dozen ailing chickens to be nursed back to health in a bathroom at the end of the journey. The old tag about him travelling fastest who travels alone has never appealed to my mother ; but then she has never noticeably been in a hurry to get anywhere. And yet she is a restless woman by nature. Her early years were spent studying the piano at the Royal Academy and taking what is known as an " active interest " in the Fabian Society. As soon as she had collected as many gold medals as she could, she suddenly discovered that she wasn't musical after all, sold her Bechstein and decided to have a child on the proceeds. Later she started to learn to make pottery ; we moved to an old stable in Hammersmith and the nights were an inferno of kilns going full blast in preparation for her first and last exhibition. She sold everything she had made, and never set a foot to her potter's wheel thereafter.

It was the same with her weaving. She learnt the whole business from carding unspun wool to the weaving of an interminable length of tweed which was made into a suit for her second husband. This period brought a characteristic amount of physical discomfort with it for those who lived with her. The sitting room of a tiny Sussex cottage was filled by a huge loom ; as there was room for little else all the dirty crockery in the house found its way on to the warp. Eventually the job was finished, my first step-father still wears the suit and it looks remarkably well in spite of the tea leaves and splashes of marmalade that must have been woven into it. But having woven a suit weaving had no further attractions for my mother. She took up something else—batik, I think it was next—learnt all there was to know about it and then dropped that too.

The only occupation that has really kept my mother

enthralled has been psychiatry. Probably because it is an unending and fascinating subject she has put her mind to it for nearly twenty years now ; she has a practice in Harley Street and when she can remember to charge a fee manages to make a living out of it. At one moment during the 1939 war she thought it might be nice to study medicine. I pointed out that as she was then 55 she would be at least sixty years old before she qualified ; to which she replied : " Yes, I know. But that'll still give me twenty years to practise in."

It was only when she realised that she was too old to begin learning about chemistry all over again that she reluctantly abandoned the idea.

The nearest my mother ever came to " settling down " was during the first two or three years of her life with my father. She met Herbert Hughes, a young Irish musician, at the house of Florence Farr, the actress, and as Herbert had no piano of his own my mother invited him to come along and use hers. They talked a great deal about music and Socialism and the Sinn Fein movement, spent hours in the Café Royal pulling the world to pieces and convincing themselves that everything would be much cosier if only it were all run by the people who wrote for Orage's *New Age*. Herbert and my mother had much in common and it wasn't long before, sitting on an upturned barrel in a Sussex pub, they decided to marry with a view to having a son who would be called Patrick Cairns Hughes.

I was duly born, on October 19th, 1908, and named Patrick after our patron saint ; it is a name I like very much and by which I would prefer to be known more often. For the past sixteen years, however, " Patrick " has been used only on official documents, by my most intimate friends and by a few acquaintances who knew me before 1929. The nickname " Spike " has

A*

stuck so thoroughly that I now despair of ever being known by anything more dignified. It dates from a time when I played the double bass in a dance band and I presumed it was the name given to all bass players by virtue of the iron spike at the end of the instrument. I learned later that it was not all bass players who were called " Spike " but that all Hughes's in the Navy were so called—a generic name for the clan, and as inevitable as " Nobby " Clark, " Dusty " Miller and " Florrie " Ford.

I kept the name for purely commercial reasons. It was ridiculous enough to remember easily, led quickly to familiarity and has proved more suitable than Patrick to my various occupations. Occasionally people ask whether it is a baptismal name, which shows how soon the gangsters of Chicago have been forgotten, and I am delighted to remember an instance when a memorandum was sent to me with the aristocratic address " Mr. Spyke-Hughes." But otherwise I have had to resign myself to being known only as Spike Hughes and the refreshing variant used by French radio announcers, " Spique Hugues."

The origin of my second name, Cairns, is rather obscure. I was brought up to believe the name was given me to commemorate a not very remote ancestor who had been Master of the Rolls and Lord Chancellor in Queen Victoria's time. I know nothing of my relationship to Earl Cairns and very little at all about him. From what I have read in the *D.N.B.* he seems to have been the last kind of person I would have liked—a dour, bigotted non-Conformist Ulsterman. He seems to have had one distinction, however ; the last sentence of his biography in the *D.N.B.* reads, quite bluntly : " He was not popular."

As far as the rest of my ancestry is concerned I know equally little. Not that it matters one way or the other ; but when I picked up the first volume of Osbert Sitwell's enchanting autobiography I couldn't help wishing that I could have dug up one or two distinguished and eccentric forbears if only for the sake of a couple of good anecdotes. The nearest I can get to it is with my mother's grandfather who was a sculptor and fought as student in Italy with Garibaldi, and even so I rather think I am confusing him with his brother who was a water-colourist.

Herbert Hughes was the eldest of six children. His father was a Belfast business man who ran a flour mill, was a tyrant to his children and had a beard which made him look uncannily like Verdi, but did not—so far as I remember—give him Verdi's air of benevolence. The six Hughes children were not born into a particularly musical family, but it soon became one. Herbert, who began his career as a boy-organist in Belfast, was the only one to take up music as a profession, but his two sisters sang and played the piano and his brother Fred, who now runs the family mill, has a pleasing tenor voice. (Fred is the father of Desmond Hughes, D.S.O., D.F.C. and two bars, who became a crack night-fighter pilot during World War II, and was christened " Hawkeye Hughes " by some fool reporter. I haven't seen Desmond since he was two years old and busy kicking the legs off a grand piano, so I can't tell whether the description fits him or not.)

My favourite uncle was always Stanley. He was an actor and played *Charley's Aunt* and *The Private Secretary* on numberless No. 2 tours. His father was originally set on putting him into the Family Business, but Stanley spent the day running up and down stairs bellowing Shakespeare until at last my grandfather decided he was quite mad and therefore qualified to go on the stage. In the end Stanley finished up in California running some sort of estate my grandfather had bought there, my grandfather having migrated to the States when he was 70 and married Ellen Boyle, the family nurse, when he was 72.

Ellen Boyle was perhaps the real musical influence in

the Hughes family. She was a charming ageless woman with a tendency to spoil children ; she had an Ulster accent like a knife dipped in vinegar and an altogether inexhaustible repertoire of Irish songs. Many of the songs she sang were published for the first time when my father issued the first volume of his *Irish Country Songs* shortly after I was born.

That first volume was dedicated to me—a fact which I learned long before I could read it for myself—and I have always taken a special pride in that dedication. Of the twenty-two songs Herbert Hughes collected and arranged in the first volume all but four are Ulster tunes. Which is why I grow very impatient with well-meaning English people who fall for the obvious charm of the Southern Irish and dismiss Ulster as " not really Ireland." When I have failed to convince them that Ulster is most certainly Ireland, and if they don't believe it they should ask Mr. de Valera who keeps beefing about Partition, then I start on the subject of Ulster music and Ulster folk-lore. The truth is that the greatest of all Irish stories, the story of Cuchulain, and ninety per cent of the loveliest of Irish songs were created by the people of Ulster. The more sophisticated South, with its Adam-built slums, its magnificent Merrion Square and Georgian country houses, with its literary associations with Sheridan, Goldsmith, Swift, Wilde, Shaw, Synge, Yeats and the rest has a more ready appeal and it is something any country twice the size could be proud of. But if we are to be parochially Irish (and we always are, except when it comes to supporting our international Rugby sides), then I feel the foreigner should know that the Wee Black North is neither so wee nor so black as it's painted. Besides, where would anybody be without the Londonderry Air ? The South has nothing like that. . . .

If I seem a little prejudiced and anxious to put forward

the artistic claims of Ulster it may well be because the first few years of my life were spent in a household where the songs of Derry and Antrim and Co. Down took the place of the more familiar nursery tales, and the legend of Cuchulain was real enough to have happened next door ; accordingly, I tend to feel sorry for those whose childhood entertainment was limited to Goldilocks and the Three Bears.

Those " first few years " were in reality no more than five ; for one reason and another my parents' marriage began to break up after that and I ceased to know anything like a normal family life. During those five years, apart from visits to Ireland, I made my first journeys abroad including one to Ostend, where I fell off a jetty into the sea, and another to Wimereux, near Boulogne, where we lived in a fisherman's cottage for some months.

Though I cannot have been more than four years old at the time several distinct experiences in Boulogne stick out in my memory. The first was the pathetic attempt made almost daily by a French aviator to fly the Channel in a primitive monoplane. Crowds used to gather on the top of the cliffs, where a wide stretch of grass served as a runway, and wait patiently in the hope that the machine would gather enough momentum to reach the cliff-edge safely and become airborne. (The principle was much the same as governs the taking-off of aircraft from a carrier.) Fortunately for the pilot the machine never reached the edge of the cliff, for if it had it would have toppled straight over on to the beach below ; the motor never got going enough to have lifted a toy balloon. I was very touched by the whole incident, or rather, series of incidents (it happened day after day), since what was evidently intended to be a Milestone in Aviation resulted in nothing so much as a first-class imitation of a bird with a broken wing. In the end the plane made a sensational flight the length of the beach, scaring the life out of me by passing ten feet over my head and making a spectacular pancake landing fifty yards away. The pilot was safe, but the machine was a total wreck and the whole affair too much of an anti-climax for the Boulogne crowds who returned home to cultivate their gardens.

This early experience of aeroplanes and first-hand evidence that human flight was obviously impossible, so far from serving as a warning against flying has had exactly the opposite effect on me. In normal times I travel by air whenever I can ; it is the most deadly boring way of getting about the world that man ever invented, but it still never loses its fascination for me. I have never learnt to fly, unfortunately, and no doubt I would make a most dangerous pilot ; but to this day I can never resist the temptation to go out and " look at aeroplanes," and I was faintly disappointed when in the early days of the raids on London the Nazi planes started to fly over Central London and I could no longer see them caught in searchlights over Chelsea.

In an ideal world all aircraft would fly at 300 feet over my head so that I could see them properly, and all aircraft I flew in would fly at the same height so that I could see the people on the ground. Otherwise one has no sensation of flight, merely of looking at a huge map sadly lacking in detail and printed place-names when one is in the air, and no evidence of the speed of the machine that is making vapour trails above one when one is on the ground.

I had two other rather alarming experiences in Boulogne, both of which (if recent researches into child psychology are to be believed) ought to have affected me adversely for life. Neither of them did so ; on the contrary, like the aeroplane business, they proved to be the starting point of two life-time enthusiasms.

One was seeing my first Charlie Chaplin film. I

enjoyed it calmly enough until the point arrived where a large man, dressed as a woman (he was the same actor who has been in all Chaplin pictures—as the overseer in *Modern Times*, the tough in *Easy Street*) crossed over a stream on a plank and fell into the water below.

I was evidently very touched by this appalling incident, for I believed it to be real and was carried screaming from the cinema.

Finally, there was the Boulogne music hall. My father, until his death in 1937, had a great passion for music halls of all kinds; even in his exalted position as Music Editor of *The Daily Telegraph* he made a point of covering the new bill at the Coliseum and the Alhambra on Mondays and would write his concise notice of acrobats and jugglers with a typical *expertise* which was the fruit of his enthusiasm for the Halls and of his personal friendship with many of the performers.

I remember only one turn of the Boulogne music hall, and my father's enjoyment of what remained of the bill was spoilt by my screaming and having to be taken out once again.

The act consisted of a couple of clowns who came on with a bass drum, a trombone and a bass tuba; and the noise they made terrified me. I read, years afterwards, how Mozart, as a child, had been frightened by the sound of brass instruments, and I understood why. A child's ears obviously hear everything on a different scale from an adult's, in the same way that walls, chairs and tables appear enormous to children; their horizon is lower than a grown-up's, too—a fact that is nearly always forgotten by parents who expect their children to be able to see over garden fences while dragging them along at an adult walking-pace; the average grown-up's walking pace is a sprint for most children under six. Parents are incorrigible in their inability to remember their own childhood, except in the wrong way—which is when it suits them.

The shock of the French clowns' brass playing was only a momentary one, like diving into cold water. Ever since then the water has been lovely and a really loud brass crescendo can (quite literally) produce a shiver down my spine. I am apathetic to brass bands as such ; they bore me because the music they play is so generally dull. But Toscanini's climax to Strauss' *Tod und Verklärung*, with the brass players apparently biting their mouthpieces to reach their fortissimo reduces me to a state of limp excitement. I know it is stinking bad music ; but the quality of the music has nothing to do with it. I get the same sensation conducting my own music ; the experience is purely sensual.

Apart from this first great impact of music on my life Boulogne also supplied me with the first opportunity of learning a foreign language. I had a quick ear, and as I was a very talkative child I learned to speak French quickly and fluently. I had to learn French, or have nobody of my own age to talk to. I made friends with a most disreputable collection of Boulonnais street arabs with whom I ran around in bare feet, beachcombing and causing my mother considerable anxiety. On one occasion I arrived home several hours after my bed time, triumphantly bearing an old piece of driftwood and a handful of inedible mussels ; I was rewarded with a sound beating. My mother was evidently not the expert child psychologist she is now, for my life has been distinguished by a notorious unpunctuality for meals and an incurable reluctance to go to bed before 2 a.m. I bear her no grudge for that beating, but I cannot help feeling that it has had some sort of effect on my behaviour.

Some time in the summer of 1913 I began to suffer from an agonising attack of chronic rheumatism in my legs. I cried incessantly at night and my life and that of my mother who tried to comfort me became a misery. A doctor, whose name I never knew, but whose existence I have always blessed, ordered me to the Mediterranean— or at least from the clay and dampness of London. My mother, showing the first signs of that restlessness which has never left her, plumped for the Mediterranean.

I tried earlier on to describe some of my mother's travelling habits. I did not mention that though she refuses to travel light, she always insists on travelling cheaply. As she has never had any great interest in physical comfort, days and nights of journeying on hard continental third-class carriages have no terrors for her. She argues that if she spends less money on getting there she'll have more to spend when she does get there. A very sound economic principle, if you are tough enough to go through with it. For my part, I have always tried to travel as near *de luxe* as possible, although, God knows, first-class travel in Britain during the past few years has been so exhausting and haphazard that one has forgotten what comfortable, civilised travel can be.

So it was that when the question arose of our going to the Mediterranean there were no Blue Trains, Golden Arrows or Simplon Expresses for us. My mother chose the cheapest, longest and, as it happened, the pleasantest route. We boarded a tramp steamer at Liverpool.

The journey was marred by one of those major tragedies of childhood which one remembers all one's life. I was greatly attached to a tiny barrel tumbler, about two inches high, which I used for washing my paint brushes in when I daubed in water-colour. I lost this precious little tumbler when I emptied it over the side, throwing the tumbler into the sea after the dirty paint water. I took the loss of this treasure rather unphilosophically. My mother recalls that I once dropped a girdle of hers into a river and comforted her with the assurance : " Well, anyway, you won't be able to lose it tomorrow." She took it well. The loss of my tumbler, on the other hand, has never been compensated for, although I have owned numerous little glasses of exactly the same size since. But I have used them to drink out of ; mine was a *painting* tumbler.

Our first stop was Gibraltar. I spent the night ashore, sleeping in a cupboard in a smelly *pension*. A Gibraltar wind had arisen in the bay and our tramp steamer had had to weigh anchor and steam off to a safer place. I have never understood why that should have happened, but it seems to be a typical Gibraltar phenomenon. Next day the ship returned and we hired a boat to take us out to her. As we neared the mooring, our Gibraltarian boatmen laid down their oars and refused to take us any further unless my mother paid them some outrageous sum. It was a difficult situation, saved only by the captain of a passing British tanker who saw that we were in some distress (my mother's protestations were evidently audible at some distance) and shouted authoritative and abusive things through his megaphone at our hijackers. I do not know what he said to them, but we were taken to our ship with speed and something almost approaching courtesy. I have had a healthy respect for the idea of Showing The Flag ever since.

At Algiers we left our tramp steamer and stayed some weeks on a hill overlooking the sea. My mother bought a bicycle while we were there and optimistically set out to ride up rough hillside roads with me on the carrier. At least, I think she bought it there. It is just possible, on the other hand, that she had brought it with her all the way from England ; I wouldn't put it past her, for she once went so far as to drag an electric cooker across the Atlantic with her in order to save the trouble and expense of buying a new one in England. When she connected it up near Oxford its consumption of current cost a fortune and deprived the neighbours for miles round of power whenever she boiled a kettle.

The combination of the Algerian hills, the African sun and my weight on the carrier proved too much for my mother ; the bicycle, wherever it had come from, was discarded and we made our excursions on foot or by tram. One journey by tram nearly ended in disaster for me. As we approached our stopping place I decided to imitate my elders and get off before the tram had stopped. Algiers trams in those days drew a trailer behind them ; I was travelling in the trailer, and as the tram drew near our stopping place I jumped off—facing the wrong direction and on the wrong foot. I fell flat on my face, and finished up with half of me under the trailer. That I wasn't made mince-meat of was due to the alarmed shouts of the other passengers which startled the driver into drawing up with a jerk.

I suffered no psychological ill-effects from this adventure ; I am still unnecessarily reckless about getting off moving vehicles and I consider the boarding of them one of the most graceful actions ever executed by the human body. The imperturbability of children in the face of near-disaster is remarkable ; I remember quite vividly how, on picking myself up from under the tram, I discovered for the first time in my life that I had a hole in my pocket. This was hardly surprising as at that time I was an ardent collector of pebbles ; but the discovery that I had lost some of them, that they made holes in pockets, made a far greater immediate impression on me than the business with the tram.

It was during this stay in Algiers that my mother first started telling me her Birthday-and-Christmas stories— stories with a special technique designed to find out what I wanted as presents for my birthday or for Christmas. The story first started at the end of a walk, under sweet-smelling pepper trees, which had led us to a cave on the top of a hill, the Mediterranean and the whiteness of Algiers spread out before us in one direction, the misty blue of the Atlas mountains behind us.

I was curious to explore the cave, but as it was no fairy-book cave (it was used, in practice, as an insanitary free-for-all comfort-station) my mother dissuaded me from entering it by telling me the story of another cave like it. Her story told of a long cave which ran into the side of a mountain and was entirely populated by small men like Lepracauns ; their business was not the cobbling of fairy shoes, but the mass-production of toys.

It was obviously sweated labour, for they worked incessantly from one year's end to another ; but at four years of age I was no Trades Unionist, and I was delighted to think of them working so hard on a job of highest priority. The cave, my mother assured me, was divided into seven sections in each of which an elaborate toy was being made in time for Christmas—tin soldiers in one, model ships in another and so on. At the end of the cave there was an eighth section, closely guarded by armed sentries who stood before heavy locked doors. Behind these doors worked The Boss and a company of picked skilled workmen.

" And what do you think they were making ? " asked my mother. The answer to that question supplied her with the information she required ; my guess gave her the clue to what I wanted for my next birthday or for Christmas. Sometimes The Boss was thought to be making rather expensive and impracticable things, like Cunard liners or self-propelled rocking horses ; but as the story was repeated I learned to make my guess more within the bounds of my mother's pocket. The formula of this story is one I recommend to all parents, provided they remember to fill the first seven sections of the cave with toys their children already possess or are unlikely ever to want.

I find, at the age I am writing all this, that it is impossible to remember what happened to favourite possessions of my childhood. It was while we were in Algiers, for instance, that the Arab " boy " employed at our hotel made me a most enchanting and ingenious popgun. It was no ordinary popgun with a cork on the end of a string, but a machine made of bamboo carved in such a way that by pulling a trigger a thin strip of bamboo was made to slap down on another and create a most satisfactory and explosive noise. It is most probable that, as my mother had no doubt collected a sackful of brass candlesticks and clay pots by then, I was made to leave it behind when we left Algiers on the grounds that it would take up too much room on the boat.

I had the popgun in Algiers ; I did not have it by the time we reached Catania in a flea-ridden boat from Malta.

CHAPTER II

SICILY

My first impression of Sicily was a disappointment. I had been told that Etna would have snow on it, if not actually be in full eruption. As we drew alongside at Catania, it was obvious that the story of Etna and its snow was nothing more than propaganda ; it was just a high, arid, brown mountain whose summit I couldn't see for clouds.

I entered a demi-paradise with a slight feeling that I had been swindled by the travel posters.

My mother has never told me of her feelings on arriving in Sicily ; but I can imagine them. All her life she has had an all-consuming love of the Mediterranean and its civilisation, of Italy and the Italians in particular. She is an erratic linguist, though (provided the foreigner to whom she is speaking can understand a medley of three imperfectly learned languages) she can nearly always make herself understood and is unperturbed if she doesn't. What she gets out of Italy is not what the Italians say but what they have done ; she is by nature a friendly and sympathetic woman, but her letters from Italy are more likely to include sketches of an odd street corner or the ornaments of a stray pillar than any anecdote of personal experience.

Her grandfather had been an art student in Italy ; her father, by profession a brewer's chemist from Stafford-shire, was a highly talented landscape painter who took a liberal amount of time off to paint in those parts of the world where there was most sunshine. My grandfather Meacham, though he never acquired any spectacular fame as an artist, had a great gift of transplanting sunlight on to canvas, particularly the sunlight of Sicily, Corsica and Italy. Charles Stephen Meacham's love of Italy remained with him long after he was too old to travel ; he was inclined to think that Mussolini was a great man (with one daughter an ex-Fabian and her sister Wendy a violent Scottish Nationalist it is hardly surprising he was reactionary in his politics), and to his dying day in 1940 he continually refreshed his Italian by reading *Pinocchio* and Hugo's more advanced conversation books in order to understand what the Rome and Bari announcers were saying on the wireless. His politics may have been a little misguided, as it happened, but I am certain that his views were dictated by a sincere belief that Mussolini was helping Italy. He had been told that Mussolini was a Good Thing and he believed it ; the main thing was that grandfather Meacham's favourite foreign country was acquiring an important status as a Power, and being a political innocent and incorrigible imperialist (which is the same thing) he was content to let things be. If Italy—according to what he had heard—was flourishing, then nothing could make him happier. I never saw grandfather Meacham after the 1939 war began, which is just as well ; his already perplexed mind must have suffered agonies at the thought of being at war with Italy.

This sudden diversion into family background would be irrelevant at this point if I did not feel that it had an important bearing on many things which come later in this book. My own love of Italy, which has been the greatest of all influences on my life, is not a matter of heredity but of tradition. If I had never actually been to Italy, I doubt if I would have inherited any great feeling for all that Italy stands for ; but when my mother, the third generation of a family of Italophiles, took me there I fell in with the family tradition at once. Our eventual route through Sicily and Italy was roughly the same as that followed by Allied troops in the 1943-45 Italian campaign ; on reflection, it seems an admirably logical route to have chosen. On the northward journey one traces the whole history of Italy in almost strict chronological order—from Sicily, the one-time Greek colony, to Pompeii and Rome, thence through Florence, the birthplace of the Renaissance, to Venice and the modern industrial cities of the north.

Not that I was conscious of any of this at the time, of course, and I cannot think that my mother had planned an itinerary of any kind, let alone mapped out an historico-geographical tour of the Peninsular and its culture. If she had any such thing at the back of her mind she was in no great hurry to put it into practice.

We arrived in Sicily and settled ourselves down in Taormina with such thoroughness that it seemed we intended to spend the rest of our lives there.

We stayed first in an hotel (which was later the Nazi G.H.Q.), then in a beautiful studio set in a garden full of orange and eucalyptus trees, where I celebrated my fifth birthday, and finally we rented a tiny house near the Cathedral.

This house was so small that our beds were ranged one above the other as in a ship's cabin ; there was a sitting room and a very small kitchen where all cooking was done on a charcoal fire. There was a small garden, too, though I do not remember that it yielded anything but a Greek toy which my mother dug up. It was a hollow pottery affair about seven inches long and shaped like a bird. At first I thought it was a cuckoo, and I looked in vain for a hole I could blow a musical note through ; but what I hoped might turn out to be an ocarina of some kind my mother decided was really a dove. And that, having discarded the cuckoo theory, is obviously what it was. The dove was cherished for many years until it was eventually mislaid in the course of one of my mother's gigantic amphibious operations when moving to or from America.

Our house was rented from a delightful old brigand of a landlord who could neither read nor write ; he signed the contract for the lease with a cross. On Sundays he made a state call on us, arriving on a donkey and wearing large gold earrings and a black velvet jacket ; he could have walked on the stage at any performance of *Cavalleria Rusticana* without exciting comment. On these Sunday visits he regularly brought with him two gifts for my mother : a pot of most exquisite honey and a bunch of flowers. He presented them with a good deal of ceremony and having delivered them, would smile politely with a mouthful of gold teeth. My mother returned his smiles and that was about the sum total of their social intercourse. The barrier of language was insurmountable at first and limited conversation to dialogue about the weather ; and when it was decided unanimously whether the *giornata* was *bella* or the *tempo* was *cattivo*, the landlord took his leave, mounted his donkey and rode away.

As in Boulogne it did not take me long to learn to speak a new language in Taormina. I picked up Italian with a strong Sicilian accent from Maria who came and cooked and washed up for us. Maria lived across the road in a house filled to overflowing with sisters and their babies, relatives and their babies and chickens and goats which must have lived in the bedrooms as there was no room for all of them in the kitchen. Maria was always in great demand down our street, for the place echoed all day with cries for " Ma-reeeee-yah ! "

I learnt more Italian, too, from an old man and his son who ran the local puppet theatre. It was a tiny little place in the main street and smelt strongly of the acetylene which supplied the lighting for stage and auditorium. The theatre, when filled, cannot have held more than thirty people who sat on long, backless wooden benches.

I made firm friends with the old puppeteer, and he ended by putting on special morning performances of his shows for my exclusive benefit. His plays had no scripts ; the theatre had been in the same family for untold generations and the stories and puppets and dialogue had been handed down from father to son. In the main the theatre's repertoire consisted of romantic plays about Turks and Saracens and Crusaders—subjects which may well have been topical when the old man's ancestors had first started playing with puppets.

The plays were not acted ; or rather, the puppets acted, but their parts were not spoken by separate human voices backstage. The puppets' movements were accompanied by Gino (I think that was the old man's name) taking the part of narrator ; sometimes he would give a running commentary on the fierce battles between Turk and Crusader, at others he would add dialogue, characterising the Turk villain in an exaggerated, gruff voice and the Christian princess in a high falsetto. His story-telling was punctuated with the Italian equivalent of the familiar mannerism of the radio commentator. But instead of saying " Well—," Gino drawled " Dunque . . ." while he made up his mind what was to happen next in a plot that had become as complicated as the libretto of *Il Trovatore*.

Gino made me a present of two superbly dressed puppets ; one of them was a fully-armed Crusader who carried a sword and shield, the other was a very expensive-looking sultan of some kind. While I was in Taormina I took these two figures to bed with me ; they were uncomfortable companions, but I would not be parted from them. Later, when I was at an English school, I regret to say I swopped them for a pot of jam or something equally functional.

Finally, I perfected my vocabulary of abusive Sicilian phrases by joining up with a gang of tough little street urchins. Our principal mission in life was carriage-jumping ; our object was to hang on to the back of carriages as they drove down the main street and to hang on as long as possible without being spotted by the driver. When we were spotted the idea was to shout rude things at him and then jump off before he slashed at us with his whip. It was an exciting, sometimes painful and always unprofitable pastime.

We made our profits not by carriage-jumping, but by begging from tourists. If our Italian failed to gain us any *soldi* then I became the spokesman in English. In spite of my looking as brown and grubby and barefooted as my confederates this ruse rarely succeeded. Instead of being rewarded as a clever little Sicilian boy, I was spoken sharply to for being a badly behaved little English boy who ought to know better.

One indignant American lady whom I had approached in this way went straight to my mother to protest. "Mrs. Hughes! Mrs. Hughes!" she panted, "do you know what your little boy is doing? He's—he's *begging!*"

My mother, I fear, merely laughed and said: "Oh, so *that's* how Patrick got those 15 centesimi yesterday! I hope he'll do better today." I had at that time an overwhelming passion for dried figs which hung on a string outside the shop next door, and my mother was delighted to think that at last I might be able to afford to buy them myself instead of bothering her for the money.

There were times, however, when I washed my face and behaved like a little gentleman, notably when we were invited to tea by Robert Hichens who had a villa above Taormina. I was very impressed by Mr. Hichens, and in after years I boasted proudly to my school-fellows that I had known him intimately since I was so high. At this date, I cannot even remember what Robert Hichens looked like, though I remember we took tea with him on a lovely terrace looking towards Etna—now, I am glad to say, wearing a snow tippet as advertised. But my early meeting with Mr. Hichens caused me to go and see the films of *The Garden of Allah* and *Barbary Sheep* safe in the knowledge that no one else in the audience was likely to have had tea with the author when they were children in Taormina. Robert Hichens (or the screen-writer of *Barbary Sheep*) influenced me to one great extent. There was a caption in *Barbary Sheep* which read: "Beware of a man who cracks walnuts in his fingers"; I have never used nutcrackers except for the most obstinate walnuts since I read that, although I have never made up my mind who was to beware of me or why.

In the arcadian atmosphere of Taormina my bedtime mythology underwent a drastic change. My mother's stories of Cuchulain, even the story about the toy-cave, seemed out of place among the eucalyptus trees and the sweet scent of orange and lemon groves. These stories belonged to a world which no longer had any reality for me after a day spent in the ruins of the Roman theatre that had been built on foundations laid by the Greeks, or on the slopes of Isola Bella set in its little bay of aquamarine.

My new hero was Ulysses. If Cuchulain's adventures could have happened next door, there was no doubt whatever but that Ulysses had stopped off at Taormina. Otherwise, I asked, how else could anybody explain my discovery on the beach of one large boot? Polyphemus can never have lived anywhere but in the grotto in the bay. I had been out to the cave in a boat and seen for myself ; the water there was thirty feet deep and so clear that you could see the rocks below you on the bottom, but then Polyphemus was a giant and thirty feet of water was nothing to him. The boot on the beach was quite clearly his ; he had taken it off when he went to bed the night before Ulysses arrived, thrown it through the mouth of the grotto and had never lived to retrieve it.

My proposal that I should carry the boot home as a souvenir was turned down ; it would be there tomorrow. It wasn't, and I was very disappointed and mystified by its disappearance.

I never tired of my mother's telling of the story of Ulysses. She made him out to be an enchanting rascal ; I was filled with hero-worship for his deeds at Troy and worried to death as each adventure of his wanderings seemed to take him further and further away from Ithaca. Before long I had so much identified myself with him that

I walked about the streets carrying a saucepan lid for a shield, a broom handle for a spear and, without warning, passers-by would become involved in a violent single combat with an imaginary Trojan.

This enthusiasm for Greece and its heroes was fostered further by the first great artistic experience of my life : my first visit to a theatre.

When Jimmy Agate warned me about writing of my childhood I went on to tell him that the first time I had ever been to a theatre I was five years old and saw the *Agamemnon* of Æschylus in the amphitheatre at Syracuse. Jimmy grunted ; but the tone of his grunt suggested that my experience was perhaps rather an unusual introduction to the drama.

I didn't understand much of what I heard, sitting perched up on a stone seat that was hewn out of the rock, but I knew the story of Agamemnon and I was deeply affected by the action. The whole performance was very real to me ; I didn't scream as I had done in the cinema at Boulogne, and I wasn't taken out, except possibly for the natural reason little boys always have to be taken out from time to time. But there can be no place in the world where the opening speech of the Watchman in the *Agamemnon* has such a convincingly realistic setting as at Syracuse.

He spoke his words standing against a background of brilliantly blue sea, and I more than half expected to see Agamemnon's ship approaching towards the Atridan's battlements when the Watchman said he'd seen the beacon; I was fully aware that we were on one shore of the very same sea that Agamemnon had sailed.

I was enthralled by the whole performance, including the blood-curdling screams off-stage when Agamemnon was murdered and the moving funeral procession at the end.

The story of Agamemnon has always been at the top of the list of operas I was going to write ; I have started several and half-finished one on the subject. If ever I settle down to writing an opera again—which is most unlikely now—it will be another *Agamemnon* and the scene I shall have in my mind will, as always, be the scene I saw in the Greek theatre at Syracuse.

We stayed some eight months in Taormina without going any further away from it than Syracuse ; Christmas came and went, together with the innumerable smaller religious festivals which the Sicilians celebrated in their own theatrical and picturesque way. The high spot of the Christmas celebrations was a big bonfire over the flames of which the bishop held a doll representing the infant Christ ; I still fail to see any connection between that ritual and Christianity, but the Sicilians have never been fussy about dressing up pagan customs to suit the purpose of the Church.

Palm Sunday, on the other hand, was celebrated in a manner more appropriate to the occasion. The entire population turned out in procession carrying not the miserable pieces of dried stuff which passes for palm in non-Catholic countries, but huge branches stripped from palm trees, and the streets looked as the streets of Jerusalem might have looked on Christ's entry.

A couple of days after Palm Sunday, 1914, my mother packed some of our belongings and we set off in a train by way of Messina to Milazzo on the north coast of the island.

On the way, my mother began to tell me the story of Garibaldi and how my great-grandfather had fought with him ; she told me that we were going to Milazzo where Garibaldi had defeated the Neapolitans and where we would see the famous fortress which the Garibaldini had surrounded and finally captured.

By the time we arrived at Milazzo, Garibaldi had taken a firm, imperishable place in my gallery of heroes, alongside Cuchulain, Ulysses and Perseus. I am afraid the fortress, after all that, cannot have made much of an impression on me, for all I remember now of Milazzo is a field covered with marigolds growing wild and called the Island of the Sun.

From Milazzo we took a carriage along the coast to reach the place which had been the final object of our journey round the island, Tindaro. My mother's reason for coming to Tindaro was to see the ruins of a Greek theatre. As usual, she had made no plans for any form of board and lodging, but she had heard there was a monastery there so to the monastery we went.

The monks took us in willingly, putting us in a guest room in a part of the monastery which was built on the edge of a rocky cliff with a perpendicular drop from the window of our room of about 200 feet to the sea below.

The Greek theatre was duly visited though not before there had been a slight misunderstanding with one of the monks. We asked him to show us the way to the famous Greek *antichità* ; he led us to the lavatory, which was certainly quite an *antichità* in its way.

While we were staying at the monastery, my mother looked out of our window and found that she could see the outline of Stromboli on the horizon ; so instead of returning immediately to Taormina, as she had intended, she decided that Stromboli might be as good a place as any other in which to spend Easter.

We set sail from Milazzo on the morning of Maundy Thursday in a boat which even my mother described as " very third-class." Our fellow passengers were all peasants who had come to the mainland of Sicily to fetch their weekly provisions to take back to Stromboli. As usual, the peasants seemed to have gone in for travelling in a big way—with babies, sacks, flasks of wine and oil, goats, dogs and chickens strewn all over the deck.

Among all the chaos and screaming and discomfort only one man on board the ship showed any signs of uneasiness and that was the captain. He explained to my mother (I had an incurable habit as a child of making a beeline for the bridge on any boat) that a gale was getting up ; the crossing would be rough. The " gale " was nothing more than a gentle breeze, and my mother—who is a bad sailor at any time—pooh-poohed the idea that we were in for dirty weather, or anything like it. But the captain was not convinced. " It may not be *cattivo tempo* for English captains," he said, " but for Italians—*cattivissimo*."

We never saw the captain again after we left port, but even so I cannot believe that he was as sick as he expected to be ; the whole set-up was a little bit too like the opening of *South Wind* already ; for the captain to have been sicker than his passengers would have been too much.

Our arrival at Stromboli started off with a champion example of cross-purpose conversation. My mother, who was very fair, was mistaken by the authorities for the wife of a German meteorologist who was expected to visit the island and was evidently overdue. We were greeted in a language the Stromboli authorities thought was German, and which we thought was meant to be English ; after some minutes, during which we managed to explain that we were not interested in the annual rainfall and that the last thing we wanted to do was to look down the crater of the volcano, it was realised that there had been some mistake. Obviously disappointed the reception committee turned on its heel and left us, announcing its intention of meeting the next day's boat and apologising for having troubled us. Heaven knows when the German meteorological mission did arrive, or even if it has arrived yet.

I went down to the beach the following day, and for the next four days afterwards, but nobody arrived who looked remotely like a meteorologist, or even like a meteorologist's wife.

Having disposed of the reception committee, my mother collected our luggage, grabbed me by the hand and set out with her unshakable optimism to find somewhere for us to stay. She scorned hotels on principle, so she never bothered to enquire whether there was such a thing at all on the island. She set course for a likely-looking house facing the sea, entered it and took rooms. She had learnt from experience that there is hardly a house, noble or humble, in the entire Mediterranean that is not willing to take in lodgers.

My mother found lodging quickly enough on Stromboli; it was the question of board that was difficult. The peasants with whom we had travelled from Milazzo were no trippers ; they had been to Sicily to buy food because there was virtually none on Stromboli. Not only did Stromboli supply almost nothing ; even if there had been anything much it would have been difficult to get. We had arrived in Holy Week, and an already underfed island populace was busy fasting.

Our landlady eventually recognised us as heathen foreigners and somehow unearthed some undercooked macaroni which lay heavily on the stomach but which served to keep us from complete starvation.

The following morning, after a night disturbed by the incessant breaking of millions of pieces of crockery—in fact it was the noise of the belly-rumbles of the volcano—my mother awoke to find that her brown shoes had been carefully blacked over. The signora explained that it was Good Friday and nobody could wear brown shoes on Good Friday, not on Stromboli.

Apart from the habit of blacking over brown shoes, the

B

inhabitants of Stromboli have peculiar Good Friday customs. We went to the church to find it crammed as full as Waterloo Station on a bank holiday. An ancient priest, wearing a cassock that had once been black and was now green, ran from altar to organ and back again in the course of his duties, singing, praying, crossing himself and apparently blessing us all although his facial expression suggested he hated the sight of everybody. His least effective activity was at the organ, a dilapidated instrument with only a handful of notes and one pedal which worked. Prominently displayed in the church was a wax figure of Christ taken down from the cross and lying full-length on a bier. The children in the congregation—and only the children, for some reason—went to this figure from time to time to kiss the wounds. They came back to their places wiping their mouths with the backs of their hands and looking slightly sick.

At the end of the service, the figure of Christ was covered over with a glass case and the bier was lifted up by the Misericordia and carried out of the church, the bearers pulling long pointed hoods over their faces as they came into the open. From this church (church A) the procession moved to another (church B) some distance away, passing on the way a similar procession carrying a figure of the Virgin Mary and headed for church A. This exchange of wax figures took place every Good Friday, and the figure from church A remained in church B until the following year, when they were exchanged once more.

Easter Day was a day of comparative feasting. As strangers we were invited into nearly every house we passed to eat dried figs and drink wine. (I was allowed one sip of wine neat, and then I was given a glass of water with a dash of wine to colour it.) In each house, too, we were shown little flower pots in which green corn was growing. These pots were symbols of Spring and Resurrection which were taken to the priest to be blessed. The islanders no doubt thought the blessing made the green corn legitimately Christian. But blessed or not, these pots were still known—after 2000 years or so—as " Adonis Gardens." Consistency has never been a strong point of the Mediterranean peoples.

On the whole, however, I found the atmosphere of Stromboli more than a little sinister, and though we set foot on none of the other Lipari islands I well understand why Mussolini chose them as sites for his political prisons. We passed one of them on the journey back to Milazzo ; it should have been the one called Volcano, for from the sea it looked like nothing so much as a Doré illustration to Dante's Inferno—an evil, grey-looking island of pumice stone which constantly belched forth large puffs of thick grey smoke. I was glad to return to Taormina and the distant serenity of Etna.

CHAPTER III

UNWILLINGLY TO SCHOOL

My mother now had a picturesque scheme to buy a donkey and cart and to tour Sicily with it peddling toys to anybody she happened to meet on the road. The plan never materialised, perhaps because she couldn't find a donkey, perhaps because she couldn't find the toys, or both. Whatever the reason, we left Taormina and our little two-by-four house in the late Spring of 1914 and began a long journey northwards. At Messina I was greatly intrigued by the idea of carrying a whole train across the Straits on a ferry ; as we had to get out of our carriage when we were sailing across I never quite saw the point of taking the whole affair on board. It would have been easier, it seemed to me, to get into an entirely new train when we got to the mainland of Italy. Nevertheless, I was impressed by the marvels of science.

Our first stop was Naples, where we were to meet my grandfather Meacham and his wife who were coming to Europe by boat from Cape Town. Grandfather Meacham had settled in South Africa about twenty years before as chief chemist to Ohlsson's Cape Breweries and made occasional trips to Europe to paint. The Meachams arrived in Naples to schedule to find the town up to its neck in a general strike, a state of affairs which apparently occurred on an average once a month. There must have been transport of some kind, however, for we found our way to Pompeii and to Capri, where my grandmother tells me (she is 90 and recalls the incident with some pride) my command of Sicilian invective completely silenced a truculent Neapolitan cab-driver. My grandfather painted like a mad thing all this time, and when he had " done " Vesuvius and Sorrento, the Meacham and Hughes circus moved on to Rome.

I found Rome bewildering. I was delighted to learn that I was seeing the Biggest Church in the World when I was taken to St. Peter's, but I couldn't take in all the business about the Pope being locked up in the Vatican. I was faintly disgusted by the thought that millions of the faithful had kissed away the foot of St. Peter's statue ; it was an unhygienic habit, and I had been strictly brought up not to touch anything with my mouth that had not been thoroughly washed first—a wise precaution in most countries, and essential in Italy. I had just had time to see the Collosseum and the hideous Vittorio Emanuele memorial (which I adored on account of its size) when my sight-seeing was brought to an end by my falling ill. I have been to Rome only once since then, and on that occasion also I was ill and spent most of the time in bed.

My indisposition, whatever it was, did not seriously inconvenience the rest of the party. As an only child I was experienced in the art of amusing myself ; I could not yet read, but I could draw and if ever my elders wished to be rid of me or wanted to go out I was given a bunch of pencils and some drawing paper and considered out of harm's way until it was bedtime. I had no fear of being left alone even in a strange house, and my mother had none of leaving me so ; whether this aptitude for self-amusement was inherent in me or had been carefully taught by my mother I do not know. To some parents my mother's encouragement of my independence might have appeared as cool, calculated neglect ; in effect, it served us both well inasmuch as I was no millstone round the neck of a young and vigorous woman and I in turn was spared the irritation of being fussed over. It was an admirable arrangement.

The journey northwards through Italy was too rapid to make any great impression on me ; Sicily I had lived in, Italy I was merely touring and many things I must have experienced are now no more than vague memories of things which flashed past the railway-carriage window of the mind.

Florence was altogether too vast a pattern for me to take in all at once, and until I visited the city again I am afraid that Florence to me meant only that place where they had houses on a bridge and delicious chocolate ices. My mother reminds me, however, that I had one great enthusiasm in Florence at that time. Whenever my grandfather went off painting I begged to be allowed to go and sit outside the Signoria with pencil and drawing paper to draw Michelangelo's David. I have no explanation to offer for this five-year-old enthusiasm, and though I feel I showed unusually good taste in wanting to draw the statue, I cannot think that it was inspired by anything more than the megalomania which had made St. Peter's so exciting to me.

Venice, on the other hand, made a far deeper impression—as one would expect it to. To a child of five the idea of water where there should be streets was a never-ending source of excitement and wonder. We lived out on the Giudecca and had to take a longish steamboat trip across the lagoon every time we wanted to fetch mail from Cook's or buy a stamp. I had little time for gondolas, which I considered an unnecessary, bumpy way of getting about, and I infinitely preferred the noise and smell of the one-man engine room in the public steamboats. I spent a lot of time trying to persuade the captains of these little boats to let me blow the hooter, but I never succeeded. An intriguing desire became an obsession which was not satisfied until we took one of the larger boats to Chioggia and a kind captain let me stand on the bridge and pull the string. The resultant shrill, steamy blast was most gratifying. Like most children I was a great creator of noise, but not overkeen on noise over which I had no control. I was frightened out of my wits on being caught in the belfry of the St. Mark's campanile at midday when a shattering peal was rung by electricity. I did not wait for the lift to take me down, but ran as fast as I could down the ramp from the top of the tower to the Piazza.

Setting them down on paper like this these appear very slender impressions to have had of Florence and Venice, but in a topographical sense they were oddly deep. Neither city was ever a strange city when next I visited it ; I can still find my way easily and quickly about both of them, recognising street corners and obscure passages which I have not seen since I was five. The first effect of

Florence and Venice, in fact, was physical not intellectual. I have only my mother's word for it that I noticed the Michelangelo David at all, and not even she would boast that I was in the least moved by all the Botticellis and Fra Angelicos and frescoes I must inevitably have been taken to see. However, as none of this travelling around was done with any idea of educating me the time was by no means wasted ; my mother was in a seventh heaven the whole time and grew to look more like one of the figures (not the pregnant one) in Botticelli's Primavera every day.

About June, 1914, we set sail for England from Genoa. We travelled on an Orient liner ; I made friends on board with the Rajah of Sarawak, who puzzled me by being white and wearing a trilby hat instead of a turban, and by the time we arrived at Tilbury I had forgotten all my Italian and had learned a rich Australian from my fellow-passengers instead.

A little while later I went to Ireland with my father and we were there when war broke out in August. My grandfather read the news at breakfast ; everybody was very gloomy and I wisely refrained from remarking on something which nobody had noticed : that for the first time in my life I had dressed myself unaided.

The war of 1914 finally broke up my mother's first marriage and prepared the way for her second, and, as far as I was concerned, a normal family life, already pretty rocky on its feet, ceased to exist. My father, who had once left us financially high and dry while we were in Taormina, now disappeared altogether and went off to the war ; it was nearly six years before I saw him again. I will not attempt to go into the rights and wrongs of the break-up of their marriage, for there must have been something to be said for both my parents ; they obviously got on each other's nerves and had done so for some time. When the split came it was no sudden happening, but the climax of a gradual process of estrangement, and if anybody benefited from the whole business in the long run it was I, for my childhood continued to be highly unconventional and entertaining.

The man who some years later became my first stepfather was a young Egyptologist called Battiscombe Gunn, universally known as " Jack," and now Professor of Egyptology at Oxford. He had lived in Paris for many years and when France was invaded he came back to England to join up ; he was turned down as unfit for anything but the stamping of identity discs. In the end this struck him and even the authorities as an unsatisfactory way of aiding the Republic, so he was invalided out of the Artists' Rifles and returned to his books.

The war did not affect my mother's habits overmuch. After teaching me to read on the roof of a tiny flat in Wardour Street she boarded me out at a prep school near Hatfield and went off to Italy again. She hadn't been in Florence very long before she decided that it would be nice to have me with her. I was given my first passport, which was one of those awkward one-page things which unfolded to the size of a table and bore Sir Edward Grey's request and requirement in the name of His Majesty, etc. Armed with this clumsy document I set out for Italy with Jack and on the way visited Paris for the first time.

We stayed in a small hotel in Montparnasse for a few days in the gloomy, oppressive atmosphere of Paris at war. The son of the house had recently been killed and his photograph was hung with crêpe ; there was hardly a family in the entire block which did not receive a casualty telegram while we were there. It was nearly 20 years before the picture of Paris in 1915 faded from my memory entirely. Probably the people suffered no greater bereavements proportionately than the people of England, but the French do not hide their feelings so well and, as a child of six, the impression I carried away from Paris was of weeping and immense sadness.

Looking back over the German War of 1939 it strikes me how few outward signs of mourning one saw among the British people ; perhaps this was because there was so little distinction between civilian and military casualties and a housewife was just as likely to be blown up by a rocket as her relatives to be killed " at the front " in a total war.

Jack delivered me to my mother in Florence and then I think must have returned to England, for my next clear memory is of living in an elegant villa outside Florence which belonged to a rich American widower whom my mother faintly thought to marry. His name was Falo ; he had two sons whom I didn't like and a roomful of model electric trains which I did. We spent the summer by the sea, at Forte dei Marmi, near Viareggio and it was proposed that I should stay on with Falo's children while my mother and he went for a trip to Switzerland. I hated the idea and I detested the Nanny who was to look after us ; but most of all I disapproved of my mother going off without me. I may have had an independent nature, but I had a highly developed Œdipus complex, and having killed off one father, as it were, I resented another being brought into the family, however rich he might be.

I went to the station to see my mother and Falo into their train, feeling very unhappy and not a little tearful. As the train started to move, however, I jumped on board and refused to get off. I was dressed only in rompers and sandals, so there was nothing they could do but take me on with them and send for my clothes when we got to Milan.

I have forgotten how Falo took this unexpected intrusion, but my mother did not seem displeased. She told

B*

me afterwards that my refusal to leave her in fact changed the whole course of her life, and that instead of staying in Italy and marrying Falo, as she thinks she might have done, she had changed her mind by the time we got to Genoa and decided to marry Jack.

Whatever the effect of my spontaneous act of sabotage on Falo and my mother I personally enjoyed the trip immensely. Falo, perhaps with some twinge of conscience, set out systematically to spoil us both and me in particular. For the first time in our lives my mother and I travelled first-class in trains ; in Zurich I was taken to The Biggest Toy Shop in the World and given a clock-work submarine that dived ; my mother was given a gold wristlet watch in Berne and I was given a large carved hard-wood bear which I carried day and night. From Berne to Paris we travelled in first-class sleepers, a form of travel which I never experienced again until 1931, when I was able to travel on the midnight train from Manchester to London as a result of being paid overtime for playing in a Manchester pit orchestra.

Travelling with Falo ought to have convinced us that there was a lot to be said for living in the luxury he offered ; but my mother had made up her mind about Jack, and I was too selfish and self-centred to think of any of Falo's gifts as anything but what was due to me without obligation on my part.

The journey *de luxe* ended in Paris, and my mother and I returned to England on our own to be met at the station by Jack.

The question of my going to school was the next thing to be settled, and it was decided to send me to the preparatory attached to the Perse School, Cambridge. I don't know whose idea it was but I always associate it with Clifford Bax. My mother and I spent a lot of time at his house in Finchley, where Clifford taught me to play chess and allowed me to play with his magnificent collection of toy soldiers ; and it was in his house that I first remember seeing the idealised prospectus of the school. The prospectus was pre-1914 so that most of the attractions offered no longer applied ; but if many of the masters, who had evolved ingenious and entertaining ways of educating small boys, had gone to the war, we were assured that the tradition had been maintained. And in any case—which was most important—Dr. Rouse was still the headmaster.

Before I actually went to the Perse there had been various experiments made in education at my expense, including a period at a kindergarten kept by two young noble ladies off the Euston Road. I learnt to weave paper mats there but failed to learn why I had to be given a ticket before I was allowed to go to the lavatory. I was also dumped in a Belgian convent in Golders Green for a short while, but I kicked fiercely against that when the nuns refused to allow my mother to give me my cod liver oil and malt on leaving me at bedtime. The unnecessary injustice of this action enraged me so much that I had to be removed and I have hated the sight of nuns ever since.

There were certain other complications at this time which concerned relations with my father. My mother had a very real fear that if Herbert should chance to meet me in the street he would whisk me off ; in consequence I was not allowed to travel alone on the bus to the Euston Road, which I was quite capable of doing and which would have saved my mother a great deal of trouble twice a day.

Exactly what my mother used for money at this time I do not pretend to know. We were obviously very poor, for we used to have one portion of food between us at Fleming's and send for an extra plate to put my share on. Dr. Rouse, however, seemed to consider me a promising child and took me as a boarder in his house at the Perse at half-fees while my mother earned her keep by teaching singing games at the prep.

Dr. Rouse, it must be said, put his money on a long shot. He knew that I had been in Sicily and that my mother had brought me up to know and love the stories of ancient Greece, so I believe he thought I had the makings of a classical scholar. He confessed this hope to me not long ago and I have always felt slightly ashamed that I should have let him down, even though he wrote that he was pleased I had " gone off like a hawk " and built myself a nest of my own. But it was a risky thing, let's face it. I was still not seven when I went to the Perse ; it would be nearly another seven years before I began to learn Greek, and anything might happen in the interval—as indeed it did.

One of the most remarkable characteristics of a child is its refusal to be impressed by things by which its elders hope to impress it. I was to be trained as a classical scholar and certainly I lost none of my passion for the Greek stories, but no amount of careful nursing and planning for the future altered the fact that my first enthusiasm was for the Rugby football I was taught to play three afternoons a week. I began to learn the violin too, from a woman with a beard which covered an abnormal deficiency of chin, but the violin did not excite me nearly so much as the idea of being a wolfcub.

I was musical all right ; there had always been music in the house (whenever we'd had a house), and I had cut my teeth on my mother's two Academy medals. One I threw into a river, the other was snatched out of my hand by a magpie. It was natural that I should learn to play something and I was given a violin because, said my mother, it's an instrument you can always take about with you, unlike a piano. The inconsistency of this remark, coming from a woman of my mother's travelling habits, did not strike me at the time ; I have learnt from experience that even a mighty Wurlitzer is something " you can always take about with you " once my mother sets her mind to it.

But for all the talk there was of the portability of the violin, my quarter-size, massed produced, Stradivarius-labelled Bohemian instrument was left behind in England when my mother took me travelling again.

This time the journey was no mere excursion to Italy or thereabouts. Within less than three months of my starting to go to school at Cambridge my mother decided it would be nice to go to South Africa to visit her parents ; so off we went—in the middle of a world war and at a time the U-boats were just beginning to get the hang of things.

We spent Christmas 1915 in the Bay of Biscay, tossed about in an undersized tub called the *Saxon* by the heaviest gale for a decade. The wind which restricted us to three knots for two and a half days blew a number of trees down in Richmond Park ; but it also spared us the attention of enemy submarines which had sunk the ship preceeding us on the Cape run. It was so rough that our two escorting destroyers packed up and waved us good-bye soon after we left Plymouth, believing that the worst that could happen to us would be that we'd turn turtle without any assistance from the enemy.

My own behaviour during the first week or so must have been intolerable. The rougher it grew the more I enjoyed it ; I ate everything in sight and slept like a log while my poor mother suffered agonies of sea-sickness. The *Saxon*, in those first few days out from home, cannot have been a very happy ship, and the general gaiety of things was not improved when a general in command of troops on board got off at Madeira and died.

By the time we reached Madeira we had left the war behind us. We sailed with all lights on and the gun on the quarterdeck became an ornament instead of the only weapon between us and destruction. My mother, like all·who suffer from sea-sickness, quickly became herself again once the sea stopped throwing us about and could no longer remember what it was like to be sea-sick. Madeira provided her with just the temptation she could never resist, the temptation to buy decorative and useless things made by the natives ; we continued our journey south with three wicker chairs of various sizes and two enormous squeaking wicker hampers which she had bought from the Madeiran pedlars who came touting alongside the ship when we dropped anchor off the island. One of the wicker hampers was given to me and remained a source of great embarrassment for many years when I returned to England. I had to go back to school with it, instead of with the more conventional trunk used by my school·fellows.

Our journey to the Cape took three or four weeks. I saw sharks and flying-fish, I saw a soldier catch a parrot fish off Ascension and have his finger bitten off as he landed it ; I saw Napoleon's tomb at St. Helena, where I dawdled so long drinking fizzy lemonade that I was very sick in the street running for the boat. And meanwhile, my mother got mumps and had to hide herself away in the cabin lest she should be quarantined and not allowed off the boat at Cape Town. (A month before leaving England I had had whooping cough and chicken pox at the same time.)

We arrived at Cape Town to dock in the most beautiful harbour I have ever seen ; my grandparents met us at the boat, drove us to their house at Newlands, just outside the city, and that very same night I was sent to bed with mumps. It was three weeks before I saw any more of South Africa than I could see from my bedroom window. I passed the time designing gigantic submarines. Though

I was an averagely bloodthirsty small boy these contraptions were noticeable for their complete absence of any warlike purpose. They were filled with vast swimming baths, tennis courts and cricket pitches, with comfortable beds and huge stocks of food.

When I recovered and began to look around me I found a new arcady. The Meachams' house, Mariedahl, was set in a small pine wood which abounded with squirrels and moles. In the garden there grew figs, peaches and quinces and on the *stoep*—the tiled terrace of a single-storied house—hydrangeas apparently grew wild and had to be cut away to allow daylight into the ground-floor rooms.

The house faced south, towards Table Mountain which could be seen over the top of the pine trees. On the north side, hidden by a hedge of papyrus, there was the brewery —an ugly building which advertised Ohlsson's Lager in huge letters on a chimney. It was near enough to be convenient for my grandfather to work in and had its own railway yard. Above all, the brewery had its own shunting engine—a small, busy machine as out of drawing as a clockwork toy which I was occasionally allowed to drive.

Having had my ambition to drive a railway engine fulfilled so early in life, I began in Cape Town to think I would like to be a musician when I grew up. For the first time after five years of wandering my mother and I almost began to have a family life again. It is true my grandfather tended to take us all off to live in tents by the seaside while he painted, but at least our base of operations was a large house with a certain amount of family atmosphere about it ; my mother, her two sisters and young brother had spent much of their childhood there and the swings and seesaws built for them were still functioning for me. Also, for the first time for many years, we were living in a house with a piano. The instrument served to revive my mother's interest in music ;

she not only began to play Beethoven and Chopin again, but she also went to hear music at the first concerts she had been to since my father's early days as critic on the *Daily Telegraph*.

I cannot form any judgment on first-hand experience, for I was too young to know much about it, but I am ready to believe that South Africa is a very musical country with first-class orchestras at Cape Town, Johannesburg and Durban.   Certainly when I was there it seemed that music flourished healthily enough and I was taken to concerts in Cape Town and at Meusenberg, a seaside resort noted for its surf-bathing a few miles outside Cape Town in False Bay.

I wish I could say that I had started my concert-going career as spectacularly as I had started my theatre-going. But whereas my first visit to a theatre took me to see the *Agamemnon*, the high spot of my first concert was nothing more uplifting than Saint-Saëns' *Danse Macabre*.   There may have been a Beethoven symphony in the programme, but if so I do not remember it, and it obviously would not have impressed me nearly so much as the simple programme-music of Saint-Saëns, with its dancing skeletons and cock-crows and the rest.   I had outgrown my terror of brass instruments by now and nothing pleased me more than the sight and sound of a full-sized symphony orchestra with gleaming copper kettledrums and tubular bells and xylophones.   I thought the conductor, Theo Wendt, earned his living in the most marvellous possible way and thereafter, whenever my mother played the piano, I " conducted " her with all the gestures and mannerisms I had copied from Mr. Wendt.   When I was alone these same " conducting " actions accompanied tunes of my own which I sang and made up as I went along.

But though I was a constant visitor to orchestral concerts my interest in music took no practical form.   I had no desire to play the piano nor any to go on learning the violin ; I just wanted to be a conductor without the trouble of doing any hard work. Not that I gave the subject any serious thought ; I was still only six years old ; but I mention it because it is an attitude that has unfortunately stayed with me all my life. I have never worked hard at anything which promised drudgery of any kind ; I have never learned to play an instrument properly ; nothing I do is done with any solid technical foundation which might ever have involved great concentration or study. Such technique as I may possess of any kind is the result of learning a job while earning a living, the outcome of an enthusiasm for something which it has *amused* me to learn or which I have been taught in an entertaining manner. On reflection, the child of six who wanted to be a conductor was unmistakably the father of the man who never learned a trade or qualified for a profession.

For a few months life in Cape Town was idyllic enough. I went to a day school at a place along the railway skirting False Bay, where they made me read *Alice in Wonderland*, a book about a little girl in whom I was not in the least interested and which I didn't understand anyway. I learnt enough Afrikaans to read the notices about not spitting in railway carriages, and I left my precious wooden Swiss bear in a train ; there was excellent bathing at Meusenberg which I did not enjoy as much as I might for I did not learn to swim until I was ten. But I had no fear of water and consequently had to be watched very carefully whenever I went near it. There were motor rides, too, around Table Mountain and trips out to Stellenbosch to an old Dutch farmhouse where we collected masses of exquisite muscatel grapes which were brought back in the dicky of the car. I sat in the dicky.

Then we started travelling again. Together with my grandparents my mother took me in one of the more elegant Union-Castle boats up to Durban. I found Durban a romantic place from the start. There was a large whaling station to be visited and the bathing beach was enclosed in a ring of steel to keep out the man-eating sharks in which the sea abounds. And then there were the Indians—snake-charmers and jugglers who charmed and juggled and played pipes incessantly on the promenade outside our hotel. I do not know exactly how many Indians there are in Durban, but there are enough for them to have their own huge quarter with mosques and bazaars and all the smell and dirt that goes with them. My mother, as usual, spent a great deal of time and money in the bazaars buying brightly coloured lengths of silk and alabaster statuettes. Once more she found herself in her natural romantic element. She had toyed with Buddhism and was delighted to find Indians whom she could talk to without having to go to India to do it.

It was at Durban that my mother decided to learn to throw pottery on a wheel. In Cape Town she had journeyed miles out into the Province to find an old Swedish woman who taught her to spin. In Durban she journeyed miles out into the hinterland to find an old Indian potter who taught her to become proficient in a new craft. The Indian lived in a hovel and wore a loin cloth and a turban ; it was all very picturesque and exotic. But Durban does not lack colour at any time ; the most common form of hireable transport is the rickshaw, drawn by a Kaffir dressed up to look like a witch-doctor wearing horns, feathers, beads, bangles on wrists and feet and a make-up of whitewash.

The influence of the rickshaw boys and a visit to a circus decided me on another profession when I was in Durban. I was going to be a clown. I made up my face with water-colour, practised falls, wore my pyjama trousers (the only sufficiently baggy trousers I could find) and behaved in a grotesque manner which made me, personally, laugh myself sick.

Then, unfortunately, the question of school raised its sombre head once more. After a long, hot, train journey through fields of maize and pineapples up into the hills of Natal my mother delivered me at a boarding school called Merchiston in Pietermaritzberg. It was a school consisting largely, as far as I recall, of wash basins and half-finished buildings which between them made the whole place smell of carbolic and mortar. I did not particularly dislike Merchiston ; .on the other hand I cannot say that I remember it with any great affection. In the first place it was a soccer school, and I was passionately anxious to play Rugby, so much so that I " cut " my soccer games as often as I could to watch, with great envy and longing, Rugby being played by the boys of Pietermaritzberg College.

My mother got herself a job as music mistress at a girls' school further up in the hills, on the way to Pretoria, so that she saw me frequently, coming to 'Maritzberg to take me on the exotically named Umzenduzi River or having me to stay with her at her school at the week-ends. The girls' school was high up in the hills, a slow winding journey by train which landed one in rolling, veldt-like country thinly populated by Kaffirs living in kraals. In the course of these week-ends I made friends with a huge, graceful Zulu, a servant at the school, who gave me beads and taught me to speak fairly long sentences in his curious clicking language.

The country was wild, though not as wild as I had expected and hoped. I was anxious to see lions and jackals, which I had read about in a series of delightful South African fairy stories, but I saw none ; however, I did see a first-class veldt fire.

Eventually I left Merchiston. Of all the schools I ever

went to Merchiston seems to have made the least impression on me. Apart from the smell and the soccer I remember astonishingly little. There was a night when a hooter was sounded for two hours on end to announce a special edition of a newspaper giving the news of Kitchener's death ; and there was the pleasing fact that my head was the wrong shape for a straw hat, which meant that I did not have to go to church on Sundays. In 'Maritzberg, apparently, God would listen only to those who wore this ridiculous and uncomfortable headgear. I blessed His choosiness.

Otherwise my period at Merchiston was singularly unproductive of either education or personal experience.

We returned to England in the *Walmer Castle* which was largely occupied by troops, a noisy, cheerful contingent of South Africans who taught me bawdy songs and spoilt me with sweets they bought in the canteen. One of their officers was Billy Millar who took his place alongside Ulysses and the rest in my collection of personal heroes. Billy Millar had been captain of the Springbok Rugby team which had toured England in 1912 and my hero-worship knew no bounds. He took a great liking to my mother and spoilt me even more than did the men under him.

CHAPTER IV

MORNING FACE

IT was mid-winter when we arrived home and I was shipped off with my Madeira wicker-basket to become a boarder in Dr. Rouse's house at the Perse again. I will not pretend that I was very happy. I was only seven years old and although I had an independent nature and could amuse myself if my mother were away from me, I did not like being without her among a lot of strange boys. I was very homesick and I missed the freedom of movement, the constant moving around to new places which had come to be what I considered the normal way of life. I cried a great deal in corners and took a long time even to begin to adapt myself to my new restricted surroundings.

Miss Rouse, Dr. Rouse's sister, took it on herself to look after the four or five children of my own age who were still in the prep school. She bathed us and saw that we washed our ears, told us stories of boys whom she had had under her care and who had become legendary figures in her own mind as they now became in ours. She was a frail, busy little figure given to talking to herself and her kindness did much to alleviate the frequent misery of life in a boarding school.

The School House at the Perse was occupied by about thirty boys. It had always had a fair complement of Indians and Chinese and other orientals ; Dr. Rouse had spent some years in India (he had been professor of Sanskrit among other things) and his school attracted boys from all parts of Asia. In addition to the more exotic figures the war had landed the Perse with a number of Serbian refugees—tough little Balkan types who had a regrettable tendency to " swank." They were more or less house-trained, but only just.

I spent about five terms in the Perse prep, showing no great aptitude for any lessons except spelling and French. I played Rugby with a certain skill, developed a passion for cricket and limited my other athletic activities to running and winning fifty-yard races at the annual sports. My behaviour at school was light-hearted, to say the least. Having once got over the initial misery of unfamiliar surroundings I refused to take anything at all seriously.

I talked incessantly in class and concentrated only on those things which struck me as having any kind of future, such as drawing and painting and acting. I took up the violin again, but showed no great skill in performance. I am convinced anyway that I was not taught well ; I was given far too many " pieces," trifling bits of nonsense with fancy titles about fairies, and my intonation must have been ghastly judging from what I have learnt since of violin teaching. I shirked my practice, for I played the fiddle to amuse myself and not to impress my teacher by neatly done homework.

My holidays were spent with my mother wherever she happened to be living at the time, which was in a different place every time we broke up. There was a flat on a top floor in Denmark Street, which we frequently had to leave when there were air-raids (our nearest shelter was in a safe-deposit under Orage's flat in Chancery Lane), there were rooms in Bloomsbury, Ealing, Richmond, in Government huts in Coventry where my mother was responsible for the welfare of a thousand tough girls, mostly from Belfast, who made munitions. One holiday I spent with an uncle near Birkenhead ; he was something high-up in Lever Brothers, which appealed to me very much as I was then going through a phase of plastering my hair with brilliantine and there were always dozens of Lever products around the house. I picked on one highly coloured fluid, which smelt faintly of peppermint, and put it on my hair. I thought I looked very elegant, until my hair went quite stiff and stuck out like a porcupine's quills. Not knowing as much French as I thought I did I had not understood the label on the bottle : it read " Dentifrice."

None of the places where I spent my holidays could by any standard be described as " home," but their variety was in keeping with the life I had lived and there was considerable pleasure to be had at school from speculating where I would go at the end of term.

Meanwhile, I had become too much of a handful for the unfortunate women who tried to teach us at the Perse prep, and I was shot up into the Big School a year before my time, to find myself by far the youngest of 300 boys. If this removal was intended as a disciplinary action, I did not notice it. I was just as noisy and inattentive in classes taken by the grotesque figures called masters as I had been in the preparatory school. The penalties were more severe, but my bottom quickly became inured to repeated corporal punishment and as I could learn forty lines of Shakespeare in half an hour it was pointless to punish me with " lines." Besides, I liked Shakespeare and I enjoyed what was intended to be a hardship.

One result of this relegation to the Big School was to give me more interesting opportunities of playing games. Junior House Matches were confined to boys under fifteen ; thanks to my being thrown out of the prep I was a member of my junior house cricket and Rugby teams before I was ten, playing with boys four and five years my senior and not getting unduly knocked about in the process. A liking as well as a certain talent for games was something of a social asset even in a small Public School like the Perse. In my own case it made for a quieter life altogether. I drew, I painted, played the violin and acted ; I was " artistic " and, therefore, fair game for all the hearties in the house as a butt for their bullying. One's artisticness came in useful from time to time ; somebody had to paint scenery and play Beethoven's Minuet in G on the violin at the end of term concert. But the usefulness of being " artistic " was limited, and the only way for an artistic child to guarantee himself a quiet life was to shine in some other sphere. Skill at games was one of two sure passports to Popularity. The other was wealth enabling its owner to give lavishly from the contents of his tuck-box. He was assured of Popularity so long as his cornucopia of zinc-lined three-ply wood did not give out. My own tuck-box was a sad little concern given me by Miss Rouse. It had originally been an Army ammunition case ; it was a few inches high, painted grey, and had rope handles at the ends. At the best of times its beginning-of-term contents was no more than a pound pot of marmalade and a half-pound jar of blackberry jam made by my mother—a most reluctant, inexpert cook who made jam for the sole reason that she had collected the blackberries during a walk on the Sussex Downs and didn't know how to get rid of them. As a means of bribery my tuck-box had very few prospects. If Popularity was to be bought it had to be bought the hard way, and not through the stomachs of one's fellows.

I can only presume that the much-covetted, indefinable thing called Popularity *was* bought, for on the whole I spent a happy time at the Perse. Or at least I will admit, on looking back, that it wasn't quite the hell one might have expected. Life at the Perse was not something you really enjoyed while you were there ; it was something which you were aware of afterwards, realising that you had been extremely lucky in having been to a school that taught you a great deal without ever advertising the fact.

As soon as war finished in 1918, the method of education at the Perse began to live up to the glamorous illustrated prospectus I had first been fooled by nearly four years before. Masters began to come back from the War, and the somewhat *ersatz* form of teaching that had been held out as a carrot in front of the donkey's nose during the war years at last came within reach.

The man who did most to put the carrot in the donkey's mouth was Caldwell Cook. He was a tall, fair man who wore cycling breeches and smelt vaguely of perfume. By modern standards I suppose Caldwell Cook would be considered " arty." No matter ; his mannerisms were a little precious, certainly, but his method was unique. He was the English master, with a love of England, a characteristic tolerance of subject races (like the Irish) and a supreme patience with his less imaginative pupils (like the English) which endeared him to all who worked with him and assured him a place as one of the great pedagogues of our age. Cook died a typical English death ; he drank himself to death after he had been " retired " from the Perse. Thanks to the administrative stupidity that set an age limit on all teachers, regardless of their ability, he took to alcohol as the only possible antidote to boredom. There can be no worse fate for a teacher than to have nobody to teach.

I do not know quite where to begin in my personal assessment of Caldwell Cook. I was ten years old when I first sat in one of his classes. " Sat " is the wrong word. One never had any impression of having " sat " in one of his classes, for one was both physically and intellectually on the move the whole time. Cook discovered that the dullest, least likely child could write verse, provided (a) that the child was given an easy model to copy ; and (b) that simple verse could be accepted as a natural means of expression. Our earliest models were the lyrics of Robert Louis Stevenson and Shakespeare and, if we were setting out to tell a story, the Border Ballads.

The exposition of these models was entertaining and involved many things besides the recital of words. The first stage was the presentation to everybody in the class of a stick, a rough-hewn baton about 18 inches long. We then indulged in a performance known as " stick-wagging." Cook would stand before us and recite perhaps a couple of stanzas from *A Child's Garden of Verses* ; as he spoke he wagged his stick to point the rhythm of the lines, to describe inflexions and emphasise phrases. His gestures were no vague "interpretations" of poetry. Each movement of the stick was as conventional as Toscanini's beat. Toscanini has used the same pudding-stirring motion in the finale of Beethoven's Seventh Symphony on every occasion I have seen him conduct. The gesture is no affectation ; Toscanini always wants the same effect and his way of getting it is to use a motion which to him most easily expresses what he wants from the orchestra. Caldwell Cook's " stick-wagging " was as consistent as Toscanini's and as vivid. When we came to the lyric in *A Midsummer Night's Dream* with its chorus :

> Philomel, with melody,
> Sing in our sweet lullaby :
> Lulla, lulla, lullaby ; lulla, lulla, lullaby :

Cook brought out the music of the " lullas " with a curving gesture of his baton. The outline he drew in the air was known as a " lulla-fish," a dolphin-like creature to be incorporated in maps which he encouraged us to draw in the Elizabethan manner. These maps were known, rather whimsily, as " ilonds " ; they invariably described mythical islands full of treasure and pirates, and the seas around them were filled with lulla-fish. My own lulla-fish had a distressing tendency to turn into whales, but I could never resist the temptation to elaborate and by the time I had finished the poor creatures were burdened with palm trees, railway trains and public houses on their backs.

With the models of R.L.S., Shakespeare and the Ballads before us, Caldwell Cook then began the encouragement of original verse. I have no definite recollection of having been told to write verse as homework ; if we were told to do so then I am sure he never thought any less of us if we failed to arrive with a lyric of some sort. From time to time, Cook published an anthology of these children's

verses which he had printed in volumes known as the
" Perse Playbooks."

Among those verses written by my own contemporaries
the lyrics which stand out most prominently were almost
invariably written by small boys who grew up to be the
least prepossessing young men. At seventeen or eighteen
these pupils of Caldwell Cook's had grown into efficient,
dull, uncharming heirs to their fathers' businesses. When
Cook first did his stick-wagging at them (between the
ages of ten and twelve) they produced completely enchanting little masterpieces based on personal experience
and observation. Cook's method, unfortunately, was not
Jesuitical enough to guarantee the ordinary child's education after the age of puberty. He knew, as all great
pedagogues know, that children are naturally talented and
that there is no art to which they will not contribute something no adult artist can contribute : the child's view of
things. If he failed to keep his children to the channel
which might have led to mature development of their
natural gifts, it was not his fault. The domestic background of so many of my school-fellows began to make
itself felt when the question of A Career had to be considered. When their children are fourteen years of age
most parents begin to think of the easiest way of not
having to pay school fees any more ; education can no
longer be considered fun, and therefore a luxury. Invest-
ments must show promise of a dividend.

I don't know whether Caldwell Cook followed the
careers of his pupils closely after their first couple of years
with him. If he did, I do not think he was unnecessarily
disillusioned to see what happened to them. His concern
was with their education at a time when they were most
likely to be creative and unembarrassed by things generally
considered a bit " soft." As far as his own work was
concerned, a new crop of children came under his influence

every year and he was happy to see what each new batch could produce.

Caldwell Cook understood Education in its best, literal sense. He translated the Latin word *educere* and to him it meant what it means in the Oxford Dictionary : to bring out, to develop, from latent or potential existence.

Our next stage with Caldwell Cook, once we had mastered the rudiments of self-expression in verse, was the playing of Shakespeare, and I believe that this part of our education in English was the most important of all. Cook knew that our peculiar ability as children to write poetry about ourselves or our immediate interests was something that would not last. His teaching of Shakespeare, on the other hand, he knew to be something likely to remain with us all our lives, either consciously or unconsciously.

No lesson devoted to Shakespeare was ever spent in a class-room. The familiar restlessness of our "stick-wagging" had already accustomed us to the idea that education did not mean incarceration in a prison of desks and blackboards. As one grew older an English lesson with Caldwell Cook meant a general exodus from the main school building, across the play-ground to a dilapidated suburban villa called Pendene House. Whose house this building had originally been I never discovered. It was Perse property and had been for years ; in most of the rooms the damp had reduced the wallpaper to mouldy shreds, and the place smelt like a cheese cloth. One room only was at all habitable, and this was known as the Mummery. Caldwell Cook had taken this room and constructed it to represent an Elizabethan stage. There was a front-stage with steps leading up to it and a curtain separating it from the back stage. There was an auditorium with benches ; there were spacious wings, and below a basement known as the " tiring house."

It was in this theatre that we learned our Shakespeare.

At the beginning of each term one Shakespeare play was decided upon. Caldwell Cook then cast it. The most likely children were given parts to play ; those who had nothing to do on the stage were appointed property masters, effects boys and stage managers. Nobody was idle, not even in the very small audience that was left over after the company had been engaged. The audience had charge of what was known as the "hammer"—a fierce, polished affair like a knobkerry which had to be banged loudly on the benches if the slightest mistake occurred on the stage.

These mistakes came from misunderstandings of Shakespeare. Our performance, which lasted for three-quarters of an hour at a time, was in effect like the first read-through of a play. But the read-through was done with action and "props." Bells had to be rung, the curtain dividing front- from back-stage pulled at the right time and if the property master let one of the characters go on without his sword or the letter to be taken from his doublet then the hammer would strike. The fact that there were no stage instructions to indicate that a letter was to be taken from a doublet was no excuse. Shakespeare had mentioned the letter in the text and it was everybody's job, including the actor's, to see that the letter was in the doublet. If the child given charge of the hammer failed to notice the slip-up then the hammer was given to somebody else.

In this way we came to know what Shakespeare was all about. The plays became something real and alive. We were encouraged in our characterisation of the parts we played and we were largely cast according to our own temperaments as assessed by Caldwell Cook. I was considered to be Wild Irish, so I was given Cassius to play in order that the Tent scene in *Julius Cæsar* should be a jolly good quarrel ; and since I was musical I was expected to know the tunes to all Feste's songs in *Twelfth Night*.

The Caldwell Cook approach to Shakespeare is something which has stayed with me all my life. Those forty-five minute readings in Pendene House have repaid me a hundred times in hard cash. I learnt in the Mummery that a Shakespeare scene told the audience who was speaking, why, where they were, to whom they were speaking and what time of day it was. When I came to write my first radio play it never occurred to me to use a Narrator. I despised the Narrator as a device because I had been brought up to believe that dialogue should explain everything, and that if a character had to be explained by an outside person then that character hadn't made himself clear.

That Shakespeare model of who-why-and-where is one that has nearly always been passed by in the teaching of radio technique. Occasionally Shakespeare is rather patronisingly described as The Ideal Script-Writer and what a pity he didn't live to work for the B.B.C. But nobody really believes that, for the next thing that happens is that the Drama Department gets cracking with special fanfares composed at great cost to the licence-payer, and Shakespeare is presented with a troop of Narrators who succeed in explaining nothing that Shakespeare himself did not explain in the text of his plays. Still, if nobody " adapted " Shakespeare for broadcasting but left the texts to speak for themselves I suppose some producer's friend would have to do without an adaptation fee.

As with everything he taught, Caldwell Cook's Shakespeare had numerous by-products. When we came to the historical plays we found that the Richards and Bolingbrokes and Johns of Gaunt needed shields if they were to look at all imposing on the stage. And so we learnt the principles of heraldry, by painting the arms of the main characters on wooden shields. The elementary rule that

no metal should be used on a metal, no colour on a colour
was so instilled into us that the travesties of true heraldry
appearing on the arms of new seaside boroughs are as
disturbing as an E Flat in the chord of C major.

In addition to teaching us English as Shakespeare used
it (our edition of the plays gave us no artificial aids in the
way of accents on the last syllable of words like "followed"
—if we didn't see that it had to be read as "followèd"
there was trouble with the hammer), Caldwell Cook
taught us to speak English of our own in a class time
known as "Speeches."

"Speeches" were designed as a free-for-all opportunity
of self-expression. A boy would get up in front of the
class, go to the platform and deliver a lecture on any
subject that entered his head. He had the free use of the
blackboard on which to illustrate with diagrams and
drawings whatever he felt he could not make clear in
words. Again it was always the least likely children who
were the most articulate. A boy who is now a parson in
India was famous for his "speeches" on decoy ducks;
other favourite subjects ranged from "What I did in my
holidays" to talks on the Norfolk Broads, modern architecture, the internal combustion engine, sailing ships and
the London Tube Railways.

These last two subjects were my own perennials. During
a holiday in Scotland I had made a sail for a boat and
sailed in it; then I read Conrad and decided to be a
pearl-fisher. Which meant that I learned all there was
to be learned about sailing ships and their rigging. My
regular talk on the London Tube Railways had its origin
in the fact that my mother would give me a shilling to
amuse myself during holidays in London. I set out early
in the morning to discover how far I could travel by tube
without coming above ground. I usually stayed underground for four or five hours, travelling backwards and

forwards and changing from one line to another. To go
by Inner Circle was strictly forbidden by the laws of the
game. I don't think I benefited very much from this
pastime beyond exercising an already highly-developed
sense of orientation.

"Speeches" were fun, whether one got up to speak or
not. As a member of the audience one always had a
chance of getting control of the hammer, and the easiest
way to do this was to anticipate the lecturer's use of
forbidden phrases.

The word " bit " was not allowed. A " bit," said Cook,
was " something a horse can't chew." There was no such
thing as " a lot " of anything—unless you happened to
find it in an auction sale. And the word " nice," except
in its proper sense, was also forbidden ; and so was " got."
Like everything that Caldwell Cook taught us these little
proscriptions had a purpose ; they prevented us getting
lazy about our own language. Not one of us who was in
Cook's class ever got out of the habit of using lots of bits
of nice easy English when it suited us afterwards ; but
while we were there the speaking of correct English
became second nature. Any tendency to use long words
where short ones would do was strictly taboo ; we learnt
to speak and write clearly and simply.

One of the principal objects of " Speeches " was to give
the child self-confidence in public speaking. As far as
I am concerned this aspect of the thing failed completely.
I had no self-consciousness during " Speeches," but I
grew up unable to utter a word in the company of more
than a few intimate friends. Any suggestion that I should
speak in public terrifies me, and I am too afraid even to
accept an invitation to talk to school children in the most
informal surroundings. On the other hand, I have never
suffered from any form of " mike fright " ; I know that
my audience may be anything from one person to five

million and as I have no proof of it either way I am completely happy in the studio.

It was no use being self-conscious at the Perse, anyway, for the whole principle of education there was based on the co-operation of the child with the teacher.

The day we first started to learn Latin we were addressed by a slow-speaking Yorkshireman whom we knew as " Tabby." He said : " I don't suppose you know any Latin. But in a fortnight from now you'll be able to speak Latin standing on your head at two o'clock in the morning. And in a fortnight from now no English will be spoken at all in this class-room. If you want to ask a question or want to be excused you'll have to ask in Latin."

" Tabby " was quite right. Within two weeks not a word of English was ever uttered in class, and I had taken good care to learn the phrase for permission to be " excused " well before the deadline for all-Latin conversation had arrived. I delighted in the words " Licetne mihi exire ? " so much and I used them so frequently that after a time I had only to raise my hand to be allowed out of the class-room without further question. It wasn't that I had a weak bladder ; it was just that I hated sitting still longer than was necessary.

I experienced some trouble with the grammar of Latin ; I have always had the same trouble with any language I have tried to speak. But grammatical errors were no great fault. Latin was a live language to us, and the more talkative we were the better " Tabby " was pleased. To anybody not brought up on this " direct method " of teaching Latin it is probably difficult to realise exactly how fluent we became in the language. We read it, we spoke it, we acted in it—less than no excuse was ever needed at the Perse to act a play of some kind in any language—and we sang in it. Our songs were Latin

c

translations of English folk-songs we already knew, brilliant unexpected idiomatic translations of things like " The Vicar of Bray." Indeed, Latin became so much a second language to us that when I subsequently visited Italy again I found myself speaking Latin without realising that it was not Italian, and feeling rather hurt when I failed to make myself clearly understood.

The same direct method of language teaching was also applied to French. For a year or so our teachers concentrated on the *sound* of French ; we were taught phonetically and a bad accent among us was a rare thing. Great trouble was taken in showing us to speak the French " u " and how to make the *sons nasalisés*. It was a simple enough method and by the time we came to learn to read and write French in its orthodox spelling we already knew how to speak the language, for we had learnt little plays and nursery rhymes by heart without ever having been concerned with the look of the language. I am depressed to find how difficult French is made for the average schoolchild. So much time is given up to deciphering a language which is not easy to spell correctly at any time, that there is no time left to develop anything approaching a tolerable accent. At the Perse we learnt French in the way we had learnt to speak English : by picking it up by ear and then coming to the grammar and the spelling.

The sad thing at the Perse was that the method which made the learning of French, English, Latin and eventually Greek into something closely approaching an entertainment was never applied to subjects like mathematics, science and geography. The truth was, I believe, that Dr. Rouse had no interest in mathematics and the rest. He was always writing to my mother to complain that my progress in any kind of mathematics was nil and couldn't she please do something about it. She usually retorted that as she could scarcely ever make two and two add up the same twice running she was hardly the person to reprove me. The correspondence between the two of them was regular and abortive. Neither headmaster nor parent could do a thing about it.

I was by no means an unintelligent child, but to show any intelligence I had to be bribed by my teachers showing a little interest in me, or at least making their subject interesting. No mathematics master I had the misfortune to work under could ever convince me that the man who tried to fill a bath with the waste pipe full open was anything but a damn fool. Nor could I, with my miserable sixpence pocket money every week, be expected to take any great interest in sums about compound interest or flashy talk about stocks and shares. No doubt there is a way to interest children in this sort of thing, but if so it was never tried out at the Perse.

On the whole, the Perse was a school where they left you alone. Every opportunity was given to a child to develop his talents ; if you showed no particular interest, then they didn't worry you unduly. This was particularly true of Dr. Rouse when I came to learning Greek. He was so absorbed with what he had to teach that he had no time to notice those who were not with him. His greatest asset, perhaps, was his enthusiasm ; and you either found it infectious, or you did not. I remained uninfected ; it was not his fault ; it just happened that at the time " The Old Man " came to teach me Greek I had another enthusiasm of my own which I considered more important than his. I have lived to regret it—in a way ; but I think it is largely a regret based on a natural desire to have cakes and eat them. I never lost my interest in Greece, and I still cherish a book which Dr. Rouse gave me when I was six—a delightfully written collection of heroic stories by Andrew Lang ; but the actual learning of Greek was something which did not appeal to me. It

meant a certain amount of hard work and there seemed
to be no short cut. Even with Latin I had found a short
cut of sorts ; it bore a relation to English, French and
Italian and I could recognise Latin words as being the
basis of words I already knew. Greek, on the other hand,
supplied me with no easy linguistic contacts, and I got no
further with it than learning the alphabet and singing
Dr. Rouse's inevitable songs.

In writing about the eight years I spent altogether at the
Perse I find it difficult to sort out exactly which of my
experiences occurred at school and which of them during
the holidays. Things happened during the holidays which
had a far more sudden and lasting effect on me than
anything which happened at school ; and yet in many
ways my private and public life, as it were, became one
and the same thing. An enthusiasm aroused or a decision
made during the holidays was inevitably developed and
affected by my return to the Perse.

During the Christmas holidays of 1919, my mother,
Jack and I went to stay with Eric Gill near Ditchling ;
my mother had known Gill since she had been a girl and
I believe appears anonymously in a characteristic episode
of his autobiography. The Gill *ménage* can best be
described as a " set-up." Its uncompromising atmosphere
of Roman Catholicism I found not a little sinister. There
was a considerable amount of splashing of holy water at
the saying of grace before meals, and there was an
interminable nightly performance of compline around a
spinet with Eric Gill taking the part of cantor and singing
plainsong in an unmusical voice.

Life in the household was frankly rather " basic."
Water froze in washbasins, bread and butter were home-
made and eaten off wooden plates ; the only lighting was
candlelight, and the members of the family were mostly
dressed in clothes that had been spun and woven in the

colony of Ditchling. It was a craftsman's home, with Gill carvings and shrines and woodcuts over every available mantelpiece, and doorway and in every corner. It was by usual standards a more than somewhat arty-crafty household, and even I (who had had no great surfeit of physical comfort) found the domestic existence a little austere. But from a purely æsthetic point of view it was no ordinary arty-crafty collection of *objets* that decorated the Gill interior ; it was a craftsman's home, but it was the home of a master-craftsman and it was no less a pleasure to live with a magnificently carved and lettered fireplace because it happened to have been done by the occupant of the house instead of by an outsider.

The Christmas we spent with the Gills was " old fashioned." There was snow and ice and no great attraction in getting out of bed in the morning, though I got up early enough to go to an eight o'clock Mass on Christmas morning. This had nothing to do with religion ; it was just that after having fallen hopelessly in love with one of the Gill daughters I had philosophically transferred my affections within a matter of hours to an Irish girl called Mollie. She would be there at Mass and I wanted to take her some handkerchiefs as a present.

I was very impressed by the ritual of the Catholic church and I liked the tune of " Adeste Fideles." The Mass seemed a great improvement on the compline as celebrated by Eric Gill, and there was nothing in his house to compare with the beauty of what must have been a shabby, tawdry waxwork crib I had seen in the church during Mass. The idea of being a Catholic was beginning to take root and though it did not flower fully until a year later it began to play a leading part in my life—if only a subconscious one.

As far as my " private " life was concerned I had rather muddled views as to what I should be when I grew up.

I had no hobbies ; I had serious occupations each of which I was determined to take up as a vocation. Some of these occupations ran concurrently as it were ; thus I found myself at one time absorbed by the idea of being a sculptor and an editor, at another I was obsessed by the determination to be a singer and a professional cricketer.

My ambitions as an editor were comparatively short-lived, and my activities were limited to two editions of a magazine called *The Studio Magazine* (registered offices : Hammersmith Terrace). The first number I wrote, illustrated and bound myself. It included poems, a leader proclaiming the policy of the proprietor and the first instalment of a serial (fully illustrated) which was never continued, not even in our next. It was my greatest desire at that time to get something into print, and as elder boys at the Perse had had verse published in *The New Age*, I too, sent numerous poems to Orage for his consideration. They were rejected, so I had to fall back on " publishing " them at my own expense.

The second number of *The Studio Magazine* was more ambitious. I produced it during a later holiday when my mother and Jack had taken a cottage near Ditchling (registered offices : Hickory Cottage, One O'Clock Lane). The move to this five-shilling a week cottage meant that I spent a great deal of time at Eric Gill's farm a mile or so away, and so my second and last venture as an editor produced a crop of distinguished contributors. Eric Gill did me a cover, Hilary Pepler (Gill's printer) wrote me a verse, and a young man called Desmond Chute drew me a couple of drawings. Desmond worked with Gill, had a flaming red beard, and later became a priest in Italy. He is also cousin to my second wife, Barbara McFadyean, but I did not know this at the time as Barbara was then only three years old and I had not yet met her.

There were no expenses involved in the publication of my magazine, so I made a handsome profit by circulating the entire edition (one copy) among my friends for two-pence a look.

Frequent contact with the Gill colony led inevitably to two things : I became a Catholic, with Desmond Chute as my godfather, and I decided I would be a sculptor. My mother, being a liberal atheist, had no objection to the former decision and was delighted by the second as it kept me busy all day. I worked diligently around Eric Gill's workshops and in due course carved a foot-high Crucifixion which I promptly sold to Pepler for half-a-crown.

I took my enthusiasm for sculpture back to school with me, and as I showed a little talent for drawing I was allowed to copy photographs of the Michelangelo David and Donatello's St. George during our drawing lessons instead of having to do birds and machine-drawing with the rest of the class.

Two new masters arrived at the Perse in 1919 both of whom dealt with children intelligently. One was a man called Hambleton, who was a good musician and a clever water-colourist with certain academic gifts. He took a liking to me, developed my interest in music by playing Bach to me, fed me with cream buns after school and gave me a plaster cast of the Venus de Milo to draw.

The other was George Lyward, who became house-master at Dr. Rouse's house. The post of housemaster at the School House was usually filled by a young man who was just about to graduate at the University and later to become a schoolmaster of some kind. The post carried on teaching duties at the school itself, of course ; it was just a very pleasant way of spending the third and fourth years of one's University career out of college—if you liked that sort of thing.

Lyward came to the House as a refreshing change after

a series of rather colourless characters whose names I can no longer remember. He was a choral scholar of St. John's College ; he sang my father's songs, was reading for a degree in Italian history and was a first-class rugger coach. The combination of these qualities and a charming personality endeared him greatly to me and I was very sorry when he eventually left.

Our first point of contact was Italy and Italian art. In exchange for the loan of a precious copy of Vasari's *Lives of the Italian Painters*, which my mother had given me, Lyward lent me some magnificent German editions of books on Italian painting. I could not read the text but every one of the superb photographs told me a story.

In only one respect did Lyward ever fall short of my ideal : he took a very superficial interest in cricket. As a Rugby coach he revolutionised our playing at the Perse. He introduced the New Zealand formation of eight forwards, a wing forward, two five-eighths, three three-quarters and full back. He was a great talent-spotter and within a season the school had beaten its great rival, Emanuel School, home and away. Lyward was a sound psychologist, what's more. The School team included a Jewish boy at five-eighths who had a talent for kicking dropped goals. When the first match against Emanuel was played Lyward offered a prize of five shillings for each dropped goal ; the cash-prize proved a great incentive and the Jewish boy cleared fifteen shillings in the afternoon.

As a junior I got my share of Lyward's coaching and took the game more seriously than ever. In the holidays at Ditchling I spent hours every day running about with a ball, all by myself, swerving past imaginary opponents, kicking imaginary goals, scoring imaginary tries for Ireland against all-comers. As far as I know, there were no spectators of these remarkable efforts, but if there had been they would have thought me completely out of my mind. As an only child I amused myself by the most elaborate forms of let's pretend, bursting into blank verse as I walked along or tying a ping-pong ball by a string to the ceiling and knocking it for imaginary sixes with a bat in epoch-making Test Matches of which I was always the hero.

I suppose I must have been a lonely child ; but it never struck me that way at the time. My phantasy world was filled with admiring, applauding spectators who were so numerous that I had to refuse them my autograph and beg them to let me get away from it all.

If Lyward contributed nothing to my progress as a cricketer he was responsible for my first taking more than a passing interest in music. Hitherto I had plodded along unsuccessfully and unindustriously with my violin playing. I was proud to be known at school as the son of the man who had collected Irish folk songs, but it never entered my head to be a musician when I grew up.

While Lyward was our housemaster he began to study the part of Hymen in Purcell's *The Fairy Queen* which was due to be performed at Cambridge in the Lent term of 1920, and I began to be interested in this new form of music which, though it was sung, was not just " songs," but opera.

CHAPTER V

BIRTH OF A PASSION

MEANWHILE, my father re-appeared in my life. He had come back from the war and taken over the responsibility (a little reluctantly, I think) of paying for my schooling.

c*

Hitherto, my fees had been paid by Jack and my mother's father, and my father's contribution was welcomed by all. It was obvious that Herbert could make very little of me when he met me again ; my mother's influence on me was strong and he had the good sense to see it, even though he may not have liked it. At any rate, he made no attempt to exercise his legal right to have the custody of me ; he was content with the doubtful privilege of footing the bill and leaving it at that.

Herbert was friendly, however. He automatically disapproved of my ambition to be a sculptor ; it had met with my mother's approval and that was always enough to set him against any idea I might have as to my future. Equally he was opposed to my being a Catholic, again because my mother had countenanced it ; although, as his elder sister was a convert, it may have been that he thought one Papist in an Orange family was enough. He realised, however, that reconversion was likely to prove an unprofitable job so he said no more about it. Instead, he concentrated on the business of dissuading me from any kind of artistic career. He had visions of me in the Consular Service and also spoke at length of the attractions of the Sudan Police (or something) and how I ought to get a rowing blue, which apparently would be a great help. As only eight people out of some 3,000 at Cambridge ever row in the Boat Race any year this did not strike me as a particularly easy way of qualifying for a job I didn't want—especially as I had never shown any great talent for rowing, but preferred sailing.

My father was not to know it at the time, but if ever he had hoped for me to take up a gentlemanly career he did the worst possible thing to achieve his ambitions for me. He came up to Cambridge for the performance of *The Fairy Queen* and took me to watch a rehearsal.

With Lyward already singing the music of Purcell's

opera to me at the House, my father's action was fatal.
He gave me the opportunity of seeing the opera come to
life at close quarters. As Lyward was singing in it, we
were all allowed to go to the theatre to see *The Fairy Queen*,
but I doubt if I would have been so attracted to opera
if I had not already seen the wheels going round. From
that moment I made up my mind I would be a singer and
appear on the operatic stage.

Though my voice had not yet broken or anything like
it, my ambition did not strike me as any less reasonable
than my father's desire that I should get a rowing blue.
As a first step I joined the choir at the local Catholic
church.

Being a Catholic at a non-Catholic school had many
advantages. For one thing there were special feast days,
like St. Patrick's Day, which carried with them dispensa-
tion from school (provided one went to Mass). For
another, one was spared the boredom of going for a
Sunday afternoon walk by serving at Benediction. I don't
think I was ever a " good " Catholic ; I tended to be
bored by non-participation in what was going on in
church. But so long as I was allowed to swing a censer
or ring a bell or sing a Mass there was nothing I enjoyed
more. I have never closely analysed the reason for my
conversion any more than I have ever analysed the reason
for my ceasing completely to take any interest in the
Church after the age of fourteen and a half ; but if I had
to have a religion then my entire upbringing, my love of
Latin countries, of music and a general feeling for the
theatrical provided as good an explanation as any other.

As a boarder at the Perse I wasn't able to attend the
regular choir practice, but I had a preview of Sunday's
Mass on Friday evenings. Our choirmaster and organist
was a round, chubby sacristan called Clarence. He had
a sharp " Cymbridge " accent, rang the Angelus, sang in a

very high alto and played appalling hymns on the carillon.

I liked Clarence immensely and looked forward to our intimate rehearsals when he took me through my part, playing the piano and piping out the more disturbing counter melodies. I cannot vouch for the quality of the singing at the church of Our Lady and The English Martyrs, but the standard of music was high, especially in Lent when there was no organ and we struggled through the *a capella* Masses of Palestrina and Vittoria.

I read music easily at sight, so eventually much of our practice time was spent up in the organ loft where Clarence played Bach to me while I pulled out the most inappropriate stops. My contribution to the performance resulted in the most deafening noise and in order to make audible his protesting " Naow ! Naow ! Not the firty-two foot ! " Clarence had to stop playing and push all the stops in again.

To my regret Clarence never taught me how to read plain-song. Its use in the choir was occasional and cropped up only at the grander Requiems. " Only " is rather an understatement, for I sang in precisely one Requiem ; it was a liturgical one in which I improvised from music I couldn't read and which lasted almost as long as death itself.

These early experiences of music were further encouraged by my mother during the Christmas holidays of 1920. I had written to tell her about *The Fairy Queen* so that when I arrived at her bed-and-breakfast lodgings in Kensington she had already lined up another Purcell production for me to see. It turned out to be *The Beggar's Opera*, but no matter ; there were Purcell tunes in it and it served to fan a growing flame of enthusiasm for the musical stage.

During the following two years I saw *The Beggar's Opera* fourteen times. I knew everybody's lines by heart and worshipped Frederick Ranalow above all mortals except V. W. C. Jupp and J. M. Gregory who were cricketers. I did not realise how firm my building up of Ranalow as an *Ich-ideal* had been until a few years ago when I had to conduct him singing at the B.B.C. I got to know him as " Fred," but it was almost more than I could do to ask him to sing his song a little faster.

My further ambitions in music were somewhat interrupted in the summer of 1921 by the revival of my determination to become a professional cricketer. I had taken six wickets for three runs in a junior house match at school and made eleven runs (two more than the total by the other side), and by the time I came to spend my summer holidays at Ditchling there was no stopping me. I lived and dreamed cricket. I saved up my pocket money in order to buy the daily papers to read the latest scores, I parted my hair in the middle in imitation of my great idol, Vallance Jupp, and during the holidays I had a season ticket from Burgess Hill to Brighton in order to take a train to get the close-of-play scores in the *Argus*.

I queued up for hours to see Sussex play the Australians at Hove, and I was an intolerable bore for several terms afterwards when I recalled how Sussex had been the only English county to lead the invincible Australian side on the first innings. I read Wisden's from cover to cover and every word that appeared in *The Cricketer ;* and my joy knew no limits when, returning to school in the autumn term, the long summer drought of 1921 had made the ground too hard for football and we played cricket in late September.

But with the coming of winter my loyalties began to be divided once more. I wrote my first piece of music. It was a simple setting of " Who is Sylvia ? " and I gave it to Robert Broome, the school music master, who put a piano accompaniment to the melody.

As I did not have piano lessons I did not directly come in for any teaching from Bob Broome. I played under him in the school orchestra, where I tore out such tunes as were ever given to the second violins, but that was about the limit of our official association. Privately, however, Bob never ceased to help me ; he later lent me books on theory, counterpoint and orchestration and whenever he came up to the House to teach would take time out of somebody's piano lesson to play and talk to me.

By the time Christmas came round again my mother had resumed her wanderings. This time she and Jack had gone to Egypt to excavate and for the first time I spent my holidays in my father's house in Chelsea. The entire family seemed to be there, including my actor uncle Stanley who was " resting " and my young Aunt Dorothy who had married an actor called Guy Pelham-Boulton. Guy was then appearing as a Chinese servant in *Bulldog Drummond* with Gerald du Maurier ; now, for some reason, he is consul in Haiti. I never got all the Hughes family's activities straight ; but then I never really knew them very well.

The three weeks spent in London that Christmas merely served to whet my appetite for the theatre ; and it was very nearly satisfied. I was taken around a great deal to shows of all kinds, including my first revue. It was called *A to Z* and they spoke highly of two new youngsters called Gertrude Lawrence and Beatrice Lillie. And, of course, I paid several visits to the Hammersmith Lyric to see *The Beggar's Opera*.

I said nothing to my father of my interest in music, as I knew he would disapprove. If I had been a budding Kreisler or a new Mozart he would have done nothing to help ; he spent the rest of his life trotting out the old line of my-son-mustn't-go-through-what-I-went-through, and I already knew enough then to keep my mouth shut on the subject. So my public show of interest in music at home was limited to playing the pianola and singing duets from *The Beggar's Opera* with a new young singer called John Goss, whenever he came to the house.

My tastes in music were already very catholic. I liked anything with a tune to it, whether it was Chopin coming out of the pianola, Handel from *The Beggar's Opera*, or " Her Mother Came Too " as sung by Jack Buchanan in *A to Z*. This broadness of outlook, which I am glad to say has never left me, was further cultivated at school by my close friendship with a French boy with the unlikely name of Kelly.

Roger Marius Kelly had arrived at the House from Paris unable to speak a word of English. He was very unhappy to begin with, and as I could speak French tolerably well I had more or less taken pity on him and tried to cheer him up. I found we had a great deal in common ; he was a Catholic, he played the violin very well and had a liking for the kind of metropolitan High Life which attracted me.

Kelly's first couple of terms at the Perse were magnificent. As he understood nothing of what went on in class he could take in only what he could see ; and what he could see struck him as immensely funny. Certainly some of the masters had peculiar mannerisms and looked pretty odd ; seen, as it were, in dumb show the whole thing was a slap-stick comedy of the most enjoyable kind to Kelly. He played the fool incessantly and when reprimanded by an exasperated monoglot master would turn to me with a puzzled, smiling, " Qu'est-ce-qu'il dit ? "

In due course, Kelly began to learn English, but he was very backward with his reading ; he learned his phrases by ear. Thus, seated one day in a community bawling-competition known as " Singing " when we had reached the chorus lines of " Strawberry Fair " we were a little alarmed to hear Kelly shouting at the top of his voice, not the words " buttercups and daisies," but " bottoms of the ladies."

From Paris Kelly brought not only lurid stories of the sex-life of the French capital, but also a bundle of popular French songs printed on broadsheets. These tunes, consisting only of words and a top melody-line, we sang and turned into violin duets ; we devoted most of our practice time to this kind of improvisation and learned nothing from it of any academic value whatever.

If my association with Kelly did nothing for my " serious " musical education, it certainly improved my French. We became inseparable companions, and I was delighted, after hearing his picturesque descriptions of Paris and glowing talk of his beautiful sister Alice, when I learned that I was to spend the Easter holidays in Florence. The journey to Italy would mean a night in Paris, and we planned a tremendous night out together.

My mother and Jack had left Egypt and had arrived as far as Florence on the journey home. It was therefore arranged that I should travel out to them, but my plan for a hilarious night in Paris was scotched by my having to escort Jack's mother on the journey to Italy.

I use the phrase " escort " advisedly, for though I was only thirteen years old I soon realised that I knew far more about travelling than my elderly companion. It was a nightmare journey, for Mrs. Gunn, not having travelled on the Continent since 1913, had not realised that the exchanges were slightly different from what they had been then. Tips to porters of 10 centimes in France and 10 centesimi in Italy led to some embarrassing scenes, but poor Mrs. Gunn was convinced they were all just a lot of greedy foreigners and that all their performance was worth was ten cents a dance. I failed dismally as a peacemaker. on these occasions, with my natural tendency to answer invective with invective in any language, and quiet was restored to the scene only when the trains pulled out of the stations where the incident had occurred.

As far as Paris and Kelly were concerned, our projected orgy was limited to a fruitless visit to a theatre to see *Les Cloches de Corneville* (there was a weekly *relâche* when we got there) and a weary trek to find a cinema that performed *en permanence*. We drank a great deal of Dubonnet, which made me unaccountably hungry, and spent an hour playing records on the slot-machines with earphones on the boulevards. I never met Alice.

Once in the train to Italy, Mrs. Gunn kept waking me every half hour or so to make sure that we had not arrived at Turin, and I comforted her by replying when we reached Melun that we were at Modane. It was a dismal journey and I was glad to reach Florence.

My third visit to Florence did more than anything to foster an interest in music which was already becoming more than a passing one. For the first time, indeed, I had actually taken my violin with me on my holidays ; I did not practise, but I played a lot—from Italian broadsheets and from an elegant edition of Corelli sonatas which had attracted my attention in a shop by its pretty cover.

But the greatest of all experiences was my first visit to an Italian opera. We went to the Teatro della Pergola to see *Falstaff*. We sat on steps in the topmost gallery which we reached after apparently buying a new set of tickets on each floor as we went up ; I was so excited that I was nearly sick at the sight of the lovely theatre, with its gilt and its rows of boxes, the heavy velvet curtain, the smell of the garlic in the audience and the sound of the cacophonous tuning-up which is peculiar to Italian opera houses. This, I realised, was *really* opera.

It is difficult, after nearly twenty-five years, to recall exactly how great an impression that performance of

Falstaff made on me, for I have seen the opera many times since. But I remember clearly that Mariano Stabile sang the name part, that "Quand'ero paggio" was encored innumerable times, that I was immensely intrigued by the pinching chorus in the last scene and that I probably saw a better performance of this Verdi opera than I have ever seen elsewhere.

The fate of Mariano Stabile, the greatest Falstaff of our time, is one of the mysteries of the war. He was reported to have been killed by an R.A.F. raid on Milan, and yet no mention of the fact was ever made on the Italian radio. As an Italian friend, working over here, said : "Fascist propaganda could hardly have failed to make something of it, because Stabile was almost a cultural monument."

Easter in Florence brought the usual amount of religious entertainment with it, including High Mass with a large string orchestra at the Annunziata and the ridiculously pagan performance at the Duomo when a firework dove is lighted at the high altar and shot out along a wire to set light outside to a huge waggon filled with fireworks and drawn by four white oxen. On the result of this exhibition of pyrotechnics (duly blessed by the archbishop) depends the success of the harvest. The fireworks nearly always go off ; if they don't, or if the harvest is bad anyway, the peasants have probably forgotten all about it by the time September comes round.

After Easter we moved out to Fiesole, to live in a little house overlooking the Arno valley. Our address was Via Giuseppe Verdi and it was from there that I made my next excursions to see Italian opera.

A visit to the Politeama to see *Traviata* was followed the next morning by a recital of the principal arias by Giulia, our landlady. She had a powerful voice which she used unsparingly to carry on conversations with her neighbours several doors away. For some reason, Giulia and her husband went off on a journey and left us in sole occupation of the house. The housekeeping was entrusted to me, as I knew more Italian than my mother and step-father, and the nightly checking of accounts with our local Mrs. Mopp was a peculiar ritual. Signora Radazza (which is a fair enough translation of Mrs. Mopp) was a toothless old illiterate with the fine classical name of Fulvia. She did the shopping for us, but as she could not write there was some difficulty with the reckoning. Fulvia could write numbers and she could add up, but she could never remember what she had spent the money on ; she could only guess at things, so that when she presented the account the figures had to be attached to the most likely purchases. She never cheated us ; she merely confused us. It was to Fulvia that I found myself talking Latin. She seemed to understand ; she was certainly nearly old enough for it to have been her native tongue.

My mother passed her time at Fiesole learning another of her crafts. This time it was book-binding, which she learned from the local barber. As with all her other manual pursuits, she learned to do the job perfectly and then threw it up. I have a copy of *Pinocchio* which she started on. Unfortunately, before she had got as far as putting a cover on it she turned her hand to something else, and the book remains as she left it—sewn but unbound.

I tried my hand at bookbinding also, but found it a dull and sticky business. I never inherited my mother's gift of concentration and single-mindedness, with the result that I spent the time in Fiesole painting water-colour landscapes, playing my violin in a pine wood, and conducting imaginary operas with a paint brush as baton. My mother set out to teach me the piano, but failed again because of my lack of concentration ; in the middle of

a lesson I would decide it was all too difficult and go
off up to the monastery to paint my favourite view of
Florence.

It was at Fiesole that I composed my next piece of
music. It was a minuet in D for the violin, and was
almost note-for-note the tune of Paderewski's minuet ;
what wasn't Paderewski was from one of Haydn's symphonies. I wrote it all out neatly in purple ink and label-
led it " Opus 2."

If I can be said to have concentrated on anything at all
it was on the purely passive pastime of listening to opera.
I spent my pocket money on piano scores of *Carmen*,
Lucia, *La Gioconda*, *I Puritani* and a whole lot more which
I lost long before I could appreciate them ; and as often
as possible I would persuade my mother to take me to the
Politeama. If she was too busy or too bored with the
idea, then I would take myself off to a matinée of an
opera in some back-street theatre.

I spent half a crown in this way to sit in the front row
of the stalls at a performance of the *Barbiere*, which
struck me as being a really comic comic-opera and I
thought it would be nice when I grew up to be a bass
and wear a funny hat like Don Basilio and get all the
laughs. I enjoyed the *Barbiere* immensely, except for the
woman who sang Rosina. She had a mouthful of false-
teeth, and the coloratura part that Rossini wrote displayed them to their fullest, most hideous advantage.
I suppose it is too much to expect a coloratura soprano to
keep her mouth shut, but I have found all through my
opera-going career that prima donnas' teeth tend to get
between me and the composer of coloratura roles. This,
I may say, in spite of the fact that I accepted the usual
ridiculous conventions of opera and its performers
willingly from the moment I first saw that rehearsal of
The Fairy Queen. I am used to Mimi looking like a

BIRTH OF A PASSION

hogshead, and I expect all tenors to move as awkwardly as wicket-keepers, but I have never felt anything less than embarrassed when confronted by the smirks and grimaces, the tongues and teeth of coloratura sopranos.

I always hoped when Hollywood took up Grand Opera (meaning the Bell Song from *Lakmé* and that bit from *Martha*) that a solution would be found ; unfortunately, the cameramen seemed to take an added delight in giving one close-ups of the epiglottis, instead of drawing a discreet filter across it all.

I wouldn't be without coloratura sopranos for one moment ; I admire virtuosity in all its forms and I can think of nothing worse than cutting " Caro nome " from *Rigoletto* or the Queen of the Night from *The Magic Flute*. It's just that I wish something could be done about the look of the thing.

I must have absorbed the Italian operatic conventions pretty thoroughly even during the few weeks of an Easter holiday spent in Florence, for I cannot recall anything in my life until then which filled me with more alarm and despondency than a performance I heard at the Politeama of *Tristan and Isolda*.

Jack was a great Wagnerite, and I was more than curious to hear some of the music he had kept telling me about.   *Tristan* appeared in the repertoire one week, so I begged to be taken to hear it.

Now *Tristan* is hardly the kind of music for a child of thirteen to cut his Wagnerian teeth on, still less if that child had come to think of opera in terms of *Falstaff*, *Traviata* and the *Barbiere*.   I was not yet interested in the orchestra ; I was interested in singing, and *Tristan* was all orchestra and no singing—at least, there was no singing of any tune the gallery could join in as there always was in what I understood as opera.   *Tristan* was a direct challenge to all that I knew as music, and I would have none of it. I came away from the Politeama confirmed in my belief that opera was an Italian art and not to be invaded by foreigners. *Fuor, stranieri. . . . !*

I will admit that I heard only two acts of *Tristan*. Owing to the Italians' highly civilised habit of starting their performances at 9 p.m. it was nearly one o'clock in the morning by the time the second act had finished. We had to get back to Fiesole and our last tram went at 1.30 ; we caught it, but even so we had to walk the last couple of miles uphill from San Domenico. On the road to Fiesole I heard a nightingale singing for the first time in my life ; the sound came from an avenue of cypresses, a clear, welcome voice after an evening of Wagner, revelling in its own virtuosity, never repeating a phrase but going on to the next part of its tune confident in the knowledge that if you liked that last bit there was plenty more where that came from. It was all as Italian as Verdi, who threw away " Celeste Aïda " and " Questo o quella " in the first few minutes of operatic masterpieces and never mentioned the subjects again.

Jack was at this time toying with the idea of settling down in Italy as curator of some Egyptian museum or other. To do so would have meant his becoming an Italian citizen ; he thought seriously enough of the idea to let his deliberations take him and my mother off to Rome for further discussions with whomsoever it concerned. In the way peculiar to our family life I was left alone in Fiesole to cope with Fulvia and fend for myself.

I did not lack company altogether, for I was able to visit a young English artist and her two young daughters in a nearby villa. Rosalind Baynes was the daughter of Hamo Thornycroft, the sculptor, and as she had had a picture in the previous year's Academy I was convinced that she was an R.A. I was a great snob about that sort of thing. Actually, Rosalind's exhibit had been no more

than a miniature of the Villa Medici ; but Princess Mary
had bought it as a souvenir of a honeymoon spent the
other side of the wall from Rosalind's villa.   To me
Rosalind was not only R.A. but also obviously entitled to
put the words " by Appointment " on her notepaper.

Rosalind also played the piano, and hearing of my
hero-worship of Ranalow dug out a vocal score of *Figaro*
to reconstruct for me the glories of the famous Beecham
production in which Ranalow and Frederic Austin had
both appeared.   Her telling of the details of a performance
which my elders still talk about was vivid enough to make
me think that I had missed something, but Mozart's
music meant remarkably little to me.   *Figaro* played on
the piano is hardly the best introduction to the work at
any time ; but the truth is that Mozart is essentially a
composer for adults, and at thirteen years of age the music
all went too fast for me to take it in.   However, Rosalind's
recital must have made a subconscious impression on me,
for when I first heard *Figaro* some years later a great part
of it already sounded familiar.

A telegram from my mother sent me careering off on a
peculiarly hot and unpleasant journey in an overcrowded
third-class carriage to Rome.   I arrived there with a cold
and just had time to see the catacombs, drive in a car to
Frascati and drop a cough lozenge from the inside of the
cupola of St. Peter's on to the roof of the High Altar
below, before I developed tonsilitis and retired to bed.
We stayed in a pension near the Piazza di Spagna which
turned out to be a kind of Communist headquarters.   As
this was before the advent of Mussolini's castor-oil tactics,
the comrades were still fairly active ; though all I saw of
their activities was the sour faces they pulled at an old
American friend of ours who came to visit me.   Poor
Margaret was regularly greeted with cries of " Sporco
borghese ! "   She may have been bourgeois, but she was

certainly not filthy, least of all when judged by her
abusers' standards.

My bout of tonsilitis delayed our return to Florence
and with it, I was glad to realise, my return to England.
It was the cricket term I was due back to and yet I
couldn't have cared less. I was hoping strongly that Jack
would take a job in Italy so that I could spend the rest of
my life there and never have to wear a school cap again.
I had been very miserable about my school cap during the
first few days of the holidays in Florence ; I had worn it as
protection against the sun, but its appearance was too
much for the Florentine street-urchins who followed me
about, pointing at it, roaring with laughter and summon-
ing their friends from side-streets with shouts of " Guarda
il berrettino ! " I thought even sunstroke was preferable
to this humiliation.

It was more than a month after term had begun that
I eventually set out for England, carrying my precious
vocal scores but minus a real conductor's baton which I
had pestered my mother to buy me. The only batons she
had been able to find were made of ebony and decorated
with silver handles and scrolls. I was not against having
one of these, but it was thought I had better wait to be
presented with an elaborate and expensive baton of this
kind by My Public at some future date rather than buy
one just then.

On the journey home I acted as chaperon to Rosalind's
children and their nurse. The children got out at Zurich
and thereafter I was responsible for the safety only of Ivy,
a girl of eighteen whose welfare I took very seriously.
Our troubles began at Bâle, where we discovered that
summer schedules had come into operation ; with the
result that we arrived in Paris late at night with no
immediate connection for England and not enough money
between us to go to a hotel. We reached the Gare du Nord

to find not only that there were no boat trains, but that the whole station was shut. Ivy and I spent the rest of the night on a luggage truck in the station yard which excited no particular comment by the scores of French soldiers on Whitsun leave who had been forced to do the same. It was a restless night, but mercifully warm ; I made friends with a Senegalese soldier who gave me a fierce cigarette and bought me coffee, and also (to ensure that I should come to no harm) introduced me to a couple of gendarmes to whose care he entrusted me. I had great difficulty in explaining Ivy to him ; I said she was *une bonne*, whereon he remarked that he thought I was a little old to have a nurse. I explained how I had come from Italy, but this only convinced him that I was Italian. As an example of clarity in conversation our *causerie* was not a great success.

Back in London I did not immediately set out to return to school. My mother, always a leading figure in my conspiracies, had arranged for me to recover from the journey by staying a couple of nights in the studio of a painter friend (a real R.A., this one).

I didn't waste much time in London. On the first evening I set off to the second-anniversary performance of *The Beggar's Opera* at Hammersmith, on the second my hostess offered me the choice of seats for two operas. One was *The Magic Flute* at Covent Garden, the other was *Faust* which was being done by the Carl Rosa at the King's Theatre, Hammersmith. I chose *Faust*—wisely, I now realise, because *The Magic Flute* is the most difficult of all Mozart's operas. Even today it is a work which I have to hear again and again simply because each new performance seems to bring out something which I missed the time before. In the right sense, *The Magic Flute* is the last music I want to hear on earth.

I sat in a box for *Faust* and applauded Marguerite

enthusiastically ; I showed good judgment in this, for the artist was a new young singer called Eva Turner and I thought she sang in the manner to which I was accustomed. As for the rest of the performance I wrote to my mother that " it wasn't bad, but the singing *WAS* different." Which, considering how homesick I was for Italy and its opera, was a very generous way of putting it.

I arrived back at school over a month late, bearing with me my vocal scores, and a harmony primer and book of 158 opera plots which I had bought in the Charing Cross Road. I was evidently beginning to take music seriously ; the opera book was my constant companion and I took it to church with me disguised in the cover I had ripped off my missal. The cover fitted perfectly and the 158 plots passed the time during sermons most profitably. I presented a figure of unusual devotion, and succeeded in betraying no surprise when, opening " The Standard Opera-Glass " one Sunday, I read the remarkable sentence which began : " Though Verdi is far beneath his celebrated predecessors Rossini and Bellini, he is highly appreciated in his own country. . . ."

My next two holidays—summer and Christmas—were miserable. My father was too busy or did not want to see me and my mother had no settled home of her own, so when term ended in July I was boarded out at a farm in East Anglia. I loathed it and eventually ran away from it, after the farmer had beaten me with his belt for unwittingly carrying some disease I didn't know about from one set of pigs to another. I packed my suitcase and set out across country to Oxford where I knew my mother was going to stay. I had no more than 1s. 6d. in my pocket, which took me as far as Cambridge. At Cambridge I took a train to Oxford ; I had no ticket, but gave the collector my mother's name and address when I reached Oxford, put my luggage in the cloakroom and started to walk the nine miles to the house where my mother was to be. She arrived there a couple of days later and showed no particular surprise at finding me there. For the rest of that holiday I was happy; I had gate-crashed my way into a charming and comfortable country house belonging to Professor Seligman, who was a doctor and anthropologist, a Fellow of the Royal Society and whose occupation fascinated me to the extent of deciding me to become a doctor—a decision which lasted about seven months.

My most troublesome vice at this time was motor bicycles. It was all right so long as I did no more than send for all the available illustrated catalogues; I did a lot of wishful-riding that way. But when I got back to school I discovered a means of hiring a machine in Cambridge, which led to a number of escapades involving the risk of serious disciplinary action if I had been found out.

By the time the Christmas holidays came round, my mother had embarked on what I believe is really her final career : she had gone to Vienna to look into the question of psycho-analysis. My father again seemed disinclined to let me spend my holidays in London, and with a shameful disregard for manners I scrounged a roof over my head from an unfortunate school-fellow, a day boy to whom I was not greatly attached. I used the wretched boy's home as a hotel, hired a motor bicycle and spent Christmas Day all by myself on the road to London. Sensing on my return that I was not really very welcome in that Cambridge house, I returned the motor bicycle, packed my things and set off for London by train.

I am ashamed to say that I can barely remember the name of my unwilling host ; I owe him more than an apology ; I owe him thanks for first introducing me to the playing of Heifetz and Kreisler, for the household I had barged into was a very musical one and there was a considerable collection of gramophone records of violinists.

In London I scrounged a succession of beds from such school-friends as had the misfortune to be on the telephone, and ended up by staying with Clifford Bax's first wife, Daphne. I had known Daphne all my life—indeed, I am led to believe that I was conceived in her studio early in 1908—and I was relieved when I finally settled down for a couple of weeks with someone I knew and who was fond of me.

I can offer no excuse for my unfortunate behaviour at this time ; I can only explain it. My mother, with her own complicated life to live, was helpless to do much for me and presumed that as my father was in London he would look after me. My father, for his part, presumed that my mother always arranged everything for my welfare. The result of this was that nobody looked after me at all. A little thought on the part of my parents would have made all the difference. At a little over fourteen years of age the only thing I wanted to do in the holidays was to be put down among all the bright lights of London and allowed to go to theatres, to hear music and have a Good Time like the other boys at school. I was starved for what is now called Glamour and in my hungering state I didn't care whose bodies or feelings I trampled over to get even the smallest taste of it. It was disgraceful and it might have been avoided, although I can't see for the life of me how—in the circumstances.

Before taking me off to her house near High Wycombe, Daphne Bax did something to appease my yearning for lights and music. She took me to see *The Immortal Hour.* This dreary piece, with its pentatonic *longueurs* and bogus atmosphere of Celtic Twilight, hardly qualifies as Glamour, heaven knows, but it was at least something I had been missing : it was opera, with singers, and a real orchestra in the pit.

When we arrived in Buckinghamshire I was fully resolved that I would write an opera, and in Daphne's house I found what I considered the ideal libretto. It was a play in verse by Clifford Bax and the subject was Aucassin and Nicolette. My " composing " at first consisted of nothing more than propping the libretto up on the piano and strumming out tunes to fit the words. I had not learned to play the piano. At school I had persuaded Dr. Rouse to let me get up early in the morning and play on his Bechstein in the drawing room next to his study. The noise infuriated him and I can well imagine why. I was " picking out chords " and my interest in the piano was purely harmonic. I could play tunes on my violin, but only the piano could give me the harmonies to fit those tunes, and I " picked out chords " with a repetitive persistence and inaccuracy which must have been maddening to the uninterested listener.

My " composition " of *Aucassin and Nicolette* began to take on a little shape, though it tended to be interrupted by my trying to vamp a song of Melville Gideon's called " If Winter Comes," which I had heard Mel sing in *The Co-Optimists* and to which I was devoted even more than " Coal Black Mammy," another inescapable tune of that Christmas season.

It was not until I returned to school that I found time to start writing down the music of my opera. I wrote it almost exclusively during Greek lessons given by Dr. Rouse and its course was interrupted only when the class burst into song with a Greek version of " The Vicar of Bray " and " Oh dear, what can the matter be ? " My otherwise undisturbed concentration on *Aucassin and Nicolette* was made possible by Dr. Rouse's own absorption in the teaching of Greek ; he took notice only of those boys who took notice of him, and as I never opened my mouth except to ask to leave the room, I gave him no trouble.

I completed the first version of *Aucassin and Nicolette*. It was in the form of a vocal score of exactly 32 pages— the 32 pages of the manuscript book I had written it in. If it had been performed it would have lasted about ten minutes, including time taken to change the scene six times.

The Lent term of 1923 was a busy one in many ways. I trained hard at the only branches of athletics which interested me, the high jump and the hurdles. I won both events in the under-fifteen age group and my record for the hurdles still stands. The event had never been run until 1923 and the following year the distance was altered from 100 yards to 110 yards.

In these I was coached patiently by W. R. Seagrove, the Cambridge and Olympic runner, who had recently become our housemaster and also played the violin nicely.

I think I deserved to win, however. Two years before we ever ran over hurdles at the Perse I had prac- tised hurdling in the garden at Ditchling in the hope that one day the event would be included in the school sports. I took up hurdling with a most uncharacteristic thorough- ness ; I studied action pictures of the great Earl Thomp- son, the 1920 Olympic champion, read books about it and apologised to the Almighty in my prayers for being so inattentive in church but please would He arrange that I won the hurdles. By the time it actually came to running the race at Fenner's I had begun to be fairly sceptical of the power of prayer and attributed my success to my own endeavours. God, I remembered, had pre- viously let me down badly in a swimming race, the final of the fives and the first round of the under-seven-stone boxing. In each of these events, however, I had lost to bosom chums so I felt no bitterness over the result. But I still felt God had let me down a bit—at least according to what my priest had told me.

During this Lent term of 1923 I began to have trouble with Mother Church. In the first place, I found that my father confessor couldn't answer very straightforward questions. I had read about doctors who had massaged the heart during an operation and brought the patient back to life. Now, I said, what happens about a fellow's soul in a case like that? Does it appear before God for a few seconds to await judgment, and if so isn't God going to look pretty silly, condemning a soul to Hell, when that soul is going to return to life at any moment and wake up from an anæsthetic?

I was told that " there are things we do not know about." It was the worst possible answer to give. I had been brought up to believe that The Church had answers for everything ; the idea of the Church being ignorant in a simple matter like the massage of the heart was something too disillusioning. Either, I thought, the Church ought to keep up with the progress of medicine or it should think up some quick answers. What it must never admit was that " there are things we do not know about." I had lapped up the most impossible fictions during my instruction as a convert, made allowances in my own mind for obvious propaganda because I knew that by believing in it I was justifying my conversion ; but this was a factual question and the Church had evaded it.

The influence of Mother Church cropped up in one other way, and it was a way which finished me as a Catholic for good and all. My father, despairing of ever being able to bring me up to his way of thinking, suddenly decided that perhaps my religion could be used to keep me in order. As a result of one of Herbert's letters to

Dr. Rouse suggesting that " Patrick's religion " might be something to work on, I was conscious of my priest beginning to work on me. I suffered moral lectures where previously my hours had been spent with him discussing the Sinn Feiners ; a friendly man suddenly turned into a schoolmaster and, as such, he became a natural enemy. The Church, which had been a peaceful retreat hitherto, a kind of playground in which education and recreation had been an entertaining mix-up, now began to spell Discipline with a large " D." I resented having my faults and bad manners pointed out to me at any time ; to have the Church do it in my spare time was more than I could bear. I remained polite in my attitude towards the Church, but underneath I was rebellious and waiting only for the day when I would be free to cock a snook at the whole set-up.

The exploitation of " Patrick's religion " was a conspiracy which I quickly saw through. The Easter holidays loomed ahead and I would be sent to some filthy farm again, probably a Catholic one this time to make matters worse. I wrote to my mother in Vienna and told her the whole story. It was an ingenuous and moving letter, describing how my pocket money had been stopped for the past two terms because some bastard had stolen my O.T.C. flute from my desk, and how I was getting sick and tired of being preached at by parents, guardians and priests. The letter's effect was immediate. My mother arranged that I should spend my Easter holidays in Vienna with her. How she managed to fix this I do not know. Perhaps it was that Herbert had by now realised that my mother's influence on me was probably the most effective, even though he openly disapproved of everything my mother did for me. To the end of his life he could rarely bring himself to be genuinely affectionate towards me ; his dislike of my mother (which was really nothing to do with me) coloured our relationship to such an extent that he attributed my every action to her. He complained always that he was never told anything of my ambitions and activities ; he was never told for the simple reason that he would have disapproved as a matter of principle. My mother and I were never very hot on matters of principle, and we preferred a quiet life. In any case, frankly, we neither of us felt that what I did was anything to do with Herbert. He had contributed little to my education except a few reluctant pounds, while my mother had gone through hell to feed and keep me during the 1914 war. Herbert, in fact, was very much out of touch with everything ; so much so that when Dr. Rouse, at the end of the Lent term of 1923, had written his usual letter suggesting that I should be removed from the Perse, my father took it seriously and agreed to the suggestion. My mother was used to getting these letters *every* term, but she had taken no notice of them. She just sent me back to school at the right time and disappeared into Europe, defying Dr. Rouse to do his worst.

And so, with two certificates for winning the high jump and the hurdles, the memory of having been captain of the team that had won the Junior House Rugby competition, a copy of Prout's book on orchestration, the score of a slightly Schubertian movement I had composed for string quartet and the first pages of a revised, Italianised version of *Aucassino e Nicoletta*, I left the Perse School for good and England for the next three years.

CHAPTER VI

NAUGHT FOR TEARS

My eight odd years at the Perse had been eventful enough, but by no stretch of the imagination could they be described as the Happiest Years of My Life. I have two recurring nightmares, and one of them (happily less frequent in recent years) is dreaming that I am back at school again. The dreadful thing is that now there is no chance of having to go back to school I am aware that I was very lucky in having been sent to the Perse, and I almost feel ashamed that I did not make more of the opportunity. I have forgotten all my Latin, I learned virtually no Greek, and yet I am conscious that those years at the Perse gave me something which probably no other school in England could have given me : it gave me a background which has enabled me to enjoy life far more fully than I might otherwise have been able to do.

If I had a son I would send him to the Perse without hesitation—provided it was the same Perse School that I went to. Unfortunately, when Dr. Rouse retired, and with him all those masters who had helped him to build up the Persean tradition of education, the school was given a scientist as headmaster and it was announced with pride that the school had acquired ten new wash-basins during the year, where hitherto it had been content to send three or four classical scholars to the University every twelve months and call it a day.

I cannot personally claim to have had a classical education or anything like it ; at least, not in the accepted sense. But during eight years at the Perse the *atmosphere* of the classics was so strong that it would have been an unusually insensitive child which failed to breathe it into its blood. It was an atmosphere that somehow permeated every subject in the curriculum (always excepting mathematics and science). Nor were the results of examinations taken too seriously. If you had any sort of feeling for English, for French, for history, your teacher sensed it instinctively and cultivated it for you. Only in this way can I possibly explain how I came to be awarded a prize for English. I wrote a most unsuccessful paper in the English exam., and yet when the annual Speech Day came round I had to go up on the platform and collect a couple of handsomely bound and embossed volumes as an English prize. Caldwell Cook had obviously thought that I liked English and therefore I should be rewarded for helping to make his life easier ; I had no academic claim to be considered a prize-winning pupil. As far as English is concerned I have grown up with remarkably little talent for its practice, and for somebody whose profession has led to the pouring out of millions of words my vocabulary is astonishingly limited. I have an insatiable curiosity as to the meaning and origin of words, but then at the Perse amateur philology was encouraged and any tendency to ambiguity severely stamped on.

Education at school was largely " fun." As a result, we grew up with very few unpleasant memories of the subjects we learned, and there was virtually nothing (with the two exceptions I have cited already) that was so dull as to have unhappy associations for one in the years that followed. The average English public schoolboy leaves history and Shakespeare and the rest behind him in the classroom. We took ours with us into our adult lives.

I made friends fairly easily at school and I had three bosum chums, one of whom is still an intimate and confidant. All three of them were Catholics and shared my own outlook on life to a great extent. There was

James Patrick Mullett, a red-headed Dubliner whom I fought bitterly on his first day at school and from whom I would not be thereafter separated until he left and went to Belgium. Jim Mullett later became a priest at the Cambridge Catholic Church, but I have not seen him since he was at school. I had a mischievous notion to visit him in his confessional and discover what kind of a penance he would give me for having made his nose bleed so many years before, but I never got round to it.

Kelly I never saw again after saying good-bye to him in Paris on my way to Vienna. He was dead set on following his father's profession as dentist and as he was a boy of considerable determination I have no doubt he went on to follow this peculiar career successfully. No child of fourteen wanting to be a dentist could surely ever grow up to be anything else, for dentistry is hardly something one would take up late in life. It is a childhood ambition realised, or nothing.

Then there was Francis Malcolm Baker-Smith who completed the Mullett-Kelly-Hughes-Baker-Smith quartet. Francis (professionally known as Malcolm Baker-Smith) is now a B.B.C. producer, but he arrived there by way of the first scholarship ever granted at Cambridge in architecture.

After three years at Cambridge, Francis got his first job. He went to Reno to build a Burgundy château for an eccentric American millionaire who had bought the castle in France, torn it down and transported it brick by brick to Nevada. Francis supervised its re-erection in America and then went off to the Pacific coast. There he passed the time as a motor salesman, as art director in Hollywood, then as art director with the Santa Barbara Repertory Company. After four years in the States he came back home to work with René Clair at Pinewood and when television was started by the B.B.C. he went as the world's first television art director to Alexandra Palace.

Francis, who stayed at school until he was eighteen, is a more typical product of the Perse than I am. His conversational Latin is fluent, and before the war it was always worth while being in a public house or a tube while he and his elder brother carried on a conversation in Latin in order not to be understood. After 1940, of course, this game lost its charm. The London public grew so used to foreign languages that a couple of rude remarks in Latin passed without comment, and the Baker-Smith Brothers could have been mistaken for a couple of Free Fighting Utopians.

How far the Baker-Smiths were " good " Catholics I would not like to say. Christopher, older by several years than Francis and myself, set out to train for the priesthood. He stalked about Rome in the dismal black garments of the *seminarista* but eventually decided it was not worth the price of all those candles, gave it up and married, to be called Father by his children instead of his parishioners.

Francis made up his mind about his relationship to Mother Church relatively early in life. Related to a Monsignor, he was sent away from the Perse for a while to attend a Catholic school elsewhere, mainly in the hope that he might become as great a dignitary of the Church as his distinguished kinsman. Unfortunately Francis had an experience at this school which wrote off whatever prospects his parents may have had of his attaining any eminence in the Church. With the characteristic, over-zealous tactlessness of so many priests the headmaster of the school broke the seal of confession. Francis had confessed to some trifling breach of school regulations to his father-confessor ; whereupon the priest jumped out of the confessional, threw off his robes and resuming the

part of headmaster, threatened Francis with expulsion
there and then. It was too late to fire Francis, however ;
he had already quit. He packed his bags and went home ;
his mother came from Kerry, but the words that rang
through his head were the old Ulster words of " To hell
with the Pope ! "

Of my less intimate friends there was a child, to whom
Francis and I were quite attached, called Marius Goring.
Marius was younger than we were ; we are all three now
contemporaries, of course, but in schooldays there was the
couple of years difference between us that made us almost
of different generations. Marius Goring, during the war,
was in fact head of the particular German department of
the B.B.C. at Bush House where I worked, but at school
he was a junior, with a mop of red hair and a fixed idea
of going on the stage. He had unusual talent as a child
and gave no hint of growing up into an expert in " neu-
rotic " parts. His first public appearance was in a play
by Walter de la Mare at the A.D.C. Theatre in Cambridge, and during his Christmas holidays he appeared
in London with Jean Sterling Mackinlay. At that time,
when he was still only ten or eleven years old, Marius
Goring could have played Peter Pan to perfection, if
some enterprising manager had had the sense to see it.
On the other hand, Marius' Peter would probably have
put a stop to the convention of casting musical comedy
actresses in the part and he would have been difficult to
follow with another boy-actor when his voice had
broken.

There was in addition to the School House at the Perse
one other large boarding house. This was called " Hillel
House," but known generally as " The Jews' House," as
it was inhabited entirely by Jews. It was in no sense a
ghetto ; it just happened to be convenient to have forty
boys of the same faith living under one roof so that Jewish

ritual, cooking and general habits could be observed with a minimum of complication.

To be a Jew at the Perse carried with it even more " perks " than being a Catholic. There were all kinds of local festivals which kept one away from school, and never by any chance did the Jews have to go to school on Saturdays. Like the School House, the Jews' House were a cosmopolitan lot. Some had parents who still spoke Russian or Polish in the home, others came from Gibraltar, and there was one very picturesque character from Syria. The Syrian was something straight out of the Old Testament, and he was greatly admired for his skill with a sling. He rarely failed to bring down a stationary rook at fifty yards.

I found many sympathetic spirits among the Jews, for they were musical and attracted by the glamour of the theatre as I was. As schoolboys they showed more talent for mathematics and science than for classics and the humanities. It may have been an instinctive racial enthusiasm that made them understand the meaning of stocks and shares better than the rest of us ; but it may also have been due to the fact that the mathematics master was also their housemaster at Hillel House and he had a reputation for being a martinet.

I made several friends among the Jews, and there was not one of them that did not go out of his way to invite me to stay in his home if I was at a loose end in London. I took particularly to one boy whose life was spent at school in waiting only for the day when term would end and he could get back to the London theatres. Dick was a charming figure, completely non-co-operative as far as Perse education was concerned, who knew all the biographical details of the leading stage stars of the day. He was in a sense the Fool of The Family, inasmuch as he played no musical instrument and when last I saw him was making a roaring success of a snack-bar off Leicester Square. His younger brother was a cellist and he had two sisters who played the violin and the piano excellently. Dick, however, shared none of their talent, and was inclined to be a disturbing influence in the home. His interest in music was confined to the appreciation of *Kitten on the Keys* and he distracted his sister Leah from her practice of more lasting classics to make her play it.

I spent a couple of nights in Dick's London home ; I was remarkably comfortable and very much impressed by my first experience of the intimacy and generosity of Jewish family life.

I do not remember that there was any suggestion of anti-Semitism at the Perse. The term " Jew " was never even thought of as an insult ; but then tolerance was something we learned very soon and very thoroughly at school. During my time there we were subconsciously educated to perceive the evils of tyranny and intolerance from the start ; to behave properly towards our fellow human beings, whatever colour or creed, was as natural to us as raising our caps to a master or to a schoolfellow accompanied by a woman.

In any case, any other behaviour would have made life impossible. In the course of eight years at the Perse my schoolfellows included Serbians, two French boys, a Belgian, an American whose Minnesota accent made us sceptical of his claim that his father was a professor of English, two more Americans, a couple of brothers from Vladivostock, and the variety of nationalities found among the Jews.

Then there were a Chinese, two Burmese (one of whom had a brother who was a billiards half-blue at Cambridge), a boy with a Welsh father and a Japanese mother (he got a cap for Wales as a Rugby international), a champion swimmer from the Argentine who introduced me to *mattè*, and a Turk who played the violin, drew well and boxed with the elegance of Carpentier.

And, of course, there were innumerable Indians. I was fag to one of them who was known affectionately as " Squash-eye." He was a great athlete but not very bright academically. When last I saw him he had been nearly four years at Cambridge and was still struggling to pass Little-go. In those days there was no need to pass this comparatively simple entrance examination before going into residence at the University.

I was devoted to Squash-eye and fagged for him willingly. He was also my favourite cricket umpire, for he had been umpire during a match with a local prep-school and had allowed my optimistic appeal for leg-before-wicket. It was an out-swinger which would never have hit the wicket, but Squash-eye gave the batsman out. The batsman was K. S. Duleepsinjhi.

My only comparable cricket memory is of being bowled for a duck by J. G. W. Davies early in the war. As Jack Davies had once bowled Bradman for a duck at Cambridge I went back to the pavilion convinced that, according to the all-important law of cricket averages, I was no worse a batsman than Bradman.

I made the journey alone across Europe to arrive in Vienna in March, 1923. If I had any preconceived idea of what Vienna would be like it was based on what I had read in biographies of the famous composers. I expected to find a Vienna of luxury and light, inhabited by aristo-crats commissioning masterpieces with the nonchalance of a pre-war housewife ordering a pair of cutlets from her butcher. The very sound of the name meant glittering musical salons and ovations for Chopin's playing, and I was a little disappointed to find that the place was known locally by the abrupt, uneuphonious name of Wien.

D*

Vienna, in the early days of 1923, was neither gay nor the city of my dreams. The rate of exchange was stable enough, but it needed a certain amount of readjustment to get used to thinking of the pound as being worth 220,000 kronen ; and it was obvious that the people were desperately poor. People in this country who have experienced nothing gloomier than utility clothes cannot conceive the drabness of the Viennese in those days when shoes were still made of brown paper and not even the *poules de luxe* had silk stockings.

Food was not short ; it was just that few people could afford the prices. This was particularly the case with the professional middle classes who were hardest hit of all. They had no foreign exchange to turn into kronen and they were not cared for by a Socialist government as the workers were. If they could afford to eat out at all then it was in a kind of communal kitchen ; if they were too poor for that, then they had to get along as best they could with a couple of rolls and a slice of garlic sausage.

Lotte, who came to teach me German, was a Jewish girl studying at the University to be a teacher. She came in the mornings bringing her " lunch " with her to eat in the tram on her way home. Lotte's main meal of the day consisted of two hunks of dry rye bread and some *leberwurst*. When we asked her if she would like some butter on her bread, she laughed, thinking that we were joking ; when she realised that we were in earnest she burst into tears.

Lotte's case was typical of thousands of her class and generation.

During the holidays I was to spend in Vienna, my father wrote from England to say that Dr. Rouse would not have me back at the Perse, and thinking that my mother's influence would be best in the end Herbert entrusted me to her care with the suggestion that I should stay on in Vienna indefinitely, learning German and eventually becoming a doctor. I was bitterly disappointed at this news because the next term was the cricket term and I was still passionately devoted to the game. In any case, I felt that studying medicine could probably wait a year or two.

However, by the time a certain amount of argument had gone on in letters between my mother and Herbert I had changed my mind altogether and decided finally that I would be a musician. My father was thoroughly bored with me by now; he had married as his second wife an actress from the Abbey Theatre, called Suzanne McKernan, and had begotten himself a daughter. He would fulfil his legal obligation to support me until I was sixteen and then he would wash his hands of the whole affair.

I can't exactly blame him; I had been no great source of pleasure to him since I was about four, and he attributed his disappointment in me to my mother. In what precise way I was to earn a living at sixteen was obviously no concern of his; let my mother worry whether I could support myself or not.

As soon as I had resigned myself to having left the Perse I allowed Vienna and its music to envelop me completely. I learned a few phrases of German quickly and began to read the posters on the kiosks. Any mention of the word *Konzert* always attracted me and I badgered my mother or Jack to translate the details. Nine out of ten of these promising announcements were of nothing more than the Viennese equivalent of the *café concert*, and after a while I learned to look for the operative word *Sinfonie* before asking what it was all about.

One particular poster excited my curiosity for a long while; it advertised what I took from the illustration on it to be a dancer who appeared in the nude. As I progressed with the German language I began to realise that the lurid silhouette of a naked woman was no mere ballyhoo ; the blurb announced that Fräulein Whoever-she-was would in fact dance in the nude, and went on to say that she was without doubt the greatest exponent of her art in the world.

I pestered my mother to take me to the cabaret where the lady's performance was to be seen in a *scena* entitled "Venus in the Fur-coat." My mother, sensing that the early stages of puberty were probably the best time to rid me of this kind of obsession, agreed that it might be great fun and off we went to a little dive on the banks of the river Wien.

"Venus" duly appeared in her fur-coat, removed it, displayed an ample bare bosom, galumphed around the stage to music and the curtain fell. It was all a great anti-climax.

After the show we went back stage, not to see the famous *Nakttänzerin* but for my mother to talk to one of the other acts, a singer calling herself "Carmen Hill." My mother had been at the Academy with an English singer of this name and it struck her as a little odd that a former fellow-student should be appearing on the same bill as a befurred Venus. Closer inspection of "Carmen Hill" revealed that the whole thing was a case of mistaken identity. The cabaret singer was a blowsy gypsy who spoke not a word of English and was obviously somebody else of the same name, though how she came to pick on a name like Carmen Hill we never discovered as our German wouldn't run to that kind of small-talk.

On the way home in the tram my mother asked me how I had enjoyed my evening and what had I thought of "Venus in the Fur Coat." I replied : "Oh, it was all right. But I'd rather see you in the bath any day."

My curiosity had been satisfied, however, and my first experience of nudity on the stage was as boring as the last, which was at a burlesque theatre down town in New York ten years later.

The great adventure over and done with I settled down to concentrate on more noble pursuits. I began a third version of *Aucassin and Nicolette*, this time writing it straight into full orchestral score.

The music of this opera was still childish nonsense, of course, but it was beginning to show a slight sense of form. Tunes began and ended in the right keys and the layout of the whole thing suggested a rapidly developing sense of dramatic contrast and the operatic stage. Aucassin's heavy father was very carefully characterised ; his part was full of villainous " Har-Har's ! " but at least his music could never have been mistaken for Nicolette's.

On the other hand, a great deal of what went on in that score could have been mistaken for Wagner's music. During my first month in Vienna I discovered Wagner with a vengeance. My first visit to the opera was to see *Lohengrin* and I so far forgot my upbringing in Italy as to see seventeen German operas before I heard a note of Verdi again.

To a boy of fourteen, experimenting with " music drama " and orchestral noises, Wagner has an obvious appeal. The naïve quality of Wagner's " drama " with its swans and dragons and general air of a pantomime transformation scene is just the thing for the adolescent. With the exception of *Rienzi* and *Die Meistersinger* every Wagner plot is cluttered up with magic and entirely impossible situations and incredible people dying of broken hearts. As a result Wagner's most plausible opera, and the one that remains the most attractive to the normal opera-goer, remains *Die Meistersinger*. Here, at least, the tricks performed on the stage are human tricks performed without supernatural aid, and if the hero dreams his prize-winning song and plugs it throughout the third act then that is not so far removed from everyday life either. As others had done with *Turandot* and *Otello* and *Figaro* and *Carmen* Wagner at last picked on a subject which could have happened, even if the action on the stage takes almost as long as it would have taken in real life.

But to me at fourteen, Wagner was the creator of a new world. To begin with, there was the huge orchestra with its rows of horns and tubas in the *Ring*, painting pictures in the orchestra pit in case you mistook the bed of the Rhine for Brighton Aquarium. Then there was the revelation that it was no longer necessary to write a long, formal tune for the singers to get their teeth into. All you had to do was to think up three or four bars at a time and with any luck they would last for four whole operas, provided you repeated them when anybody on the stage mentioned the person or subject with which the *motiv* was associated. And as all Wagner characters are constantly telling the same story over and over again—in case you missed the point the first time—these snippets of themes come in for full employment and theatrical security.

However, at an age when I was not troubled by operas which began before tea instead of after dinner, Wagner was a constant source of excitement. I frequently fell asleep during performances, but no harm was done ; on waking one had only to keep an ear open for the next *leitmotiv* and catch up with things from there. It was a foolproof method and nobody in the audience could ever complain that there was no tune to whistle on the way home. Take the big Siegfried theme, for instance, the one that recurs in Wotan's Farewell, in the Funeral March and every few moments in the last two days of the *Ring*. Anybody can whistle that tune, and when you think you're stuck and can't remember how it goes on you suddenly realise that you've got just as far with it as Wagner ever did, because he couldn't get any further with it either. Even in the famous quintet in *Die Meistersinger* Wagner never lets you down. He starts off with one of the most beautiful phrases a composer ever invented, a phrase which looks like going on for ever like a soaring Verdi ensemble. It lasts twelve bars until Wagner suddenly remembers he mustn't enjoy himself too much ; at the unlucky thirteenth bar back comes the wretched plug-number and the magic is broken. He has kept faith with his public and given them a stunted tune to whistle ; but he has broken all faith as an artist who created a lovely tune and never had the courage or ability to go on with it.

In recent years I have lost all interest in Wagner. As I admit his genius so I recognise that he was the greatest musical menace that ever lived ; his influence is inescapable in the same way that Hitler's influence has been inescapable. In the same way that you and I can directly credit Hitler with the fact that we have to queue for a bus, so must Wagner bear the responsibility for so much of the music of the past fifty years, for the fat, stodgy musical thinking that has obscured what should be a clean, clearly defined art. It had been such an art up to his time and no doubt it will be again ; but the infection still hangs around in the blood-stream of Western civilisation ; and while the Italian tradition survived until the death of Puccini, while the public shows an increased inclination to turn to the music of the Russians, of Debussy and Sibelius and the younger English school, the Wagner-coccus has yet to be cleared away.

Wagner himself admitted that he had to " learn " to compose as though it had been a foreign language. What was he, then, if he wasn't a composer ? A dramatist ? Hardly. A good dramatist would not have been so repetitive and long-winded, nor so humourless and unoriginal in his plots. Wagner was a phenomenon that cannot be explained ; he bears as little relation to the general current of music as the popular crooner bears to the normal standard of singing. Both are Things ; both attract fanatical supporters who are blind in their enthusiasm and have neither ears nor thought nor feeling for anything else.

Until crooners came along there was never in the history of art any person so utterly obsessed by one interest to the exclusion of all others as the Wagnerite. Go to Covent Garden during the Wagner season and you will see a gallery filled with so-called " music-lovers " who will never listen to a note of music unless it is written by The Master. The operas of Verdi and Mozart, the symphonies of Mozart, Haydn and Beethoven are a closed book to them. They do not like Music ; they like only Wagner, the man who confessed that music was not a natural form of expression to him.

Wagner certainly must have something about him, but it is no longer for me, I fear. And in justification of my dislike of him I will submit that it is surely no more unnatural to regard a certain kind of music with disgust than it is for some people to be sick at the thought of eating oysters. Oysters, to non-eaters of oysters, are not fish ; to me Wagner is not music. It is a Thing, and great fun if you're a conductor, which I am not.

The music of Wagner, now I look back, might have done irreparable damage to me in Vienna. As it was, it succeeded in luring me away from Italian music for several years, if not altogether, at least to such an extent that I felt rather guilty if I caught myself enjoying the kind of music I knew instinctively to be my kind of music.

Wagner, his music, his philosophy, his sense of the *kolossal* fitted in perfectly with my fourteen-year-old out-look on life. I began to take myself and my music desperately seriously. I not only affected a bow tie, but began to plan a musical trilogy on an heroic theme, the theme of Cuchulain. The problems of putting this Irish story on the stage would have been immense ; as dramatic highlights there was Cuchulain driving a chariot as a boy, and fighting a duel in a stream up to his waist. I proposed to overcome these problems by having a character on the stage telling us what was going to happen, then dropping the curtain and letting the orchestra describe the scene, and when that was over having a character tell the story of events the audience had had to miss.

Fortunately, I got no further with the Cuchulain trilogy than designing the sets and inscribing an elaborate title-page for the full score with an imposing dedication—always essential preliminaries to any work I planned to write. The spanner thrown into my neo-Wagnerian works was thrown by Richard Strauss.

The music of Strauss not only upset my mental apple-cart but affected me physically as well. Just as, for my first Wagnerian experience, I had picked on *Tristan* in Florence, so my introduction to Strauss was by way of *Elektra*. There could have been no less fortunate choice of starting-point.

I knew nothing of modern music ; I had not even heard a Strauss symphonic poem. The noise and clatter of *Elektra* hitting my uneducated ears fascinated me in the way a snake fascinates a rabbit. I was terrified and helpless.

The psychological and æsthetic effect of *Elektra* combined to produce a first-class ulcer in my stomach ; the ulcer provided a Viennese specialist with admirable material for a paper in a medical journal (I was apparently rather young for a complaint of this kind) and convinced my mother that mind influenced matter in the most peculiar fashion.

I was certainly in a most irritable state so far as my

domestic relationships were concerned. I could behave myself if I were alone with my mother ; I could behave myself if I were alone with Jack ; I could not behave myself if I were with the two of them together. I had an Œdipus-complex that stuck out like a sore thumb and the experience of *Elektra* and its psychological horrors about did the trick. The result was the ulcer, a diet and an entirely changed outlook on music. Richard Strauss became my god, and a setting for voice and orchestra of a sonnet by Masefield became a tone poem entitled *The Pit and the Pendulum* overnight. I scored for an even larger orchestra than before, including no fewer than six bassoons who were scheduled to make the most blood-curdling noises.

The first shock of *Elektra* is now no more than a memory ; I have heard the work since and it strikes me as singularly unhorrifying, though probably the best opera Strauss ever wrote. There is, however, one thing about that performance in Vienna which has indelibly impressed itself on my mind and that is the personality of the singer who played the title part.

Her name was Marie Gutheil-Schoder. It is a name that will mean nothing to those who do not know Vienna, but Gutheil-Schoder was an unusual figure even in a State Opera company which included such singers as Lotte Lehmann, Elisabeth Schumann, Jeritza, Richard Mayr, Leo Slezak, Richard Tauber and Alfred Piccaver

Marie Gutheil-Schoder, when I first heard her, had already been 24 years at the Vienna Opera. She was over fifty and had the figure of a girl of sixteen ; she had a voice, and she had a first-class musical brain, she was a dancer and a superb actress.

When Arnold Schönberg first introduced his string quartet with the vocal finale in 1908, it was Gutheil-Schoder who had had to sing while Felix Weingartne stamped and roared in protest in the concert hall. When Schönberg's *Erwartung* was first performed on the stage in 1924 it was Marie Gutheil-Schoder who learnt the impossible solo part.

I saw Gutheil-Schoder in all her most famous parts, with the exception of Donna Elvira in *Don Giovanni* which she had given up because she felt her voice no longer did justice to Mozart's music. I saw her often as the slim, boyish Octavian in *Rosenkavalier*,* playing the part with an elegance which would have shamed an artist half her age, revelling in the rich Viennese dialect of the comedy in the last act with the finest of all Barons, Richard Mayr.

I saw her as Carmen and realised for the first time that here was a part that cried out for acting and so rarely got it. I saw her as Salome, a terrifying performance of vicious petulance, evil and seductive in the way she danced, in the half-sulky, half-commanding way she sang " I want the head of Jokanaan," and passionately beautiful in the last great monologue.

Marie Gutheil-Schoder was not a beautiful woman. She had the rather shapeless, plastic face of an actress who assumed the appearance of the character she played. There seemed little physical resemblance between the woman who was Elektra and the woman who was Salome, and there was no resemblance whatever between either of these and the Gutheil-Schoder who was Octavian.

Her versatility as an artist took her outside the sphere of opera into films and into the mimed dancing of Strauss'

* If you should chance to read the H.M.V. booklet which accompanies the recording of *Rosenkavalier* I hope you will not take it too much to heart. In the first place it states that Hugo von Hofmannsthal died in 1932, whereas he died in 1929 ; and then it goes on to say that when the opera was finished and due for performance " Gutheil-Schoder canvassed anxiously for a part." This is a characteristic inaccuracy. Marie Gutheil-Schoder wanted not " a " part, but the only part she ever could or did play, the title-role. " I must say," wrote Hofmannsthal to Strauss, " that as far as performance is concerned she is the only possible person to be considered, and she has the figure for it too."

ballet, *The Legend of Joseph*. In this ballet she played the part of Potiphar's Wife, and though there was little real dancing in the part, Marie Gutheil-Schoder dominated the stage in a way that shamed even Karsavina when the great Russian appeared as guest star in the ballet in Vienna, though it is only fair to state that the elastic of Karsavina's pants broke and she had to dance with one hand holding them up for most of the performance.

To celebrate her 25 years at the Opera, Gutheil-Schoder appeared as Elektra ; it was the part that pleased her most and appealed particularly to a group of us enthusiasts who haunted the famous fourth gallery, the " Vierte Galerie " at the top with its wide promenade and bright exit lights under which we could follow our scores.

The Vierte Galerie sent a huge bouquet that night and we got a special bow from the stage at the end. We were a " claque," I suppose, but our only reward was our love for a great artist.

Miss Laelia Finneberg, who studied with her, is almost the only person I have met in England who remembers Marie Gutheil-Schoder, though visitors to some of the Salzburg Festivals may have seen her productions of Mozart. When she finally retired from the Vienna Opera she became a *régisseuse* and a brilliant one. She had grown up in the great Mahler tradition in Vienna, a tradition so strong and so much alive long after Mahler's death that I heard members of the Vienna Philharmonic (which is also the Opera orchestra) asking themselves how Mahler would have made them play a particular passage. She knew the opera stage inside out ; she knew the singers' problems, she knew the musical problems and she knew the whole racket well enough to blend the music, the singing and the acting into as near a perfect whole as a human being could.

In the three great Strauss roles of Elektra, Salome and Oktavian she had no equal. When Strauss came to London with the Dresden Opera Company just before the 1939 war I reminded him of Gutheil-Schoder. The occasion was a mass Press interview and I succeeded in getting the old man into a corner and talking about music in German to him. He had begged us not to discuss politics, but he came very near to it himself when he remembered his time as director of the Vienna Opera. There was a very distinct note of regret in his voice when we got to talking about Gutheil-Schoder and her Strauss performances. "Ja, das war eine schöne Zeit," he said— and he knew only too well that those lovely days would never return under the Nazis.

Now that she is dead, nothing remains of Marie Gutheil-Schoder. Even if she had made gramophone records they would have served no useful purpose for it was not her voice that made her great. All I can hope is that if any one of my three daughters grows up to be an opera singer I shall be able to remember the way Gutheil-Schoder would have done things. For there is no performance of *Elektra*, of *Salome*, of *Carmen* or of *Rosenkavalier* that I have seen since those days in Vienna which I have not instinctively compared with her appearances in these operas.

I have seen no other Elektra who so moved me by the desperate fury with which she looked for the buried axe, who faced Clytemnaestra with such defiance and pride and who recognised Orestes with such overwhelming joy; I have heard no Salome so full of unconquerable desire at the words "Ich will den Kopf des Jokanaan," nor so pervertedly satisfied by kissing John the Baptist's mouth; I have heard no such mischievous boyishness in an Octavian's voice as in the scene where Octavian dresses up as the Viennese servant girl and refuses wine with the

coy " Nein, nein, i' trink ka Wein . . . " ; I have seen no
Carmen cut the cards with such superstitious belief in
fortune-telling.

And off the stage ? I never met her. But I wrote once
to say that I had dedicated an opera to her, and ever
afterwards Marie Gutheil-Schoder would write me postcards from the towns in which she was appearing. These
very personal little notes from the singer, telling me how
she was getting on with *Erwartung* and asking after the
progress of my own work, made me the envy of the Vierte
Galerie. I confess I took the whole thing very much for
granted ; I knew that was how Marie Gutheil-Schoder
would behave. She was no *prima donna*, except in the
sense that she was so obviously the First Lady of Vienna.

CHAPTER VII

WICKERSDORF

WHEN, after a few weeks in Vienna, it was finally
decided that I should be a musician I was put in a tram
and sent up into the hills below Grinzing to see a composer
and teacher. His name was Dr. Egon Wellesz, an authority on the history of opera and himself the composer of
several works for the stage. I found him a charming
man who spoke English well and lived in a lovely villa
with a garden full of cherry trees. I went to see him
mainly to get what one might call a " directive " from
him, to get his advice on my future career and to hear
whether he approved of the musical education I was
likely to get at a school to which it was proposed to send
me in Germany. When I arrived at Wellesz's house he

was busy scoring his opera *Alkestis* and I made a mental note of the fact that as his handwriting was very neat I would write nice neat scores too, in future.

Wellesz saw from the undisciplined manuscripts I brought with me that I had enthusiasm, if nothing else ; so he recommended that I should learn a little more about composition at the school in Wickersdorf. I suggested hopefully that I might be allowed to go to the conservatoire at Leipzig, but the idea was not highly thought of. I realised then that Leipzig was no longer the place it had been in the times of all the great composers I had read about. No, Wickersdorf would do admirably, and as for my future—well, obviously the best thing would be to be a critic.

The idea of being a critic had never passed across my mind, although my father had been on the musical staff of the *Daily Telegraph* for nearly fifteen years. Wellesz, however, was something of a realist ; he knew that one couldn't earn a living as a composer and I was clearly not a virtuoso of any kind, so I had better earn my bread and butter writing about music.

Wellesz sent me off with the names of a couple of books on harmony and orchestration and the instruction that I should hear as much music as I possibly could—good, bad and indifferent.

I obeyed this instruction to the letter. I went to the Opera three or four nights a week, and when it closed down for the summer I transferred my interest to orchestral music played in the open air of the old Imperial Palace gardens. In this way I got through quite a considerable repertoire ; I didn't understand half of what I heard and I certainly didn't know if I was hearing a good performance or not. But I followed most of the music with scores borrowed from a library and began to learn something about the workings of the orchestra.

In August of 1923, just when the mark exchange was beginning to go haywire, I set off to school at Wickersdorf. Of all the eccentric experiments in education in which I had played the part of guinea-pig Wickersdorf was the most peculiar. It was a co-educational school built in the middle of the Thuringian Forest, a seven-mile walk uphill from the nearest railway town of Saalfeld, and so completely isolated that I have wondered how, while there is a place to hide in like this unending forest of pine trees, any of the Nazi war criminals can have been rounded up by the Allies at all.

Although I went to Wickersdorf willing to try anything once, I found very quickly that I did not like the co-educational system. After eight years at an English public school it was strange and irritating ; if a girl happened to annoy you there was no come-back. She demanded equality of status, but pleaded helplessness if you wanted to punch her head as she deserved. And I missed the games I had been brought up to like.

There was always plenty of exercise at Wickersdorf but I found little pleasure in it. I was not greatly attracted by swimming in an ice-cold lake, still less did I like beginning the day at 6 a.m. with half an hour's gymnastics practised naked in a pine forest. That sort of thing was very picturesque and Wagnerian in its setting, but I preferred my body to acquire health in a less direct way, playing a game which demanded a certain amount of skill, and had a definite result at the end of it to show that there had been a contest between two teams no matter how ridiculous the laws of the game may have been. There was no sport at Wickersdorf ; even a sporadic game of soccer, played mainly by children who knew few of the rules and none of the art of the game (they had never seen it expertly played), came under a heading of *Körperkultur*. I realised afterwards how typically Teutonic it all was.

A game which London gutter-snipes will play between lamp-posts with a tennis ball had to have a high-sounding purpose ; enjoyment of the game *qua* game was discouraged ; one played and attended Sport in order to be Fit. I quickly saw that there was no future in this sort of outlook, and for the first time in my life I actually " cut " games.

I was very non-co-operative at Wickersdorf altogether. I soon discovered that as a musician I could be regarded as a " specialist," so that whenever there was any official suggestion of my doing something I didn't want to do, I just disappeared to do some composing. Uncongenial pastimes were arranged in an alarming way by the authorities. On half-holidays you were expected either to go for a five-mile walk, or dig potatoes. Since neither occupation struck me as having any connection with a normal school life I pretended not to understand the instructions. I was sick to death of pine trees and *die Natur* and I could see no point in breaking my back lifting potatoes merely because it would help the Community.

Wickersdorf was full of the Community Spirit. The bread we ate was home-made, and the soup was always made of home-grown cabbage. I do not recall that we ever ate anything else. Each teacher gathered around him (or her) a group of pupils known as a *Kamaradschaft*. In an English school this *Kamaradschaft* would have been the nucleus of a House and would inevitably have led to inter-House competition. At Wickersdorf the *Kamaradschaft* ate together and talked together and kept very much to itself. To have suggested any form of competition, athletic or otherwise, between one *Kamaradschaft* and another would have been against the Community Spirit.

In a characteristically restless way I belonged first to one *Kamaradschaft* and then to another. I started out in one headed by a German South-West African doctor who

wore Tyrolean shorts and spoke English. I eventually
settled down in one run by a Dutchwoman who taught
English and had once acted with Mrs. Patrick Campbell.

I was attracted to Dr. Garter's group in the first place
by the presence at his table of a beautiful girl called
Irmgard von Holten. She was very aristocratic, squinted
slightly and I fell hopelessly in love with her. During our
English lessons I found myself acting opposite her in
Arms and the Man ; she played Raina and I played
Sergius. But I got nowhere with Irmgard, so I transferred
my affections to a girl called Bacci (Italian for kisses.
I don't know how she got the name). Bacci played the
part of Louka ; she was the daughter of a famous Berlin
Communist agitator and held forth on the iniquities of
the aristocracy as represented by Irmgard von Holten.
However, Bacci did nothing to alter my natural indiffer-
ence to politics ; the only change I underwent was the
purely geographical one of shifting myself from Dr
Garter's table to that of Bacci's *Kamaradschaft* mistress
Frau Schuylenburg, the Dutchwoman who had been with
Mrs. Campbell and was taking us through our Shaw.

As I had gone to Wickersdorf primarily to work at
music I took comparatively little part in the general
education there. I remember that there was a properly
rigged-out theatre and that most of our English lessons
were held in it. There was no need for me to attend these
English classes, of course, but I liked the idea of reading
Shaw ; the German children were all so expert at
English that it never really struck me that the classes
were held for their benefit as a language lesson and not as
an excuse for play-acting for me.

There was plenty of music at Wickersdorf. The place
swarmed with teachers of harmony and counterpoint
singing, piano and violin. It was an austere musical
life, presided over by a little man with a beard and a bald

brown head. His name was August Halm and he looked
like something from a Dürer drawing. Halm was a great
one for Utility Music—which is the best way I can
describe the grim string quartets which he composed for
his pupils to play. These works were highly contrapuntal,
their mood was ascetic and they completely lacked charm.
They were faithful expressions of their composer's personality, for Halm never smiled.

I found him a stern, unsympathetic teacher of composition who did nothing to make music entertaining. He
was not interested in my enthusiasms, and while he taught
me score-reading from Haydn string quartets and early
Beethoven symphonies, he had no comment to make on
Haydn's style or Beethoven's orchestration. It was a
severe, Gothic outlook on music which was completely
foreign to my nature.

I found a more congenial spirit in the master who
taught me harmony and counterpoint. He was a Jewish
pianist called Appelbaum, and I managed to divert his
attention from the work in hand enough to explain music
which puzzled me. Thus we got around to the scores of
Richard Strauss and the piano music of Busoni. Appelbaum had none of Halm's damping effect on my enthusiasms ; indeed, he encouraged me by taking part in the
performance of two short pieces I had written for violin
and piano.

There was one daily ritual at Wickersdorf which worked
havoc with my still undeveloped appreciation of music.
After prancing about in the nude among the pine trees
every morning, we trooped into the main hall for breakfast. I was always ravenously hungry by then, but before
we were allowed any breakfast Appelbaum would perform
a Bach Prelude and Fugue from the book of the Forty
Eight.

I have no doubt it was all meant as a tonic for the soul

and to stimulate mental discipline. The only effect it had on me was to make a note of Bach's music unbearable for nearly ten years afterwards. Perhaps it doesn't sound a hardship, but some of the preludes and fugues in the second book of the Forty Eight are pretty long at any time. On an empty stomach they were torture.

What composing I did at Wickersdorf I did in the seclusion of my room and I showed none of it to anybody. There seemed to be nobody there who was interested in opera, and with the regularity of Nat Gubbins' cat, I was " with opera " again.

This time I caught a bad dose of Celtic Twilight. Frau Schuylenburg had lent me some Yeats plays and a book by Fiona Macleod. My homesickness for Ireland (a country I barely knew) and the mysterious lights of the pine forest combined with Yeats to set me off in a welter of pseudo-Irish romanticism. I wrote my name in Gaelic on the title-page of my score, composed poems about the Land of Heart's Desire and vowed that I would henceforth turn to the legends of my own country for operatic inspiration.

The upshot of all this was a couple of scenes, composed and orchestrated (I always wrote direct into full score), of a great music drama entitled *Deirdre*. The libretto—all my own work, of course—bristled with" thou " and "wilt" and " yon flow'ry vale."

In addition, I passed the time with sketches for a tone poem entitled " Eireann " and a string quartet which was later to be orchestrated and called " A Gaelic Idyll." And there were numerous " Faery Songs " and settings of Ernest Dowson and Yeats for voice and orchestra. I found the manuscripts of these outbursts recently and one look at the score is enough to see that I cannot have had the faintest idea what any of this music would have sounded like. And, frankly, I still don't know for I have never written such uncompromisingly " modern " music since. I'm relieved to think that *that* particular child didn't grow up to be the father of the man all right.

After a couple of months at the place I got bored with Wickersdorf. It must have been a fairly easy-going concern, for I do not remember anybody saying that I shouldn't take a train and go off to Dresden in the middle of the term. My object was to go and visit A. S. Neill, the famous Scots founder of a number of very free-and-easy schools for " difficult " children, whom I had met in Vienna and liked enormously. Neill, with a huge repertoire of funny stories, was the most instantly likeable person a child could ever meet and I had a half-hope that I could move to his school at Hellerau, just outside Dresden.

I set off with a rucksack and a Tauchnitz copy of *The Perfect Wagnerite* and travelled into Saxony, going by hard third-class, changing trains innumerable times and arriving in Dresden late at night. I was just in time for the last tram to Hellerau, but when I got there I found I had no idea of Neill's address. Passers-by proved unhelpful and it was very late by the time I had asked the last of them ; and it was certainly too late to begin knocking at people's doors in the hope that I might eventually strike Neill's house that way. So wrapping a flimsy mackintosh around me, I parked myself on a seat by the side of the road and settled down for the night. It was October and fortunately not very cold, but I got to learn everything there was to learn about the way the stars rotate around the sky by watching them during a restless night. I believe I slept a little, but at dawn I was up again and on my round of enquiry. I eventually found Neill having breakfast in typical surroundings ; there was an Irishman there and a young German composer ; there were numberless middle-aged women, the child from next door, the gardener and his family, a Dutch architect and a Czechoslovakian cabaret artist. My unheralded arrival in this *ménage* interrupted its normal life in no way, and excited no comment. I had come to see if Neill had a school, I said, and if he had then I'd like to join it.

Just at that time Neill did not seem to have a school—a most unusual state of affairs with him, for he usually managed to start them at once wherever he went. At this moment, Neill was at a between-school stage and was busy writing detective stories in which all the mysteries were solved by a psycho-analyst along purely Freudian lines. They made improbable reading.

I don't think Neill would have had me at his school anyway ; he considered me quite mad because I listened to modern music. To Neill there were two types of person beyond salvation : those who listened to modern music and those who climbed mountains. At this stage, I am inclined to agree that both these pursuits are pretty lunatic ; the mental exercise of the one strikes me as being as boring as the physical exercise of the other.

I stayed in Hellerau a couple of days or so, long enough to look over the huge and well-equipped Dalcroze School there and to pay a visit to the Dresden Opera. I sat in a box at the Opera, not, unfortunately, to hear an opera performance but to attend a symphony concert by the excellent Staatskapelle.

I could afford a seat in a box because the German exchange was by now beginning to get completely out of hand. So much so that The Situation in Dresden was beginning to get Serious. Riots and strikes were threatened, so it was thought best for me to get back to Wickersdorf and thence return to Vienna. Another journey, punctuated by hours spent in the middle of the night in junction waiting rooms (the German transport system, even after the R.A.F. had been at it, can't have seemed so different), brought me to Wickersdorf to find that the mark was another million or so to the pound more than it had been when I left Dresden. Indeed, in the village of Wickersdorf itself an efficiently working barter system had already been started ; eggs were exchanged for milk, and bread for potatoes. Money, unless it was foreign— guilders, dollars or pounds—was worthless.

Without shedding many tears I left Wickersdorf school for Vienna. I spent a night in Saalfeld in order to get my passport put in order. A stamp was put on it by a decrepit town clerk which entitled me to leave the province of Thuringia. For this I was charged 2,700,828,000 marks. It looked very well written down—mere figures were not to be trusted—and my passport showed the receipt of *zweimilliardensiebenhundertmillionenachthundertachtundzwanzig-tausendmark*.

I spent a very comfortable night at the main hotel in Saalfeld and my bill the next morning added up to less than I had paid for a cup of coffee the night before. I arrived back in Vienna in glorious October sunshine, having finished with schools for good and feeling unusually exhilarated to be home again. For Vienna, by now, had become home ; it was a city which contained everything I wanted in life—two opera houses, concerts, a musical atmosphere which was inescapable and a people who spoke and behaved in a way I could understand.

Though the School Leaving Age in my case was roughly fifteen, I did not have to face a hard world and earn my living in it. There was nothing I could earn my living at, anyway. I became a full-time student of music.

CHAPTER VIII

REUNION WITH VIENNA

I was sent to live with a Viennese family, where I would not only continue to learn German but where my piano would be out of my mother's earshot. I had a pleasant room in a flat overlooking a garden, about a quarter of a mile from where Wagner had once lived with some housemaid or other. The family was Jewish-Hungarian and consisted of an elderly couple, two sons and a daughter. There was also a very aged companion called Frau Schlesinger who was convinced that the entire world was going to pieces. Her evidence for this belief was in the newspapers where she constantly read of earthquakes in Japan and hurricanes in America ; she was in a state of perpetual alarm at the idea of radio (as who isn't ?) and was sure that the number of train accidents, suicides and murders she read about were all part of the Inevitable Catastrophe.

Of the three children, the elder son Leo had been a soldier and was now an unsuccessful commission agent of some kind. He worked mostly at home, in a room stacked with rubber stamps and imposing headed notepaper belonging to the various firms with which he dealt. Leo was something of a cynic ; he didn't think The Revolution had done much good ; he said it had been too like an evening at the opera—with intervals for refreshment between the shouting.

Paul, the younger son, was an engineer who lived in a room which looked like a junk-shop ; it was in reality devoted to a huge and complicated crystal set on which he once heard the Savoy Orpheans broadcasting from London, but which mostly provided indistinct performances

of café music and English lessons from the local
station. Frau Schlesinger could never be induced to go
near Paul's room ; the sight of him at work, twiddling
knobs, with headphones on his ears and an ecstatic expression on his face was more than her already gloomy
philosophy could cope with.

The daughter of the family, plump and unattractive
except for a friendly smile, married a widower who lived
two flats above ; he was a professor and ostensibly the
official translator into German of the works of Romain
Rolland. The professor's son was a lad of thirteen and
a constant menace to me. He played the violin and would
come downstairs with his instrument in order that I should
accompany him on the piano. Our performance of the
only piece he knew—Toselli's *Serenata*—was execrable, for
I was no pianist and the boy's intonation was unbelievable.

In the flat immediately above there was the sort of
pianist who always lives in the flat above : the one-piece
pianist. She was a young lady I never met ; but she
was evidently a tryer. She refused to be defeated by the
difficulties of Strauss' *Voices of Spring* and her daily practice
was devoted to this waltz to the exclusion of all other
music.

I contributed more than my fair share to the general
din of 25, Einwanggasse. I went to Egon Wellesz for
composition, and to a married couple who tried to teach
me harmony, counterpoint and the piano. With the
husband I did not progress very far ; I have always
wanted to run before I could walk and I failed to concentrate on fundamentals, which bored me. I wanted to
know how to write modern harmonies, not old ones.

As a piano pupil I was even less successful. I never
practised and I didn't like the woman who taught me.
She was a hard-faced blonde who wore boots which laced
up to her knee, and I spent my practice time picking out

E

harmonies which her husband was trying to teach me to write without my ever going near a piano.

I didn't last very long with this couple, as their patience was exhausted long before mine. My lessons with Wellesz, on the other hand, were something I enjoyed immensely.

Wellesz had a great gift of teaching without letting his pupils know it. He encouraged my enthusiasms, but kept them in check if they threatened to get out of hand by leading me imperceptibly along a more disciplined path.

I went to Wellesz twice a week, and our lessons began either with his playing through something I had just written, or more often in discussing something I had just heard. As I went to the Opera almost every night, the questions we discussed were usually operatic. Sometimes the questions would lead to the study of a Wagner full-score ; at others, to the instrumentation of *Carmen* or the analysis of a scene by Richard Strauss. If in my own work I showed a tendency to keep the music and drama too much on the same level, then Wellesz would teach me about dramatic contrast and orchestral light and shade.

Being a composer himself, Wellesz played me a great deal of his own music in illustration of his points. He had been a pupil of Schönberg and was also author of a biographical study of The Master. But his music took very little after that of my " musical grandfather." Wellesz, the authority on Byzantine music and baroque opera, had a cosmopolitan outlook on music. He went to the Aztecs, to the Persians and the legends of Greece for the subjects of his stage works. His *Alkestis* had for its libretto the only book for the opera stage by Hugo von Hofmannsthal which had not been set by Strauss, while Jakob Wassermann had provided the libretto of the

Persian *Princess Girnara*. He had evolved his own action
for a ballet of *Achilles on Skyros* and later himself adapted
Euripides for his two-act opera on the *Bacchae*.

This catalogue of Wellesz's own work is given here to
show something of the type of man who was my teacher.
If he had happened to concentrate on chamber music or
symphonic poems I have no doubt I would have done the
same ; my capacity for Freudian identification was such
that Wenceslas' page was a non-conformist by comparison.
The fact that Wellesz composed operas and showed a
marked preference for subjects which had been the bedtime stories of my infancy made the devotion of pupil to
master doubly intense.

Wellesz's own music, I may say, was a complete
contradiction of his personal character. He was as gentle
and charming a being as one could wish to meet—away
from a piano. But when Wellesz the Composer took
charge of things and began to play through a new work
for the benefit of visitors the transformation was astonishing. Wellesz, the cosmopolitan, had no use for the piddling
dynamics and whispered utterances of the Schönberg
school. He was whole-heartedly devoted to the Russians
and the French and began where Stravinsky had left off
in *Le Sacre du Printemps*—only louder.

His music was the music of a man who was fully aware
of what was going on in the world, and if he looked for
his inspiration in the stories of antiquity rather than in the
gossip columns of the *Police Gazette*, like his contemporary,
Hindemith, then it was because Wellesz had a strong
lyrical streak in him. Some years later I saw *Alkestis* and
Achilles performed as a double bill on the stage ; both
opera and ballet " came off " in performance in a way
I would never have suspected from hearing their composer
play them to me. If the music was never highly original,
at least it was never dull and some of the orchestral

noises, picked up from the orchestral masters of all nations, were extremely effective.

My natural catholicity of taste suffered nothing at the hands of Wellesz. I had a habit of arriving at my lesson with a new score I had just bought and asking him to play it for me and tell me what it was all about. One morning I turned up with a copy of Zez Confrey's *Kitten on the Keys*. Wellesz never turned a hair, but proceeded to play it for me. He gave a creditable display until we reached the Trio. This we discovered on analysis had been lifted bodily from a tune in *Carmen* ; so we turned to a score of Bizet's opera, found the place where the tune occurred and went on from there to study the use of brass instruments in *Carmen*. Twenty-one years later that morning's lesson bore fruit when I did a programme for the B.B.C. on the orchestration of *Carmen*. I didn't mention that but for *Kitten on the Keys* I might never have got round to it at all ; my reputation for flippancy is bad enough already. But my enthusiasm for *Carmen* does in fact date largely from that incident.

Wellesz, like the good Viennese he was, had to spend his time getting the Germans to put on his operas—in Berlin, Mannheim, Dessau and Münster. Vienna, overflowing with the most exquisite traditions, was the centre of " advanced " music in the early 1920's. It was the headquarters of the Universal Edition, which published everything any member of the Schönberg school chose to write. And yet any music later than Richard Strauss had virtually to go underground.

Following the *Skandal* of Schönberg's Second String Quartet in 1908 a Society for Private Performances was formed to enable composers to hear their new works without being interrupted by hecklers like Weingartner. Even after a World War and a revolution the Viennese public still did not make much sense. After 1918 Vienna became the capital of a Socialist republic, but it showed few signs of learning much of liberal methods. The prejudice against " new " music was largely based on anti-Semitism.

True, the City of Vienna made Freud a freeman of the city, but the anti-Semitic faction was a vociferous body. At one time the wave of anti-Jewish feeling became so great that Vienna University students demanded the dismissal of all Jewish lecturers and tutors. It was only when they realised that this would leave them almost entirely without tuition of any kind that they stopped their nonsense and decided to behave. Vienna was ripening for the Nazis in 1923 ; I was only surprised that Hitler didn't pluck the fruit long before he did.

The Vienna Opera was state-subsidised and it did things on the grand scale, so long as there was no question of departing from tradition. Anybody who was anybody at all in the world of Central European opera came to sing or conduct at the Staatsoper. But it was a heartbreaking set-up for the local Viennese composer. The " novelties " put on each season were as drab as any " duty " works could be, written by untalented members of the orchestra or by some obscure but venerable old gentleman who turned out an opera every few years merely because he had long been in the habit of doing so.

Thus it happened that when Schönberg's fiftieth birthday came to be celebrated a festival performance was put on of his opera *Die glückliche Hand*. The leading part was sung by a member of the State Opera company, but the performance took place at the Volksoper—a poor, unsubsidised institution which came under new management on an average three times a year.

Berg's *Wozzeck*, an opera by a native of Vienna, was played on sixteen different German stages, in Prague in Czech and in Leningrad in Russian before it reached

Vienna five years after its first performance in Berlin.

Vienna to the Viennese artist, in short, became very much like Ireland to the Irish : a nice place to be away from. The Viennese, who had driven Mahler away from the Imperial Opera, intrigued and counter-intrigued until Strauss resigned the post of Director of the Staatsoper. Reinhardt went to Berlin ; so did Schönberg, so did Bruno Walter, so did nearly everybody of any talent in music, in the theatre, in films, until there were more than 100,000 Viennese living in the German capital.

In 1933 they had to drift back again. " The rats," said Egon Wellesz, sadly, " are boarding the sinking ship."

From the point of view of the foreigner, however, Vienna could not have been more enchanting. At fifteen years of age I was not greatly troubled by the attitude of the Viennese to their talented fellow-citizens. There was so much music to take in that the non-performance of a new opera here and there passed by unnoticed. I was puzzled by the subscribers to the Philharmonic Society who whistled and stamped at the *répétition générale* of a concert performance of Stravinsky's *Sacre* ; but I presumed that subscribers to such societies all over the world were bound to behave like that. Besides, a good *Skandal* made me believe that Vienna had not lost all its character as a Musical Centre.

If, as a student, I lived in an atmosphere of New Music and Lost Causes in Vienna, I realise now that it was the *normal* artistic life of the city which brought the unforgettable things. I may have been excited at the time by hearing *Sacre* played by the Philharmonic Orchestra ; today I would trade every note of that score to experience again a particular Sunday morning concert conducted by Weingartner in which three symphonies were played— by Haydn, Mozart and Beethoven.

I went to that concert because I made a habit of going

to hear the Philharmonic before lunch on Sundays.
Wellesz had told me to hear as much music as I could,
and I carried out his instructions faithfully. In this way
I became acquainted with the repertoire and with such
novelties as happened to turn up from time to time. But
above all I came to accept something very near perfection
as an everyday occurrence. And I have paid in full since
then for this early, casual acceptance of high standards in
music by having to suffer the unspeakable mediocrity
of the average British performance—the average British
performance not of new works, for the British orchestral
player reads unfamiliar music better than anyone in the
world, but of the standard classics. Lacking any tradition
or (to use a recently fashionable phrase) any " continuity
of policy," British orchestras bring the same atmosphere
of hit-and-miss which characterises their reading of new
works into the performance of works which they should
know backwards.

Thus, long before I was sixteen years old, I was
thoroughly steeped in an eighty-year-old, uninterrupted
tradition of orchestral playing by an orchestra which in
the lifetime of its own members had played whole seasons
under Nikisch, Mahler, Weingartner, Walter and Strauss.
The Vienna Philharmonic was like a Stradivarius violin :
something on which even the inexpert performer could
always make a pretty noise, and on which the virtuoso
could play in a manner really worthy of his gifts.

During my time in Vienna the Philharmonic instrument
was played on by virtuosi. From Weingartner I heard the
classics and unfamiliar works like Berlioz' *Harold in Italy*
(a piece which nobody apparently intends ever to perform
again in my lifetime, for I cannot see that hearing one
performance in 23 years can be considered a very promising outlook).

Weingartner, perhaps because he posed as a composer

himself, had little sympathy with the music of his contemporaries. I do not remember hearing him conduct anything later than Brahms. On the other hand, one could have wished for nobody better from whom to hear Haydn, Mozart or Beethoven for the first time. Weingartner's performances of the symphonies of these composers was everything that the term " classical " implies. The conductor himself, standing erect, economical in his gestures, unvarying in tempo or nuance between one performance and another, was the figure of Authority. It was not for nothing, one felt, that Weingartner's edition of Beethoven was the Authorised Version of the symphonies, read and digested universally. The Editor practised what he preached, and gave to the music something which he could not pass on in the form of a correspondence course—a sense of style, the realisation that early Beethoven was not late Haydn, but early Beethoven.

Richard Strauss, the unsurpassed conductor of his own music, tends to be forgotten as a conductor in his own right. But now I try to think of exactly what it is that Strauss conducts, I can think of nothing but his Mozart. However, even if I ever heard him conduct anything else it is his Mozart which stands out most clearly in my memory and which has remained with me as a natural standard of Mozart performance.

Strauss' Mozart, unlike Weingartner's, was not confined to the concert hall ; Mozart, after all, was an opera composer and Strauss had begun life as conductor in an opera house. So while he did astonishing things with Mozart symphonies Strauss was at his best and most devoted when he conducted performances of *Cosi fan tutte* and *Figaro*.

As an interpreter of Mozart's music Strauss was most curiously contradictory. His own scores are largely

" mush," with a dozen instruments wandering up and down the chromatic scale in the background, signifying nothing. Clarity is the last thing to look for in a Strauss score, and not even Toscanini can convince the hearer that there is really any important musical wood behind all those trees. Knowing this it was all the more astonishing to find that Strauss could bring an unusual clarity to the music of Mozart. And since he was dealing with the clearest music ever composed, this was really something.

There was something additionally contradictory about Strauss and his Mozart. Strauss, the composer of *Elektra* and *Salome*, seemed to fight shy of the dramatic Mozart. He seemed attracted only by the charming Mozart ; he spent his time on *Cosi fan tutte* and *Figaro*, not on *Don Giovanni* or *The Magic Flute*. He got every ounce of brilliance out of the " Jupiter " symphony and his performance of the last movement was like the shower of golden rain that Zeus used to get Danae into " trouble." When he came to the great G Minor symphony again, it was the charm that Strauss looked for, not the drama. There was no academic justification for his finishing the minuet movement with a repetition of the Trio ; if Mozart had wanted it that way, no doubt he would have told us. And yet, in performance, the effect was undeniably charming. The paradox of the whole thing was that, by ending the movement in G major, instead of G minor, the dramatic return to the fundamental key of the symphony was emphasised by the finale which followed. The effect was even more startling than the composer had intended, and heaven knows Mozart's intentions were clear enough.

Strauss' devotion to Mozart's operas was in the Viennese tradition. Twenty years before, Mahler had started something by performing Mozart on the stage as if he were a great composer and not just a purveyor of

E *

pretty little arias. That tradition had been handed down and persisted at the Vienna Opera through a world war, a revolution and the incredible political complexities peculiar to all operatic institutions.

Even now I do not think I have ever heard a perfect performance of a Mozart opera. I have heard fine singers, but they haven't understood Mozart ; I have heard intelligent singers who could act and obviously knew what Mozart was all about, but the noise they made with their voices was dreadful.

I have been to Glyndebourne, and returned in the depths of depression at what I heard. I have always enjoyed myself at Glyndebourne, but I am not certain that half the success of opera there was not due to the long dinner interval. Critical faculties tend to disappear after a lot of hock ; the second half of the performance always sounded better than the first, as a result, and in any case there was the inescapable magic of Mozart.

But since returning from those Glyndebourne evenings I have played over the gramophone records of *Figaro* and *Cosi fan tutte* and *Don Giovanni*. Heard in cold blood, in a world without hock and where even three pennyworth of Algerian wine is no longer obtainable at 8s. a bottle, they are singularly lacking in glamour. Only Salvatore Baccaloni, as Leporello, has both voice and a sense of style. The English singers in the company have good diction and one can hear their appalling Italian only too well in consequence, while the German artists, especially the men, are as vocally unattractive as any men could be who once thought it would be nice to sing like Richard Tauber. In the average Glyndebourne performance shouting is passed off as virility and a form of operatic crooning as a substitute for *bel canto*. (Tauber, I may say, has been one of the finest of all singers of Mozart in his day and his Don Ottavio was an unforgettable experience.

An ill-advised gramophone company has deleted his
recording of "Il mio tesoro," which was a model of
phrasing and easy singing.)

I despair of hearing the perfect Mozart opera performance from the Italians ; the music was written too soon
for them. Opera in Italy begins with Bellini, even though
it was an Italian who started the whole business in the
sixteenth century. The Germans just don't make the
right sort of noise.

Which makes me think that the Mozart I saw in Vienna
was probably as good as I shall ever see. Mozart was an
Austrian, and the Viennese alone have ever impressed
me as having the right temperament for the music of
a composer to whom Italian was a second language and
yet who was not an Italian composer in the sense that
Verdi or Donizetti was.

The Viennese, for all that some of them may claim to
belong to Gross-Deutschland, are citizens of a buffer state.
They possess the giftedness of the Germans, and the
charm and grace and sensitivity of the Latins. Their
dialect is still full of eighteenth century French phrases,
and their accent is soft and musical. They have absorbed
all that is best in Western civilisation but without losing
their national character. Their nature is cosmopolitan
but they are more devoted to their home town than any
American song-writer.

Mozart, a typical child of the Age of Reason, was a pure
Austrian—as likely to cry with homesickness for his
native land as to write to his father proudly announcing
that he was an *Erzengländer* (an "arch-Englishman")
when the last siege of Gibraltar by the French failed in 1779.

The performances of Mozart's operas in Vienna were
in German, of course ; so far as the libretto was concerned
there was never any question of whether the productions
were "Italian" or not in the narrow sense.

But the essential " Austrian-ness " of *Figaro* and *Don Giovanni* I have never heard better brought out than with the Vienna cast which included Elisabeth Schumann and Richard Mayr. These two, the Sophie and Baron Ochs of numberless performances of *Rosenkavalier*, were at their best in *Figaro*. Elisabeth Schumann, dark, attractive to look at and with a charming and miraculously clear, accurate voice made the most enchanting Susanna one could imagine. She had all the wit and sense of fun the part demands ; she was good-humoured with Cherubino and she was a perfect maid to the Countess ; and above all she had an indefinable dignity. Susanna may be only a servant, but she has the kind of dignity peculiar to good servants. Elisabeth Schumann had all the natural grace and manners one would expect from somebody who served the greatest lady on the operatic stage : Mozart's Countess.

In *Don Giovanni*, Schumann sang Zerlina—a sharply characterised study of a bewildered and occasionally frightened peasant girl. If Don Giovanni had been a celibate he could scarcely have resisted her, the way she sang in " Là ci darem la mano " or knocked an audience cold with " Batti, batti " and " Vedrai carino."

There was one other exquisite Schumann-Mayr partnership, even more delightful than that in *Figaro*. One or two nights a week the Vienna Opera company took a small orchestra and cast over to the Redoutensaal in the Hofburg. Here, in a long room with walls covered by priceless Gobelin tapestries, they performed opera on a " chamber " scale. A small stage had been constructed at one end of the auditorium (lit, naturally, by huge chandeliers) and the repertoire consisted of *Figaro*, *Così fan tutte*, *The Barber of Seville*, Weber's little comic opera, *Abu Hassan* and Pergolesi's *La Serva Padrona*.

It was in the Pergolesi opera that Schumann and Mayr

excelled—she as the busy, dominating servant-turned-mistress, he as a richly comic, grumpy old man who was helpless in the face of her frontal attack. They were not only both first-rate singers ; they were first-rate actors.

Only one of Mayr's performances was well-known outside Vienna, his Baron Ochs in *Rosenkavalier*. But he was a very much better singer than that part ever allowed him to be. His finest roles were Figaro, Leporello and—though it had a less immediate appeal—Sarastro in *The Magic Flute*. This performance was a superb job of sustained bass-singing and I am not certain it was probably not the greatest of all his roles merely because it was the most exacting. I am sorry Mayr never lived to sing " Isis and Osiris " with Toscanini at Salzburg, for that would have been an unforgettable experience.

The Redoutensaal was the perfect setting for the four operas in the repertoire ; they were all set in the eighteenth century and seemed to have grown out of the very walls of the room. In addition to operas, the Staatsoper also presented intimate ballet in the Redoutensaal as well : a delightful sequence of dances to Ravel's *Ma Mère l'Oye*, Stravinsky's *Pulcinella* and divertissements to music by Johann Strauss, Lanner and Richard Strauss' suite of dances by Couperin.

The performances in the Redoutensaal were in addition to those at the Opera, for singers and orchestra were a large enough company for the Staatsoper to be in four places at once—with opera in the Hofburg, opera in the Staatsoper, the ballet on tour and the main body of the orchestra playing Philharmonic concerts elsewhere.

The idea of an orchestra of the standing of the Vienna Philharmonic playing music by Johann Strauss and Lanner is something that shocks the average British " music lover." The Viennese, however, do not subscribe to the idea that music must only be " serious " to have any

æsthetic value. Not only was the Philharmonic concerned with the Strauss divertissements in the Redoutensaal, but it gave regular concerts of music by the Strauss
family, Waldteufel, Gung'l, Lanner and Suppé. The effect
of this on me was to provide me with another set of
standards which cause me to be bad-tempered unless they
are maintained.

For years, as a radio critic, I have agitated that the
B.B.C. Symphony Orchestra should let its hair down
enough to play Strauss waltzes in the original, full-
orchestral version. During the war the B.B.C. did go so
far as to include some Strauss in programmes of " popular
classics." But the result had an effect of musical slumming. In Vienna, the Philharmonic played Strauss
waltzes and polkas because it was a normal thing to do ;
the B.B.C. did it in a typically patronising way, showing
off to the public as if to say, " We're quite human at heart,
really—honestly, we're just like you."

Though it made a change to hear a British orchestra
playing a Strauss score in full, I found very soon that I
preferred my Strauss tunes played by small groups of
Jewish fiddlers from Mile End Road. At least they
played as though they *believed* the music was worth playing,
whereas the B.B.C.'s Music Department so obviously
didn't.

I am afraid my attitude to the question of the performance of music in general makes me very poor company
among my acquaintances (as distinct from my friends),
and I am considered a hypercritical bore. But what am
I to do ? After all, I was brought up to hear Johann
Strauss played by the Vienna Philharmonic conducted by
Bruno Walter ; how can I possibly be polite if the B.B.C.'s
performances do not begin to approach even the Vienna
café standard ? Nobody can blame the B.B.C. for not
being Viennese, but at least one feels they might take the

trouble to listen to some of Bruno Walter's recordings, if
only to get the *tempi* right.

There is in the B.B.C.'s mental make-up a curious
streak of obstinacy. They will give credit where credit is
due ; they will maintain that Walter and Toscanini are
great conductors, as though the Corporation and nobody
else had put them on the map. But never will they admit that
there is anything to be learnt from outsiders, however
distinguished. Instead, they say : " Yes, that's very nice
of course, but this is the way *we* do it." And two years after
Toscanini's recording of Beethoven's Eighth Symphony
has been available to the public the B.B.C.'s conductors
are still drooling away obliviously, dragging their slow
lengths along in the first movement as though it were a
stately minuet instead of being marked " Allegro vivace
e con brio."

I do not expect the hack English conductor to be a
Toscanini, but if he will not bother to translate the
Italian expression marks and tempo indications then it
looks rather as if Toscanini has lived in vain. Perhaps
I am wrong, but I rather imagined that artists like
Toscanini are sent by Providence to leave the world a
better place and bequeath us higher standards of per-
formance, so that music in general might benefit.

The Jewish fiddlers from the Mile End Road find
inspiration in Kreisler and Heifetz, and work like slaves to
play better if they possibly can. But the B.B.C.'s conductors remain unaffected by example and have no sense of
competition. Naturally not—the B.B.C. is a monopoly
and their jobs are safe so long as they do Nothing Irregular
which would be likely to concern the Head of Staff
Administration.

But I cannot help feeling that British musical life and
standards would be better for a little more of what I call
the Elman Spirit. When Mischa Elman had " arrived "

and was already settled down in America, his father was
asked by a London concert agent to send Mischa over
here for a tour.   Father Elman's reply was : " Send
Mischa to Europe ?   Against whom shall he play ? "

If I have clear memories of Weingartner and Richard
Strauss conducting the Vienna Philharmonic, of Weingartner conducting as director of the Volksoper and
Strauss as director of the Staatsoper, I find the richest of
all my musical experiences in Vienna to be the most
difficult to define, the least easy to connect with any
single incident.   Where Weingartner and Strauss have
passed into history, Bruno Walter crashed into my
musical consciousness when I was fifteen and has remained
in it ever since.   I have heard Walter in Vienna, in
Salzburg, in Berlin, in London and in New York, and I
find it almost impossible to sort out one performance from
another of the concerts and operas I have heard him
conduct in two continents during the past 23 years.

With the exception of Toscanini, Bruno Walter has been
the most important musical figure of our time.   There is
no question of comparing these two conductors ; they are
complementary and one should be grateful that they and
we have had the fortune to be contemporaries.   In
private life they are friends ; in public life they have
co-operated—as co-conductors in Salzburg and New
York.   If I wrote, a moment ago, of the Elman Spirit
then I find myself having to take it all back.   Between
Walter and Toscanini there can never be any competition,
for each has something the other hasn't got.   It is not a
question of one conductor performing music " better "
than the other ; they belong to different worlds ; one is
typically Latin, the other typically Jewish.   Toscanini is
a classicist.   Walter is a romantic.   The main thing they
have in common is a unique devotion to music.

As Toscanini did not enter into my musical life until 1931 I do not want to embark on any detailed discussion of his conducting at this point. Bruno Walter, on the other hand, was the focal point of every musical season I experienced between 1923 and 1939. Where Toscanini has been a spasmodic stimulant, Bruno Walter has come near to being a staple diet.

The German language has an almost untranslatable phrase to describe Bruno Walter's conducting ; it is the word *Musizieren*. Literally, the word means " to make music." In Walter's case it embraces far more than that. He does not " conduct " an orchestra ; he plays on it, caressing the music and moulding each phrase with the care and love and air of somebody who is creating the music as he goes along. Walter's way with the more brilliant passages in Mozart is no less brilliant than any other conductor's ; but his essentially romantic nature makes a Mozart slow movement a unique experience. He brings a rare richness and gentleness to the phrasing of Mozart *cantilene* which is without parallel among present-day conductors. But there is never any question of Walter, because he is romantic at heart, destroying the essential elegance and classical nature of Mozart. He brings all that into his performances, too ; but he also manages to perceive the depth of Mozart where other interpreters miss it and pass it by.

Bruno Walter's way with the slow tunes of Mozart is no more a question of over-romanticisation than Kreisler playing the slow movement of the Beethoven concerto. Fritz Kreisler is gifted with a singing tone and a beauty of phrasing which leave one convinced that Beethoven had that sort of playing in mind when he wrote the concerto. It is no less " classical " for being extremely beautiful.

Just how unmistakable is Bruno Walter's personality was proved to me shortly before the war when I tuned in

to a concert broadcast from Hilversum. The orchestra
was in the middle of the Allegretto of Beethoven's Seventh
Symphony. The tune " sang " in such a peculiar way
that I had little doubt as to the identity of the conductor.
And when, in the finale, the tempo began to run away
with itself I was even more sure of the man who was in
front of the orchestra. At the end of the work the
announcer confirmed that the symphony had been conducted by Bruno Walter. Toscanini would never have
allowed that finale to get out of hand ; equally, not even
Toscanini could have put what Walter put into the
Allegretto.

To the onlooker, Walter does not appear an easy
conductor to play under. His beat is vague and indeci-
sive ; but his musical personality is so strong that there
has never yet been an orchestra which has failed to respond
to him. Whether Walter's methods are different at
rehearsal from what they are at a public performance I do
not know, for I have only ever seen him in a packed
concert hall or opera house. But whatever his method
there is no doubt about the result ; from Bruno Walter
one hears exquisitely sensitive *Musizieren*, whether he is
conducting *Figaro*, *Rosenkavalier* or *Walküre*, or leading the
orchestra from the piano during the course of a brilliant
solo performance of Mozart's D Minor Piano Concerto.
Always there is that same fanatical devotion to music,
the same joy in making music whether it is a Mozart
symphony, Mahler's *Song of the Earth* or the *Emperor
Waltz* of Johann Strauss.

My early experience of and subsequently unshakable
devotion to Bruno Walter's conducting are again something which make me an intolerable companion when
confronted with performances which fall below the
standards he has set for me.

In 1933 I sat in Queen's Hall with Egon Wellesz to

listen to a performance of the "Jupiter" Symphony under a famous English conductor. This interpreter, notorious for his eccentricities, was in a more capricious mood than usual. He decided that it would be nice to have the Minuet played with down-bows instead of phrasing it as Mozart had written it. The effect was frankly monstrous ; the long graceful phrase that Mozart had written sounded perilously like a mazurka and was entirely and ludicrously pointless.

Wellesz and I looked at each other in astonishment. Eventually Wellesz turned to me and said : " Sehen Sie, Pat—dass ist nichts für uns die Bruno Walter kennen." And with those words—" that sort of thing won't do for us who know Bruno Walter "—we left Queen's Hall and went out for a drink. I got very drunk.

I don't think I would have minded all that monkeying about with the " Jupiter " half as much if the conductor had *always* done it that way. But he hadn't, and he never did it that way again. It was not ignorance. It was just sheer mischievous, immoral, indefensible exhibitionism ; it was doubly unforgivable as the conductor had a reputation for being a great interpreter of Mozart.

Next morning the notices referred to a " typically brilliant performance of the ' Jupiter '." I went straight out and got very drunk again.

Music critics, as a race, bore me oppressively. The dramatic critic earns his living in the main by reviewing new theatrical productions. The music critic is forced to write week after week of the same old pieces of music, because whereas the theatre exists on the presentation of new plays, the concert and opera world relies almost entirely on a repertoire. The music critic finds little relaxation in the pursuit of his profession ; he cannot skip from the discussion of Alban Berg to an estimate of the importance of Jerome Kern in the way that a dramatic critic's weekly column may include notices of *Hamlet*, a couple of farces and a new musical comedy.

The narrowness of the music critic's professional world leads him all too often into becoming an obsessionist. The weekly column cannot be filled eternally with notices of a recent performance of the Emperor Concerto. A good week in the theatre may bring six or seven novelties ; in music it is a good year that brings six unfamiliar works, let alone six that are at all interesting and worth writing about. Still less frequent than first performances of new music are good performances of familiar music which justify printed discussion. A Toscanini, a Bruno Walter, a Menuhin or a Szigeti doesn't crop up all that often.

And so the music critic inevitably falls back on his obsession. Topic A in some cases may be Wagner, or it may be the ladylike music of the Benjamin Britten-Michael Tippett school. In either case the reiterated rolling of logs does not make for entertaining reading, and one opens one's Sunday paper with regular foreboding. In my family one famous musical column is known as " ITMA," for nine times out of ten the critic's subject is That Man Again, Wagner ; while if another column omits to mention the name of Mr. Britten at least once in the course of any discussion of any kind of music we feel that the music of Britten stands not where she did.

For some ten years I was music critic on a London daily paper, and I hope sincerely that those days are now behind me for good. I enjoyed hearing music for nothing ; my trouble was that I enjoyed music. If I heard a bad performance then I never had sufficient space in which to say so, and in any case I wanted to forget it, not draw attention to it. And if the performance had been especially good, then I still didn't want to write about it. A " rave " notice is difficult enough to write at any time ;

in the postcard size notice printed by a daily paper, it was impossible. Nothing is more embarrassing to read than a string of superlatives the next morning, for no sub-editor ever leaves one enough space to qualify one's enthusiasm. Most of my notices of Toscanini's Beethoven concerts came out looking like Hollywood blurbs and made me wonder how I had come to forget the adjective Stupendous.

At fifteen years of age, however, I thought it would be fun to be a music critic. I had no ambition to be a particularly distinguished one, though I hoped at least to be an important one whose presence at concerts would be pointed out in hushed tones.

One evening in November, 1923, I went to the Vienna Opera to see the first performance of a one-act opera by Alexander Zemlinsky based on Wilde's *Birthday of the Infanta*. I was fully conscious of its being An Occasion, for not only was I attending a première for the first time in my life, but Zemlinsky was Schönberg's brother- or father-in-law, and that made it all Very Important.

I made a lot of notes during the performance, went home, wrote my notice and mailed it to the offices in London of *The Sackbut*, a monthly magazine originally edited by Peter Warlock, published by Curwen and known to be interested in international musical events.

My notice of Zemlinsky's opera had neither shape, insight nor a sense of proportion. I generalised madly ; I used terms like " expressionism " and " impressionism " without knowing in the least what they meant.

At one moment I went off into a detailed description of the orchestration of an unimportant *motiv*, at the next I dragged in a string of names to show whom the composer was *not* like.

It was a masterpiece of uninformed amateurishness and I believe I must have felt rather ashamed of it even at the time, for I kept the whole thing quiet until it was published in *The Sackbut* of February, 1924.

The article appeared, flattered by a most elegant display, and it had my name on it. I was a Music Critic. Q.E.D.

When I say that it had my name on it, it bore the name under which I continued to write for some time afterwards. In order that my father should not know what I was up to in Vienna I called myself " Patrick MacHugh." I have no doubt that this Irish paraphrase of the family name did not deceive Herbert in the least, but anyway he could not complain that I was letting the name of Hughes down in the world of music criticism.

I plucked up enough courage to take the February copy of *The Sackbut* and show it to Wellesz. Egon reproved me for my inaccurate generalisations about music (he resented being lumped together in one of my catalogues with Cyril Scott and Arthur Bliss), but he did so in a friendly, parental way and we went on from there to a nice lesson on the elements of music criticism.

Even if he had not had my welfare at heart I doubt if Wellesz would have discouraged my writing in *The Sackbut*. I was a useful contact for him and in the months that followed I managed to get paragraphs in here and there about his own musical activities.

I fear I am giving an impression of immense precocity by referring gaily to my activities as a " music critic." In point of fact, that first notice in *The Sackbut* was virtually my first and last attempt at *criticism* for several years. For the rest, I merely reported such musical events as had occurred or were projected in Vienna along with odd bits of gossip about the latest work of Schönberg and his school.

These reports appeared in *The Sackbut* when they reached the size of an " article," or in that journal's

weekly off-shoot, *The Musical News and Herald*, when they
were no more than paragraphs. I cannot remember how
much I was paid for any of these contributions, nor even
if I was paid at all. At best I cannot have received more
than could be paid by a postal order, but in any case I was
strangely indifferent to financial rewards for my labours.
My reward was the pleasure of seeing what I had written
actually in print.

The music I wrote about was music I heard in the
ordinary course of my concert-going and nights at the
opera. If my report was not printed then there was no
harm done ; the whole thing was speculative, and I
looked on it as nothing more than valuable experience.

I did receive one assignment, however. The Vienna
correspondent of *The Times*, who was not particularly
interested in music, commissioned me to cover a concert
of British music to be performed under a visiting British
conductor. I went willingly and feeling full of importance
sat in one of the boxes in the Musikvereinsaal where I had
hitherto heard music only from the standing-room place
at the back of the hall. My " notice " consisted of little
more than a 300-word story of what was played and how
it was received, but it was published in *The Times* before
I was fifteen and a half with the date-line " From a
Vienna Correspondent." I had written at last for a daily
paper.

Encouraged by *The Times'* description of me as " A
Vienna Correspondent " I next succeeded in crashing the
columns of *The Daily Telegraph* under the very nose of my
father. I did not give Herbert a chance to disapprove for
I sent my paragraphs direct to Robin Legge, the music
editor whom my father later succeeded.

I wrote as before under the pseudonym of " Patrick
MacHugh " but the name never appeared in the columns
of the Saturday music page of the *Telegraph*. Robin

Legge re-wrote my contributions and incorporated them in his own column, though occasionally I was credited as "A Vienna Correspondent" who had supplied the information.

There was one highly important by-product of all this journalistic activity, far more satisfying than the honour of writing without payment or the pleasure of seeing my words in print. I found myself on the list of dead-heads at the Opera and the concert halls.

I could present a printed (not engraved) visiting card which bore the words : "Mr. Patrick Hughes—Contributor to *The Sackbut, The Musical News and Herald,* etc., etc.," and the managerial offices of the Opera would let me have a comfortable seat for all but the most well-booked performances.

The management never went so far as to send me tickets ; I had to fetch them from a commissionnaire at the stage entrance where they were left by the Intendant. I had reverted to the use of my proper name on my visiting card, sensing that " MacHugh " would have been too difficult. As it was the commissionnaire had his own way of coping with Hughes, and alternated quite indiscriminately between " Hoog-hez " and " Toog-hez."

My access to such *Freikarten* as were going led to another important experience in my musical life ; it was not just that it cost me nothing to get into the Staatsoper and sit in the stalls or a box, but it meant that for the first time since my arrival in Vienna I was actually *seeing* operas as well as hearing them.

I had the same sense of bewilderment at seeing what actually went on in *Don Giovanni* as the famous bass-player who took a night off to see *Carmen* and was staggered to find that all the time he had been playing " pom-pom " in the orchestra pit they were singing the Toreador song on the stage.

But though there was a generous number of tickets available for Herr Toog-hez I never completely deserted the promenade of the Vierte Galerie. Whenever there was an opera which I wanted to follow with a score I went upstairs and stood under the exit lights to do it. As a dead-head one could never be certain in which part of the house one would be sitting, and a score was useless in the stalls. Sometimes, knowing what to expect, I took a chance on getting a seat in a box for an opera I could follow with a score. I sat in a box for a performance of *Parsifal* and I was very glad I hadn't decided to hear it from upstairs. I fell asleep frequently during this revolting work which seemed to be longer than Holy Week and Lent together. As I am not a horse and cannot sleep standing up, *Parsifal* would never have done in the Vierte Galerie.

In spite of the luxury of being able to sit down at the Vienna Opera, I am still happiest hearing opera in the circumstances of the top gallery of the Staatsoper.

When, as a critic, I had made friends with Mr. Barrand and Mr. Reynolds at Covent Garden I found it no longer necessary to scrounge a seat from them to see an opera after the official Press night. They gave me a pass which entitled me to wander at will at the back of the stalls-circle, where I could see to read my score, go out to the " Nag's Head " for a drink if I was bored, or walk round to the side and watch the conductor and the orchestra.

The stalls-circle promenade at Covent Garden lacks a little of the camaraderie of the Vienna Fourth Gallery ; there is virtually no social intercourse there and certainly no *claque*. Indeed, on most occasions the solitary figure of a man in tails absorbed in the score of *Falstaff* or *Turandot*, apparently preferring to stand although there are empty seats, is a sight that causes a puzzled raising of eyebrows among seated customers. But to me it is the most natural and pleasing way of going to the opera and I can no more get out of the habit than a professional sailor can get out of the habit of calling the floor " the deck."

I feel I would always have enjoyed Glyndebourne more if I had been able to stand up and move around during the performances ; at the same time, as I never remained sober through any Glyndebourne evening that I remember, perhaps I couldn't have stood up even if I had been allowed to. Alcohol and the conviction that Mozart is the greatest of all composers combined to make every visit to John Christie's opera house a Do. It was only when, sober and critical, I subsequently heard the recordings made by the company that I felt rather resentful and annoyed at having been so successfully taken in.

During the winter musical season in Vienna of 1923-24 I discarded all thoughts of the Celtic Twilight I had been so enthusiastic about at Wickersdorf and settled down to spend several hours a day composing my first serious opera. Every opera I had ever started, of course, had been my first serious opera for, like a new love-affair, " this time " was " always different."

On this occasion, however, I persevered longer than hitherto. It was a one-act opera called *Agamemnon*, and I dedicated it to Marie Gutheil-Schoder with a flowery tribute to her art in German on the title page. Well, not " the " title page exactly, for I wrote and re-wrote the first five minutes of the work about four times, each time, of course, with a clean title-page. My dedication to Frau Kammersängerin Gutheil-Schoder was inspired solely by my admiration for her as an artist, for there was never any part in the opera which would have suited her to play.

As one-act operas go, *Agamemnon* was an ambitious little piece. I had found some manuscript paper with 42 staves on it—two more than Strauss had needed for

Elektra—and I began my orchestration where Strauss had left off. I filled every one of the 42 staves, and the visual impression one had of one of my louder *tutti* passages was of a flock of sheep having walked across the page leaving their droppings behind them. While the orchestra I proposed to employ was gigantic and unusual, the actual music written for it was commonplace and familiar. A study of the score of *Agamemnon* today is like reading a musical diary in detail. Whatever opera I went to see at night found its way into the pages of my score the following day.

A page full of gongs and general pandemonium was the result of hearing Strauss' *Woman without a Shadow* ; the sudden use of a small group of instruments was directly traceable to a performance of *Ariadne auf Naxos* ; a visit to a concert of modern French music would produce an alarming rush of harp glissandi and whole-tone scales.

The scene which gave me most trouble was the opening. The curtain rose (after two bars from the orchestra—as in *Elektra*) on a dimly lit stage, with the Watchman on his tower waiting to sight Agamemnon's fleet returning home. Because I had remembered this scene so vividly from the performance of Æschylus' play at Syracuse ten years before, I was particularly anxious that it should be a knock-out. It was this opening which led to all the re-writes and new title-pages. Eventually I solved the problem ; the solution was a noise which I recognise today as the opening of Strauss' *Alpine Symphony*.

For all that the music of *Agamemnon* was derivative, the opera (as far as I got) had a certain dramatic shape to it. There was " atmosphere," there was contrast, and I used an uneconomical orchestra to build climaxes at the appropriate time. It showed that while I was as imitative as a monkey of other composers' mannerisms, at least I had picked up some of the fundamentals of opera construction. I had passed through an Italian phase, a Wagner phase and a Richard Strauss phase in just over a year ; with the writing of *Agamemnon* there were so many influences at work that it was impossible to say what sort of phase I was in the middle of. Consequently, there was comparatively little clear-cut characterisation ; no character could be consistent if she was to be Clytemnaestra as seen by Debussy one day, Puccini the next and Strauss the day after that. In my own mind Clytemnaestra never varied ; I had built up her character in the libretto, half of which I had invented myself, half based on a German translation of Æschylus ; I knew what manner of woman she was, all right, but I was far too characterless to keep to the musical point in attempting to paint her portrait. She was not a portrait ; she was a kaleidoscope.

If *Agamemnon* had ever been performed as I envisaged it I might have made a packet out of it—as a synthesis of Famous Operas of All Nations, or Fifty Different Composers in Fifty Minutes. Not even a cinema organist at his mighty Wurlitzer ever paraphrased so much by so many in so little time.

CHAPTER IX

SIGHING LIKE A FURNACE

THE composition (or compilation) of *Agamemnon* was seriously interrupted in the Spring of 1924, not so much by my indulgence in an orgy of music by Richard Strauss on the occasion of his 60th birthday as by a single item in the Opera's programme for the Strauss Festival Week. Vienna certainly went to town in the old man's honour.

Strauss had resigned from the directorship of the Staatsoper but there were obviously no hard feelings, for there
were gala performances of every known Strauss work in
the operatic repertoire. *Rosenkavalier* was played with
Lotte Lehmann, Elisabeth Schumann, Richard Mayr and
Marie Gutheil-Schoder ; *Elektra* and *Salome* both with
Gutheil-Schoder ; *Ariadne* with Jeritza and Maria
Ivogün ; even the early *Feuersnot* was revived and put on
with an all-star cast.

The papers were filled with essays and photographs and
tributes ; there were anecdotes of Strauss the composer,
Strauss the family man and pamphlets on The World
Significance of Richard Strauss and his Art in Relation
to the Universe and International Economy. The City
of Vienna presented him with the Belvedere Palace to live
in, named at least one street after him, picture postcards
of the composer were sold by the thousand in tobacconists'
shops and there was a general air of festivity mixed with
a solemn Teutonic preoccupation with the *Weltanschauung*
of everything and everybody to do with Strauss which
would have delighted Beachcomber.

Strauss himself conducted most of the performances,
dressed in white tie, tails and a head waiter's black waist-
coat. My nearest glimpse of him was during a concert by
the Vienna Philharmonic when I sat at the back of the
orchestra and watched him conduct his *Sinfonia Domestica*.
On the conductor's rostrum Strauss has great charm ; he
was the son of an orchestral player and has an unusual
fellow-feeling for the orchestral musician. Strauss,
senior, was a horn player and a brilliant one who distinguished himself during preliminary rehearsals of the
first performance of *Die Meistersinger* in Munich by blowing
loud and irrelevant notes on his instrument to protest
against what he considered a sacrilegious attitude towards
music.

Strauss, junior, did not inherit his father's aversion to Wagner for I have heard him conduct a lovely performance of *Tristan* in my time ; but he grew up with a special affection for and understanding of horn players. In the Festival performance of the *Sinfonia Domestica* Strauss enjoyed himself hugely, quickening the tempo in the final section just to see whether the horns could play their passages. They could, for the Vienna Philharmonic's horn team is without a rival. The valve-horn was not invented in Vienna for nothing, and Strauss grinned enchantingly when he heard the immaculate sound which came from Prof. Stiegler and his colleagues.

There was only one performance at the Staatsoper during the Strauss Festival for which the magic of the name of Toog-hez failed to obtain a free ticket, and that was the world première of the composer's ballet *Schlagobers*. I can only think that a ballet with the title " Whipped Cream " was written as a gesture to Vienna ; it not only sounded like occasional music, but it was occasional music written by a composer who had written himself out. Strauss at sixty was just about ticking over ; the engine was making the same sort of noise as before, but it never revved up and it certainly didn't take anybody anywhere. Even I, to whom Richard Strauss was a demi-god, recognised this and was prepared to deny him thrice.

By virtue of a certain amount of persistence and flourishing of cards outside the Intendant's office I was given a seat in a box for the second performance of *Schlagobers*, and, as I usually did when the Staatsoper coughed up two seats, I took my mother to see the ballet.

As an art-form ballet was new to me. I had seen most of what the Vienna Opera Ballet had to offer but I had little idea as to whether it was good or bad. I only knew what the tops of the dancers' heads looked like from the Vierte Galerie and what their faces were like from the stalls when I saw their performances " on the house."

My mother, on the other hand, had been what is now known by that dreadful term " balletomane " for years. She had seen the first Diaghileff season given in London ; she built up Nijinsky for me as a legendary figure to such an extent that when I met his daughter years afterwards I could hardly open my mouth for awe. She had written a long article in the *Windsor Magazine* on the training of dancers from childhood at the Imperial Ballet School, she had met Karsavina, and was so overwhelmed by her first experience of *Le Sacre du Printemps* that she remembers nothing between the fall of the curtain and buying hundreds of violets in Covent Garden seven and a half hours later.

Judging by the ballet I have seen since, the Vienna Opera Ballet was a competent body. The individual dancers had charm but no greatness, though they would not have suffered by comparison with some of the cavorting I have seen from the Monte Carlo company. They had their own classical tradition and they stuck to it. If, by Diaghileff's standards, some of the dancing was insipid in *Scheherazade*, the first few minutes of *Carnaval* were worth going a long way to see. They did Gluck's *Don Juan* well, for it was their own creation, and their natural Viennese charm came out in Mozart's *Les Petits Riens* and in the interpolated *Blue Danube* included in *Die Fledermaus*. Otherwise it was a typical Opera Ballet, although there was a higher percentage of dancers with individuality than one usually finds in such cases.

The prima ballerina was a girl called Fräulein Pichler, who was married to an Englishman, was very blonde and extremely competent technically. There was Hedi Pfundmeyer who mimed well as Potiphar's Wife in Strauss' *Legend of Joseph* when the part wasn't being taken by Karsavina or Marie Gutheil-Schoder, and who had an absorbing interest in new music—an interest which took her travelling in search of first performances of new operas and ballets.

Then there was a blonde Hungarian girl called Maria Mindszenty who became something of a film star and whose name I first heard in the buffet of the Vierte Galerie being spoken of very highly by a young man my mother had met at tea and brought along to the ballet. His name was Robert Speaight and I never discovered what he was doing in Vienna at a time when the theatre was not particularly exciting.

And finally there was a youngster, dark and quite fascinating to whom I was attracted when I was fourteen, and head over heels in love with when I was fifteen ; she was called Tilly Losch.

The only reason I mention *Schlagobers* at all is because Tilly Losch was in it. I had seen her in *Carnaval,* as Laideronette in *Ma Mère L'Oye,* in *Don Juan,* as Ida in a delightful Hans Andersen ballet by the Danish conductor, Paul von Klenau, called *Little Ida's Flowers.* When she appeared in *Schlagobers* I developed my first magnificent obsession. I had thought actresses were very nice before and probably dancers too ; but never until now had I lost any sleep over one.

Tilly (I can call her that because I grew to know her well a long time after) stopped the show in *Schlagobers* with a short solo dance as " Princess Teablossom." It was a pseudo-Chinese affair to music which suggested rather surprisingly that Strauss was aware of something having happened in music since 1910. Even if I hadn't been so fascinated by Tilly Losch on the stage, I would still consider that dance the most intelligent bit of music in an otherwise pretty drab ballet. As it was, Tilly and the music for the " Prinzessin Teeblüte " combined to change my whole outlook on music for a long while afterwards.

As a composer I deserted opera for the dance.

My love for Tilly Losch may have been forlorn enough as far as personal relationships were concerned, but the inspiration of my new muse led me to pursue a more practical musical course than I had previously followed. In after years it was my ballet that was performed before my opera.

Around 1924 it was the fashion in Vienna for prominent dancers to give dance recitals. Thus when Karsavina came as guest artist at the Opera she took time off to present a programme with her partner on the well-equipped stage of the Konzerthaus. It was billed as a *Tanzabend* in just the way that Kreisler presented a *Violinabend*.

Tilly Losch had given one of these recitals earlier in the year with the *premier danseur* of the Opera Ballet as her partner. The Opera Ballet didn't offer much in the way of male dancers but Toni Birkmeyer was a considerable cut above the rest of them. He was that rare thing among male dancers, a Family Man, and he came to London to dance as Tilly's partner in Cochran's revue *Wake Up and Dream*.

I regret to say that I didn't see the Losch-Birkmeyer recital for the simple reason that I didn't know anything about it. But I did get to hear about it and actually saw the programme of the music they danced to. I was intrigued to see that the repertoire included a piece by Bartók. Tilly, I could see, had her head screwed on the right way; she encouraged Modern Music, and I was quite convinced I was a Modern Musician, if not actually *the* Modern Musician she had been waiting for all her life. She would, of course, give another recital the following season.

In fact, Tilly Losch did nothing of the sort. But the possibility that she might do so started me off on writing my first piece of dance music.

F

I gathered up the score of *Agamemnon* carefully and put it away in a folder. That it has remained in the folder ever since is neither here nor there. I left off in the middle of a bar with the violins playing away merrily as an introduction to some important pronouncement by the newly returned Agamemnon. There had previously been a great choral climax of welcome and as I had no idea what the hell Agamemnon was going to say in reply to this public demonstration of loyalty it seems as good a place to have left off as any other. And there, one might say, the matter rests at present.

I sat in my room surrounded by picture postcards of Tilly Losch and in a fever of white-hot inspiration composed four dance movements which I strung together and called *Tanzsuite No. 1*. The suite, which in performance would not have lasted longer than three minutes altogether, was scored for what I considered a " practical combination " of instruments : flute, oboe, bass clarinet, piano and percussion. The music was extremely dissonant and angular, for I was going through a most " advanced " phase at the time having just begun to discover Stravinsky and Bartók. Tilly Losch I knew was well up in the latest developments of music so it never occurred to me that my music would not appeal to her. In any case, even if my inspired *Tanzsuite* contained no bar of what I now understand as music, it was written competently enough to pass as a fair example of the noise fashionable in the early 1920's. I was much more a Child of Our Time then than I have ever been since.

When the *Tanzsuite No. 1* was finished (there was never a No. 2) I sent the score to Tilly Losch with an appropriately humble and flattering dedication. Fräulein Losch acknowledged its receipt with a charming and noncommittal letter without ever suggesting what a bore I must have been to her, and I slept with the letter under my pillow every night until it became so crumpled that I feared it would fall to pieces altogether.

Encouraged by the apparent success of my first essay in dance music (Tilly, after all, had not actually said she would *not* dance to it), I decided to keep on writing in this idiom. I became even more practical in my choice of medium than I had been with the somewhat eccentric quintet of the dance suite and wrote a dance for piano.

I called the piece *Grotesque*. A more honest and descriptive title would have been *Music composed after hearing the Allegro Barbaro for piano by Bartók*, for it was no more or less original than that. If Bartók had not written his piece first, then mine might have passed as an average example of the superficially rhythmic novelty of the period ; as it was, there was no question of excusing the similarity between the two compositions on the ground that one was " influenced " by the other. *Grotesque* was very near to actionable plagiarism albeit the plagiarism was unconscious.

As I was no pianist *Grotesque* was free of all technical difficulties ; I had already long ago determined to play the piano for nobody's amusement but my own—a very easily fulfilled ambition if you play the piano badly.

Grotesque, however, *looked* difficult on paper ; but when the accidentals had been sorted out it was easy enough and by no means ineffective. I personally liked it well and sat down to compose a contrasting companion piece which I called *Noon by the Sea at Taormina*. This was highly impressionistic. I had recently had my first experience of the piano music of Debussy and I set out to paint a sound-picture of distant midday bells and the hot Sicilian sun sparkling on the sea ; my childhood memories were still very vivid.

Fortunately, as there was very little that could be called music in this second piece, the question of derivativeness or plagiarism never arose. I doubt if anybody could ever have traced any particular influence on the composition for the piece, written in 8-4 time, ranged from *pp* to *pppp* in its dynamics and was consequently almost inaudible.

But I was very pleased with my two piano pieces. I made a fair copy of them and without saying a word to Egon Wellesz, to whom I dedicated them, I sent the MSS to a London publisher who specialised in " modern " music, together with the score of the *Tanzsuite No.* 1.

After three months' careful reflection the publisher wrote to say he would accept them. The news arrived in the post on October 18, 1924, the day before my sixteenth birthday.

I was to get a royalty of one-sixth on each copy of the two piano pieces after 250 had been sold ; the dance suite was to be kept in manuscript and I would get a royalty on each performance.

To date some 33 copies of the piano music have been sold (the two movements were published in one volume) and the dance suite remains unperformed to this day.

I am still very curious about those 33 copies, and I would give much to know who bought them. My friends certainly didn't, for I gave them all presentation copies gratis. I was never unduly perturbed by the lack of financial success of my first published music. I was reconciled to what I considered a normal state of affairs by the experience of Jack with his books on Egyptology. He inclined to write books on the use of the subjunctive in Coptic which fewer than a dozen people in the world could understand, and as they were all colleagues of his he sent them free copies automatically.

My two piano pieces were eventually published in December, 1925, price 3s. By that time I was so ashamed of them and their whimsy title of *Pictures Unframed* that I never dared send a copy to Wellesz. I had them most elegantly bound and have never willingly shown or played them to anybody. *Pictures Unframed* is a secret between me and the unknown thirty-three who bought those copies at the official retail price.

To confess one was the composer of two published pieces of music by the time one was sixteen is faintly indecent and I feel I ought at least to try and explain, if not excuse, my precocity. In the first place, was it really an unnatural precocity? The average age of students in the early days of the old English Universities was fourteen or so. The physical development of children has not, I imagine, changed very much through the ages ; their intellectual development is mostly a matter of fashion and nobody can lay down definitely that such-and-such an age is the right age for a child to be writing music or painting pictures.

Having come from an English public school, where I had suffered apple-pie beds and been the victim of various sadistic practical jokes because I wrote music, I found it difficult to believe that I was not laughed at when I told an enquiring Viennese lady that I was a Composer. In Vienna they were used to children writing music and a few years before my arrival there Erich Wolfgang Korngold had had an opera performed at the Staatsoper. Korngold had been only twelve or so, whereas I was already fourteen and had not yet written an opera at all. I began to feel, in fact, that I was rather a backward child.

Music, alone of the arts, is one that can be practised without experience of Life with a large L. Painting and literature are primarily arts which depend upon external things or at least upon the artist's reaction to external things. Music on the other hand can be created for its

own sake ; one need not have had tó go to bed with a
woman to write a violin sonata. But one must have had
some experience of human beings to write a novel and
seen the countryside to paint a landscape.

The Viennese attitude towards composers still at the
stage of puberty was summed up in Schiller's tag about
" Früh übt sich was ein Meister werden will." My only
trouble was that I exercised myself early enough and
never became a Meister. (On reflection, all Schiller said
was that he who *wants* to be a Master starts early. He
didn't say that by starting early one would necessarily
become one.)

Living as I did in a different part of Vienna from my
mother all this time, there was no direct parental super-
vision of my everyday life. I was very fond of my mother
but she had the wisdom to see that I was far better left
alone. Or shall I say that she knew only too well that I
was impossible to live with and that for the sake of her own
quiet life I was far better off in a home—so long as it was
somebody else's home and not hers.

We saw each other when we wanted to, not because
there was no escape from it. I do not want to give the
impression that my mother was callous and indifferent to
the welfare of her only child. She has never been a
disciplinarian, and a normal family life is completely
foreign to her nature. She behaved with me in a way that
would shock the majority of " normal " mothers, but by
her very eccentricity, or perhaps even lack of method, in
bringing me up she succeeded in leaving me with
uniquely happy memories of childhood.

Though I considered myself independent of any
maternal influence at the time, I realise now that my
mother chose my friends for me with great care while I
was in Vienna. I picked up one or two friends for myself.
There was a young Hungarian homosexual called Benno,

who made passes at me in the Vierte Galerie. He was blond and looked like the Prince of Wales ; his attentiveness dwindled, however, when he realised that the charm of his blue eyes meant nothing to me compared with the beauty of Tilly Losch.

Then there was a rather moth-eaten Italian marchese who had met Richard Strauss and actually owned some of the Master's manuscript. The marchese was friendly enough until we fell out over the question of Mussolini's castor-oil treatment of Italian Communists. My friend's lurid description of the effects of the treatment, instead of converting me to the ideals of Fascism, as he hoped, merely revolted me. This was the first and last time that politics and ideology have ever interfered with my personal relationships.

As regards their moral character the friends my mother picked for me were not always much better than those I chose for myself.

There was an American singer called Dwight whom my mother had come across somewhere, and he, I should say, was as queer as a goat. Even after eight years at an English school I was virtually innocent of the mysteries of pederasty ; no doubt that sort of thing did go on at the Perse but I was always too busy having a " crush " on some local girl of my own to notice. When I was fifteen and " certain advances " were made I remained entirely ignorant of what it was all about ; my instinctive weapon of self-defence was a recital of the charms of Tilly Losch and it never failed me. I was quite unconscious that advances were being made or that I was expected to react in any way, but I bored my assailants so successfully that I was left in peace, though a little hurt and puzzled that I was no longer asked out to tea as frequently as I had been.

I would not say that Dwight was without his points.

If it hadn't been for him I might never have heard Battistini sing. That great Italian singer came to Vienna to sing less than four years before he died. I could not get into the Opera to hear him so I had to be content to go with Dwight to hear him give a recital. Battistini was nearly seventy but the voice was still there, a miracle of that easy singing so rightly called *bel canto*. He began to get really warmed up in the second half of his programme and when he came to Falstaff's little aria, " Quand'ero paggio," he was magnificent. I did not need Dwight to tell me that I was hearing probably the best singing I am likely to hear in my lifetime. I was too young to have heard Caruso or Scotti or any of the other legendary figures Dwight used to tell me about, but the tales he told remained firmly fixed in my mind. In recent years I have been able to hear the pre-electric recordings of Dwight's idols and every word he said about them has proved to be true. Dwight knew a good singer when he heard one, all right. I've often thought it was a pity he was such a bloody awful singer himself.

On the whole, however, my mother produced quite respectable people for me to play with. The fact that they were all very much older than I was (they could scarcely have been younger) did not perturb me. I had finished with school and people of my own age and preferred the company and conversation of my elders ; I looked and behaved more than my age and I had acquired a certain *gamin* authoritativeness on Vienna and its ways which intrigued adults paying their first visit to the city. I knew the cafés and the bus routes and how to get home after the last tram had gone ; I had become more or less bilingual and could argue with waiters and taxi drivers to good effect.

Physically and emotionally I was no different from any other child of my own age. I may have looked eighteen, but I was more frightened than flattered when I was accosted by a tart in the Prater who sidled up to me wearing a red cloche hat and dangling a large handbag by the handle (unmistakable badges of office at the time) and whispered coyly in broad Wienerisch : " Kommst, mit na' Haus' ? " I guessed the good lady was inviting me to go home with her, but I wasn't absolutely certain. My mother, after considerable thought, decided that I had in fact been accosted and could barely keep a straight face in telling me so. I was given a long and interesting description of prostitution, its dangers and advantages and would I please repeat the actual words used by the *Freudenmädchen* as they were obviously something every psycho-analyst should know.

Intellectual precocity, as distinct from early physical development, is something which can either be encouraged or controlled and is almost entirely a matter of environment. As one who had been precocious in his time I was horrified not long ago to hear the fourteen-year-old child of a famous English actress complaining loudly in a theatrical club (long after he should have been in bed) that the claret he was drinking was not up to the standard to which he was accustomed at home. And yet I should have known that such precocity doesn't last for so very long. At fourteen one may behave as if one were 25, but by the time one is 22 things have caught up with themselves. Like water, one's age finds its own level sooner or later, and one even lives in hopes that on reaching the age of 80 one will not be mistaken for 102 but for 45.

My own precocity between the ages of fifteen and sixteen did not, I like to think, make me entirely intolerable company. My preoccupation with music (considered normal by the Viennese) was a little surprising at first to those American and English grown-ups who were my mother's friends in Vienna ; but after a time they began

F*

to regard it as a natural phenomenon, and if I appeared
to be a half-breed Viennese alley-cat they merely presumed
that was what happened to people like me in the circumstances. Besides, I was not entirely unreliable as a guide
to the artistic life of Vienna. Flourishing my professional
card in the Intendant's face I scrounged two seats for the
Redoutensaal and took an English resident's wife to see
her first Mozart opera. She and her husband had been
very kind to me during a time when my mother was away
from Vienna and I repaid the debt characteristically in
the easiest way I knew. The resident's wife appeared to
be delighted by this introduction to a world she never
knew existed and asked me to tea several times afterwards
when her husband was away from home. I thought she
was very pretty in a blonde English way, but for all my
precocity I was still a couple of bars behind Young
Woodley and did not avail myself of an opportunity
which would undoubtedly have led to an interesting
initial experiment in amorous intrigue. Mrs. Chatsby,
on thinking it over, was probably a very dangerous woman;
she came from Camberley, and it is very unlikely that she
liked Mozart at all.

Though the phrase was not in vogue then I was what
is now loosely known as " sophisticated." If the verb
" sophisticate " is used in the OED sense of " to make
artificial " then I was sophisticated. I was *not* sophisticated in the sense of a more recent definition of the word
which I quote from the *News of the World* :

> Asked by the magistrate if she knew the meaning of the word
> " unsophisticated," Miss Dawn replied : "I don't know.
> Someone who is not a prostitute I suppose."

And that, I think, finally puts the term in its place.

CHAPTER X

PURSUIT OF HAPPINESS

I HAD two particular friends in Vienna to whom my mother originally introduced me. Lionel Penrose and Adrian Bishop were both at least ten years older than I was and had recently come down from Cambridge. They nicknamed me " Percy " for a reason I have never discovered and I was devoted to them.

Lionel was in Vienna looking into the business of psycho-analysis. At Cambridge he had been a brilliant mathematician and gained a half-blue for chess. His chess career had evidently begun early in life, for when Lionel was fourteen he composed a problem which was printed in an Australian journal with the comment " Hats off to Wizard Penrose ! "

Like many mathematicians, Lionel was also a musician. He composed remarkable tunes which could be played from left to right and right to left, and when turned upside down were the same as right way up. These little pieces were full of added complications and ingenuities in the form of accidentals which were sharps if played one way but flats if played another. Occasionally he varied things by composing two musical palindromes to be played together.

Lionel had one great musical enthusiasm which was Mozart ; and it is largely due to him that I acquired my own enthusiasm for this composer. I first knew Lionel at an age when Mozart meant remarkably little to me ; I thought the tunes were pretty but at a time when I was obsessed with richness of orchestration Mozart's clarity left me unmoved. Lionel, rightly, would listen to none of my objections but made me sit down beside him at the piano and play Mozart symphonies arranged for four hands. By playing Mozart in this way I began to find things in the music which I had missed as a mere listener. The fact that Mozart began to mean anything at all to me at sixteen was, I fear, just another symptom of precocity ; for Mozart is essentially a composer for adults. However, as my precocity took the form of getting a lot of things *out* of my system some years before they were due for evacuation, it was only natural that I should get one or two things *into* my system before their time. Mozart was one of them.

It is one of the great paradoxes of music that Mozart, who died so young, should be a composer whose work is fully understood and interpreted only by unusually experienced and mature musicians. The technical difficulties of his music are virtually nil ; if you can play scales and arpeggios in tune then you can play Mozart—on paper. But it is the very simplicity of Mozart that is so deceptive and which confuses otherwise first-rate performers who (*a*) treat him in a cold and aloof manner, or (*b*) treat him with a desperate over-seriousness.

The two worst performances of the first movement of the G Minor Symphony I have ever heard were given by two otherwise impeccable conductors. Toscanini lent on the opening theme like a drunkard leaning on a bar, stressing notes in a way that would have suited the beginning of the Brahms Fourth Symphony perfectly but which never began to make sense as Mozart. That Toscanini, with his remarkable gift of seeing the end of any given piece of music right from the first bar, should decide that this famous first subject must be so pulled out of shape as to be almost unrecognisable when it is first heard, is something I have never been able to understand. If Toscanini is convinced that the first subject does not begin until the third bar of the movement, how does he justify Mozart using the first and second bars as important figures in the development section ? I can only presume that the Glorious Uncertainty of cricket has its counterpart in music, and that Toscanini is as likely to have a blind spot about Mozart as Jack Hobbs was to be bowled for a duck.

Serge Koussevitzky's performance of the G Minor Symphony is even more remarkable. He starts the first movement *rubato* and approaches Mozart's indicated *allegro molto* somewhere about the ninth bar, having got there with a neat turn of speed which bears no relation to anything whatever. The famous Boston conductor has put all this on gramophone record for anybody to hear. It makes complete and utter nonsense. Heaven knows Mozart wrote a lot of peculiar and ambiguous letters with a lot of dirty words in them to his cousin, but when it came to writing music he wrote the instruction "allegro molto" at the beginning of the movement because he wanted it there and not somewhere at the bottom of the first page of the score.

I have cited two instances of what well-known conductors can do to Mozart. What nine out of ten rank-and-file conductors do to his music is nobody's business. On the one hand we have the semi-amateur English conductors who have not yet learnt that all Mozart first movements marked *allegro* must be taken at a peculiarly Mozart tempo to make sense at all ; they are pointless played *presto* merely because the notes are easy. On the other hand there is a school of German conductors incapable of understanding the meaning of the word "andante." One of these gentlemen, highly boosted in the *Radio Times*, recently dawdled so lovingly over the slow movement of the G Minor symphony that he had to be faded out for the nine o'clock news. If he had spent more time at school learning the meaning of simple

Italian words he would have known that "andante" (moving smoothly) is not the same thing as "andato" (gone bad). This conductor's drooling over the slow movement of the G minor was *andato* all right. It stank.

I think the main trouble with the performance of Mozart is the absence of a universal tradition, the sort of tradition which most conductors respect when they come to Beethoven, Wagner and Verdi. Interpretive artists in general tend to "discover" Mozart with alarming suddenness some time in their careers. They are inspired by the discovery of A New Angle, and in most cases this results in a distortion comparable to Shakespeare recited without regard to the punctuation. Otherwise excellent violinists over-emphasise simple phrases in Mozart concertos in a way they would never dare in the Bruch concerto. Almost always it is a question of misplaced emphasis on notes which need gentle treatment.

This habit of "leaning" on Mozart tunes is about the only tradition that has been handed down at all ; I cannot think where it comes from, unless it is a legacy from the nineteenth century which could never make up its mind about Mozart.

After Bruno Walter only Szigeti consistently performs Mozart to my satisfaction ; both are mature musicians with an instinctive sense of Mozart's peculiar style and of Mozart's peculiar *sound*. Toscanini, nine years older than Walter and old enough to be Szigeti's father, is oddly inconsistent in his interpretation of Mozart ; his natural genius leads to unforgettable performances of *The Magic Flute*, the Haffner and Jupiter symphonies, but always at the back of my mind I have a feeling that Toscanini is just beginning to discover Mozart. Toscanini, usually infallible where a composer's style is concerned, approaches Mozart with over-enthusiasm. Walter and Szigeti perform Mozart with the sureness of touch and graciousness of the aristocrat ; Toscanini, by comparison, is a *parvenu*, and his inability to distinguish between Good Form and Bad Form on occasion leads to musical gaffes and embarrassing incidents such as his treatment of the G Minor symphony.

I will not pretend that even with Lionel's guidance to help me I began to take in Mozart all at once. At fifteen I was a text-book example for psychologists of the power of Identification. Lionel liked Mozart, therefore I must like Mozart because I liked Lionel. By being a copy-cat (which is a more colloquial term for Identification) I satisfied my psychological leanings and incidentally absorbed Mozart's music and its performance in a way which I began to appreciate only many years later. All I have written about the way Mozart was played in Vienna is purely retrospective ; I was completely unaware at the time that I was going through a unique experience ; and in any case, precocious or not, I was far too young to have been able to make more of it than I did. As with a breast-fed baby, the advantages of being suckled are as great after being weaned as they are before. I lost my milk-teeth and grew up with a fine lot of second teeth firmly set in the music of Mozart.

Adrian Bishop was a direct contrast to Lionel. His real name was Frank, but—with the characteristic erudition of his school fellows—he had been nicknamed Adrian at Eton on account of his resemblance to a character in *The Ordeal of Richard Feverel*. In appearance, Adrian was not unlike a young Oscar Wilde ; he was a Dubliner, the son of a director of Jameson's whiskey, and had all the wit and charm and spontaneous irresponsibility of his native country. From Eton Adrian had gained a scholarship at King's College, Cambridge ; he was a gifted classical scholar who somehow failed to fulfil the promise everybody expected of him and he struck me even then as being undecided what to do with his life.

In between his time in Vienna and the 1939 war Adrian went to Persia as an education officer in some way connected with the Anglo-Persian Oil Company. In the late '20s he was back on leave and I met him at Lord's where he had arrived after spending a hilarious day in an open taxi emitting high-pitched " peeps " whenever he saw a Rolls-Royce. His greatest moment that day was on Westminster Bridge where his " peep " so startled a man driving a Rolls in a top hat that the hat fell off and was crushed under a tram.

It was eight years before I heard from Adrian again, and then I received a postcard from him to say that he had become a monk in an Anglican Benedictine monastery. His monastic career was short-lived, however, and it was not long before John Betjeman produced him in London—an older, stouter Adrian but as amusing and endearing as ever. When war came Adrian was swallowed up in one of the M.I. branches of the War Office, the one dealing with the Baltic countries.

After the 1914 war Adrian had somehow found himself mixed up with the war of intervention in Russia. He was remarkably reticent about his experiences and appeared only to recall that the Russians he was fighting with had invented rubber women to satisfy the desires of sex-starved troops. The rubber woman, which could be inflated when required, or deflated for transport purposes, was considered to be more economical to carry around than the old-fashioned brothel or *bordelle mobile*, which I once heard nicely translated as " Whores' Artillery."

Adrian and Lionel, the one gay and Irish, the other a Quaker with a mathematician's imperturbable, logical mind proved delightful companions in spite of the disparity between our ages. From Adrian I learnt the rudiments of eating and drinking and talking ; from Lionel I received a characteristic sympathy for my adolescent emotional problems and enthusiasms. From both I acquired a very necessary sense of proportion. I had a tendency to regard myself over-seriously, to write desperately melodramatic one-act plays and to pick up the worst possible mannerisms from superficial acquaintance with the work of Franz Wedekind. Adrian and Lionel laughed me out of my *Sturm und Drang* and would stand no nonsense from me. They announced frankly if I was being a bore—which was often—but because I loved them both very dearly I took their advice to heart with good grace.

I wish sometimes that I had the chance to live through my fifteen-year-old experiences of Vienna again at leisure. It is not that I did not appreciate the experiences ; it is just that they seemed to tumble over each other in such a short space of time that I find it difficult to sort them all out twenty years afterwards.

By the Spring of 1924 Vienna had almost become a metropolis again, a capital without a country, but a capital nevertheless. A League of Nations loan was beginning to set the place on its feet and the city had an air of prosperity about it even if, as the Viennese maintained, things were only improving from worse to bad. I do not think the impoverished middle and professional classes were much better off than before, but shoes began to be made of leather instead of paper, brand new tram-cars were put on the streets, there were late buses running throughout the night (a sign of the revival of night-life) and the municipal railway actually had trains running on it for the first time since it had been built— before the 1914 war.

Whatever the truth of the economic state of Vienna, the city offered an attractive artistic life. Internationally famous artists started to put Vienna into the itinerary of their tours again, and during the season which had produced Battistini for me I heard Fritz Kreisler for the first time. Nor did Kreisler do things on the cheap ; he returned to his native city to give a concert consisting only of three concertos. He gave a recital as well, but his appearance with the Philharmonic was an unforgettable delight. Some years later I had to listen to a peculiarly boring German pianist holding forth on Kreisler's " lack of integrity." Herr Icks held that Kreisler had sold his soul, that he played only café music and had committed the crime of being a success in America.

That Herr Icks' only ambition was to be a success in America stuck out a mile. He had been to the States and flopped ; later he returned to America. Knowing in what contempt Herr Icks held the American public I asked his son how come. Herr Icks Junior had no illusions about his father. He said : " Pappi only dislikes America when he is a failure ; this time he is a success. He played in a cinema last month."

As for Fritz Kreisler's " lack of integrity," it amounted to three superb performances of Mozart, Brahms and Beethoven in one evening the first time I heard him. As far as I'm concerned Kreisler can become a crooner for a living if he wants to, though I can't help feeling that would be a pity. He showed promise as a fiddler—of the café type.

With no threat hanging over me of having to go to school in the autumn the Vienna summer of 1924 was an enjoyable time. The Opera packed up at the end of June, Wellesz took himself off to his lakeside villa in the Salzkammergut and I was left with nearly three months in which to pass the time more or less as I pleased. In the company of Lionel and Adrian there were excursions into the Vienna woods to eat wild strawberries and to swim on the banks of the Danube and in the pool at

Schönbrunn. The city itself, with its warm, civilised climate, its incessantly playing fountains, the flowers planted in the baskets of lamp-standards in the Ringstrasse and the rich green of the lime trees was a fairyland where last trams seemed to leave far too early and cafés to close inhospitably soon.

Barbara read that last sentence over my shoulder and tells me—with the intimidating authority peculiar to wives—that I spend altogether too much time in pubs. I do not deny it ; nor can I promise her any hope of losing the habit. It is not that I have an abnormal craving for alcohol or any particular aversion to my wife's company ; it is just a habit which started in that Viennese summer and ever since then has played a dominant part in my social existence ; it is certainly too late to try and alter my ways now.

It was the Viennese café which was the scene of my first awareness of a social existence. The Café Kremser, just over the road from the Opera, provided my earliest experience of club life. I wrote my letters there, I read English, American, French, German and Italian papers there searching the columns of each for news of the musical and theatrical activities of each country. It was in the Kremser that I was first surprised to discover that *La Vie Parisienne*, in addition to its delicious drawings, also featured a first-class column of music criticism by a writer who was obviously a great supporter of Schönberg.

If the English pub does not offer the comfort and convenience of the Café Kremser, if I cannot go round to my local to read a four-page supplement of the *Corriere* devoted to the first performance of *Nerone*, at least it provides similar opportunity for the discussion of trivial and significant topics with friends one has arranged to meet and with casual acquaintances who happen to drop in.

Perhaps the greatest charm of the English local,

regularly patronised, is the certainty that one is bound to meet somebody there whom one knows, together with the uncertainty of never knowing which of one's familiar drinking companions is likely to turn up at what time on any given evening. The good English pub at its best has been described as the " poor man's club." To me it is more attractive than most clubs. There are fewer bores, for one thing, and being free-for-all there is always a chance of striking up a new and unexpected acquaintance-ship with a stranger who has never been to the pub before and is unlikely to come in again. I have met some odd people at the Savage Club, heaven knows, but even the Savage bar cannot confront me with a Scottish tinker walking his way leisurely from Portsmouth to Dundee. Perhaps my meeting with the tinker is not the sort of thing that happens every day in a London saloon bar ; on the other hand, it is only in a pub that it can really happen at all.

I came across the tinker one evening in the early '30s, a tall, wild-haired man with clear blue eyes and the skin of a medlar. He had come to England because he thought that to " go abroad," as he called it, would make a change from wandering ceaselessly around the High-lands. Time mattered nothing to him and he genuinely had not the faintest idea how long it had taken him to travel from Scotland to Portsmouth. He had just walked until he got there, and having seen the English Channel, he had set out for his native country again. Though he was independent of normal human relationships, the tinker was not a lonely man. He made friends easily, on the road, in the pubs, in the doss-houses where he passed the nights, and his conversation consisted largely of anecdotes and character sketches of the people he had met on his journey through England. He was unusually observant and stored up his experiences in his mind, not so much to talk about in company as to reflect upon when he was alone.

At closing time, he asked me the way to Shepherd's Bush. I was a little puzzled by his request ; Shepherd's Bush was scarcely on the way to Scotland from Sloane Square. The tinker explained that he liked the sound of the name of the place, and thought he would like to go and see it. I showed him the road and with a God-be-with-you in Gaelic he set off into the night, walking with the grace and strength of a panther.

I have no great desire to return to Vienna at present ; in the first place I lack the courage, for neither Vienna nor I are the same today : Vienna has no Opera House any more, and I have no pancreas worth mentioning. But looking back on that Viennese summer of more than twenty years ago I find myself oddly wishing to live through it again in preference to any other period of my adolescence. I believe it is because, at fifteen and a half, I had a capacity for the enjoyment of my surroundings and the people in them that I have never really had since. I still have enthusiasms, but they are enthusiasms for things which have become an established part of my life ; I am still able to be bewildered by the greatness of *Otello* and *The Magic Flute*, but it is a bewilderment which largely reassures me of something of which I am already unassailably convinced. I hear *Otello* and each time I say " This is terrific ! " And each time I have to add : " As if I didn't know."

But in Vienna people, sights, sounds, the very sunlight of the days and the warmth of the nights in the open air were things I was discovering for myself for the first time. If I had a Faust-like opportunity to recapture my youth I would sell my soul not so much for the chance of being physically young once more as for the ability to enjoy things and experiences for the first time again.

If I were suddenly confronted with the prospect of living through the summer of 1924 again there is perhaps only one incident which I would wish to turn out differently : my visit to Budapest.

My mother and I went there by steamer from Vienna. The Danube flowed swiftly. On occasion the Danube can be blue and beautiful ; this time it was yellow and muddy and so far from its stream helping our paddle-boat on its way the river seemed to cock a snook at us and arrive in Budapest a long way ahead of us.

The journey to Budapest was long, hot and monotonous ; after the first five thousand churches set on hills or among villages in the flat country on either side of the river the scenery became a little repetitious. But the boredom of what should have been a picturesque and romantic voyage (see any guide book) was completely forgotten when we came within sight of Budapest. The sun was beginning to set, throwing the city's buildings into sharp purple silhouette, a thousand lights began to flicker along the riverside and the Hungarian capital looked almost as beautiful and unlikely as anything ever imagined by Eric Maschwitz.

The illusion continued for several hours. We drove from the quay to our hotel in an open horse-drawn carriage, and spent the evening wandering from café to café listening to gypsy orchestras. I have since acquired a passion for gypsy music ; I know nothing about it beyond what I have read in Walter Starkie's *Raggle-Taggle* and in my blind, uneducated enthusiasm I prefer the Rumanian form to the Hungarian. In Budapest, however, I was less impressed by the gypsy music itself than by the orchestras' astonishing virtuosity in performing all (or all but one) of Liszt's Hungarian Rhapsodies by heart. I may have heard some first class *csárdás* during the evening, but if I did then the memory of them was successfully wiped

out by the Liszt rhapsodies and tzigane versions of two
tunes which were frequently requested by the citizens of
Budapest at that time : " Why did I kiss that Girl ? "
and " Yes, We Have no Bananas." Nevertheless, the
gypsy musician let loose among the music of Tin Pan
Alley is not to be sniffed at ; though he plays a foxtrot
for money offered by a sophisticated patron of the café,
the gypsy personality and tradition are clearly discernible
among the ensuing toil and sweat. I remember that
" Yes, We Have no Bananas " was decorated with some
astonishing paraphrases and cadences.

I went to bed happy after this evening in Budapest,
but the following morning I developed an uncontrollable
dislike of the place. The sun was shining, the girls in the
streets were the prettiest I had ever seen in any town ;
like the Viennese the Hungarians were going through a
bad economic time, but still the women were exquisitely
dressed. They had a natural elegance which was not
hampered by lack of money to spend on clothes ; they
just threw a scarf round their necks or a handkerchief over
their heads and made the average Parisienne look like a
ragbag.

But in spite of the beauty of the city and its girls
Budapest suddenly defeated me. I found that I could not
make myself understood. I spoke German only to have
people turn their backs on me ; they understood German
well enough, but Hungary had been an independent state
only a few years and I was speaking the language of their
former oppressors. It may have occurred to me to try
speaking English, but I doubt it ; I have always been
very obstinate about speaking English in any foreign
country, preferring to experiment with a " neutral "
language like German or French or Italian. I might have
been happier if I could have found the remotest connection
between Hungarian and any other language I had heard of,

but there was none; and it was no consolation or great help to be told that Hungarian is very closely related to Finnish.

I spent three hours queueing up and being messed around in the police station to tell the authorities that I had arrived, and after lunch I went back and spent another three hours telling them that I had decided to leave. With my passport finally in order I returned to Vienna, by the fastest train I could catch. The Budapest which had begun by hitting me like a midsummer night's dream was left behind me and I felt the relief of awakening from a nightmare.

With the prospect of any revival of comfortable travel in Europe growing increasingly remote every day I have lived to regret my impatient flight from Budapest, for it is the one city I have ever visited from which I never got my money's worth. My experience of gypsy music is limited to what I can hear on gramophone records, which is no more than enough to whet my appetite for an excess of it. I know that if I went back to Budapest I might not hear all I expected, but I cannot help feeling there might be an occasional *csárdás* among the gypsy virtuoso performances of "The Lambeth Walk" and "Who's afraid of the Big Bad Wolf?" (which is bound to have been imported by the Russians who adore it and judge most modern Western music by its standard).

My mother stayed on in Budapest to see a famous psycho-analyst called Ferenczi and on her return to Vienna we left for Venice. This revival of travel with my mother was due to her husband having gone to Egypt some months before to do some excavating; Jack was expected to return to Europe late in September, and as his boat was to land him in Venice my mother, who always suffers a little from train-fever, decided to be there to meet him in good time. We arrived in Venice at dawn on a hot day in the first week of August.

CHAPTER XI

VENICE—SALZBURG AND BACK

WHEN I had first been to Venice, as a child of five or so, it had impressed me largely as being a place with one or two buildings and a lot of water. Ten years later I began to discover that the view formed in childhood was rather out of perspective. Hitherto I had been intrigued by Venice ; this time I fell in love with it completely. I realised that the canals smelt, that the mosquitoes knew no pity and that the darker *calle* had not been cleared of refuse since victory over the Byzantine Empire had been celebrated on V-Day, 1204. But I have little patience with people who habitually belittle Venice, for I believe them to possess neither sight nor hearing, only an over-developed sense of smell. There are few cities in the world which so well repay unguided exploration of back streets and deliberate avoidance of famous monuments. Away from the Piazza San Marco and the bar-fly atmosphere of the Hotel Danieli, Venice can be a city of a thousand unexpected delights and rewarding curiosities.

In the unfashionable districts of the city one may encounter picturesque local festivals unmentioned in Baedeker, half-hidden churches containing unfamiliar Bellinis and above all one may eat and drink exceedingly well.

Lionel Penrose turned up in Venice while I was there and together we discovered a tiny *trattoria* (it couldn't be called a restaurant) where there was one table under a fig tree in a small rectangular walled garden. Meals were served only at midday, for in the evenings the table was removed and the garden became a skittle-alley. The owner cooked the food and waited on us ; the service, in consequence, was not over-rapid, but as the *padrone* boasted a particularly powerful brand of white wine made by his brother in Sicily and costing only a few pence a litre, any delay in the arrival of the meal passed unnoticed. My mother had brought me up never to drink water in Italy and at this time I had a strong head for liquor ; which was just as well, for Lionel and I used regularly to get through three bottles of the inn-keeper's Sicilian wine—at least one of them by the time lunch arrived on the table.

Back-street shopping in Venice had its charms as well. I had two favourite shops ; one was a dark, smelly little music shop near the Rialto which specialised in mandolins, Italian foxtrots printed on broadsheets and the latest cacophonies of Casella and Malipiero. The other shop was one I went regularly to look at without ever going inside it. It was a men's hat shop kept by a man who obviously knew the value of French as the Language of Fashion. The hats in his window never changed, but the labels advertising them did. If a particularly revolting-looking hat was described one day as " L'ultimo chic," the same hat on the following day would bear another ticket advertising it as " tipo très." When last seen the hatter was beginning to experiment with English ; his tickets bore such resounding phrases as " très coktail " and " princ of vales."

Venice would not have been Venice without its cosmopolitan colony of homosexuals. They abounded on the public beaches of the Lido, but such passes as were inevitably made at me were repulsed with the technique that never failed. I showed them picture postcards of Tilly Losch and was thereafter left in peace, to be referred to in their conversation as " he " instead of " she." It was a distinction I appreciated, though I have a feeling it was intended as an insult.

If I spent my days lying in the sun on the Lido or wandering through the alley-ways of Venice, my holiday was by no means without its musical experiences. There was opera at the lovely Fenice, where one expected the audience to be dressed like a Guardi picture and where the orchestra, which included several small boys in short pants, made more noise tuning up than it ever made during any of the operatic climaxes which followed. And there was the naval wind band every evening on the Piazza.

This band was one of the most astonishing I have ever heard. It was conducted by a little white haired martinet in uniform who looked and beat time like Toscanini and drilled his players into a remarkable state of technical efficiency and virtuosity. It was no band to play a few popular " selections " and leave it at that ; it would play a whole act of *Traviata* at a time and then continue with Beethoven's Fifth Symphony.

On the occasion of the visit of the British Mediterranean Fleet to Venice, the Piazza band launched out into a special arrangement of Elgar's Enigma Variations. The sailors in whose honour it was played were mostly dead drunk and well out of hearing, and the smarter English visitors were out on the Lido at the Excelsior or gallivanting around Venice on one of the treasure hunts with which the younger children of peers made the Venetian nights hideous ; but the gesture was not lost on me. I stood reverently listening to the band, trying to make something of the music of a composer who was completely foreign to me and feeling greatly relieved when it was all over and the Enigma were followed by the Dance of the Seven Veils from *Salome*.

Perhaps it is too much to expect to be able to appreciate Elgar in such circumstances ; a naval band, however brilliant, is hardly the medium through which to hear the music of a man who was a fine orchestrator. On the other hand, I first made acquaintance with a large part of *Otello*, *Ernani* and *Manon Lescaut* on the same Piazza and what I heard presented no difficulties. It was all music which came naturally to me and which I understood instinctively.

Even today, twenty years after my first introduction to English music, I still have the greatest trouble coping with works which my contemporaries consider to be master-pieces of the English Renaissance. I can manage Elgar for he is so thoroughly professional in his technique and his blatantly pompous vulgarity ; I can even suppress my nausea on reading his instructions to play *nobilmente*, though I feel it is up to the listener, not the composer, to decide whether a tune is " noble " or not, especially as Beethoven was content to ask for no more than that the slow movement of the Ninth should be " Adagio molto e cantabile." But for the rest I beg to be excused from the interminable rhapsodies on folk tunes, the dullness of " contemplative " slow movements and awkward, self-conscious heartiness.

It is an astonishing thing, this lack of genuine virility in so much English music. Elgar, with all his faults, had guts ; one always felt that here at least was a man who had been to bed with a woman and liked it, who thought about the English countryside in terms of rolling hills, rich trees and haystacks where he could roll about with some wench and no questions asked. It is this Elgar, frank and genuine one moment, moody and introspective the next, who stands head and shoulders above his countrymen, the Elgar who wrote the Rondo of the Second Symphony and some (but not all) of *Falstaff*.

The Elgar who really gets me down is the composer of the opening of the First Symphony. Here the nobil-mentality gets out of hand a little too much. Yes, yes, I know it's " sincere " ; but sincerity does not excuse

music though it may easily explain it.   " Sincerity " is a
term of justification to which English critics are touchingly
devoted. They would rather hear my German pianist,
Herr Icks, floundering about his Steinway, dropping
wrong notes as the R.A.F. dropped incendiaries, because
his Beethoven is " sincere " (and inaccurate), than hear
Heifetz playing a Wieniawski concerto.   But then
most English critics are determined never to enjoy music ;
to play something correctly and in tune is rather bad form;
it shows that somebody has bothered to acquire a technique.   In England, of course, music comes primarily
from The Soul ; only the blundering amateur is " sincere"
and above suspicion.   The professional plays music only
for money ; it does not occur to anybody that he makes
money because he knows his job and has devoted a life-
time to learning that job thoroughly—and, maybe,
sincerely.

But perhaps I am prejudiced. I have never learned a
job myself and therefore I detest amateurishness in others ;
I will pay money to watch amateurs play cricket, but I
will not accept a free seat to hear them make music.
And, being an amateur, I hope nobody will question my
sincerity on this point.

Though my introduction to Elgar's music in Venice
may have puzzled me, and the Enigma Variations have
lived up to their title a little too literally I was not down-
cast by the experience. Within a few days of the event
I had packed a suit-case and set off for Salzburg to attend
the International Contemporary Music Festival.

This somewhat grotesque occasion began characteristically for me. I arrived in Salzburg at about 5.30 in the
morning, had breakfast in my hotel and, as the first concert
of the Festival was not until the evening, went to my room
for a few hours' sleep.

When I awoke my watch showed seven o'clock. I had to

walk downstairs as the lift was not working and on
reaching the dining room was told that there was no food
ready for half an hour. I asked for an evening paper, but
the porter explained that the evening editions had not yet
arrived. With nothing to eat and nothing to read I took
a short walk outside the hotel. It was raining, a wet
Salzburg rain making a grey twilight and falling noisily
into the swift, yellow Salzach. I went back into the hotel
where the porter offered me a morning paper ; I refused
it, having already bought one on the station when I
arrived. What about dinner ? A little early for that, it
seemed, but breakfast would be ready in twenty minutes.
I smiled indulgently ; I was no stranger to Austrian
humour and the porter was a friendly soul.

When the time came I went into the dining room and
asked for the *piccolo* to bring me a drink. My request
caused no great surprise, but it was regretted that the
wine boy would not be there until 12 o'clock—when
lunch would be served. I was about to say that this was
carrying a joke a bit too far when it dawned on me that
things were a little haywire. Outside, the street lamps
were being put out and it was growing lighter. I looked
at my watch which showed 7.30 ; I would have to hurry
to get to the concert. It was not until I reached the lift
(which was still unattended) that I realised what had
happened. There was no point in going upstairs to fetch
my mackintosh yet ; I had overslept exactly twelve hours.

I began to doubt if I had in fact overslept, however,
and to wonder whether it was not all an interesting instance of relativity when I picked up a morning paper and
read a notice of the concert which I still half-believed had
not yet taken place. If I had *not* overslept then it would
mean I would have to hear the music the critic was writing
about ; and that, according to his views, would be sheer
hell. My prayers that it was today and not still yesterday

were answered, however ; in the evening I went to a concert and it was by no means the same one I had read about. But it took me most of the day to catch up with myself.

The least important aspect of Contemporary Music Festivals in the '20s was what we knew as the " contempt-ible music " itself. The International Society which organised these annual jamborees was presided over by Edward Dent, and the choice of an Englishman as presi-dent was a wise one. Nobody else could have coped so diplomatically with a regiment of crackpot foreign composers, with their ceaseless complaints that their works had been mislaid or misplayed or insufficiently rehearsed, that a rival had been given a better place in the programme or that incompetent players had been engaged with the deliberate intention of ruining their masterpieces.

Dent dealt superbly with every situation, staving off international crises with a few tactful words in three languages, comforting the dejected, humouring the aggres-sive and politely ridding himself of the bores (no mean feat in a small town full of modern composers).

It was generally agreed that the most tiresome part of the day was when there was music. The composers represented at the Festival were interested only in their own music, while the rest of us were not all that much interested in anybody's music at all. There was a certain amount of discreet partisanship among the audience. While there were no actual cheer-leaders it was noticeable that the biggest applause for Patagonian work would come from the Patagonian listeners. It was all a little like the Olympic Games, and but for the presiding influence of Dent might well have been as typical as the Olympiad of the brotherhood of man.

The social life of the Festival, on the other hand, was really rather pleasant. There were excursions to swim in the lake of Max Reinhardt's palace at Leopoldskron ; there were trams (if anybody had thought to use them) to take one to Berchtesgaden ; there were innumerable restaurants and beer gardens.

One of the riverside restaurants was the scene of one of the more ludicrous incidents at the Festival. A party of us, including Harriet Cohen, lunched there one day and when we had finished our meal asked the proprietor if Miss Cohen might be allowed to play on the restaurant piano, a suspicious-looking upright of no known make.

The proprietor regretted ; perhaps the other customers might object. But as at that very moment the other customers got up and left, leaving us the sole occupants of the room, this seemed a very poor excuse. We pleaded again ; after all Miss Cohen was a world-famous *Künstlerin* and the proprietor should feel honoured. At last, after several minutes, the proprietor gave in. He looked furtively over his shoulder towards the door then turned to ask what Harriet Cohen would play.

She replied, "Just a little Bach." The proprietor appeared to be none the wiser ; then clasping his hands as if in prayer he said : "All right—but *please*, not if it is political ! "

Harriet Cohen contrived to be the life and soul of the Festival ; she even managed to enliven the dreary business of the music on one occasion by arriving during the interval of a concert with an enormous basket of flowers which she distributed among members of the audience. It was all in aid of nothing in particular, but it was a most refreshing gesture.

Whatever impression the music of that Salzburg Festival may have made on me at the time, it did not last very long. Indeed, my only musical memories today are of incidents more or less unconnected with the official programme. There was an enchanting performance in the local puppet theatre of Mozart's *Bastien and Bastienne* and a revealing recital of Debussy songs by an exquisite French singer called Claire Croiza. I went to hear Mme. Croiza out of politeness to Edwin Evans who suggested that the concert might interest me ; I stayed to be fascinated and to wonder where these lovely songs had been all my life.

And finally, there was a nightly performance at the Mirabelle by Paul Hindemith and his brother Rudolf. The Hindemith brothers, as members of the Amar Quartet, worked overtime at the Festival playing string quartets of all nations ; when the evening's work was over they sat down to improvise German marches—four hands at one piano. These marches were excellent parodies and most popular with the Mirabelle's clientele. The proprietor of the Mirabelle evidently did not share the same horror of " political " music as the owner of the riverside restaurant. Otherwise he would have known that the sort of music the Hindemiths played in fun was exactly the kind of thing the already active Nazis took seriously.

On the whole, I returned to Venice having acquired a pretty light-hearted attitude towards music. I had heard Milhaud's setting of the *Catalogue des Fleurs* and decided that English literature offered little in the way of a text for witty vocal music to rival the first page of the British passport, with its rolling preamble of " We, George Nathaniel Curzon of Kedleston. . . ." Within a few days of returning to Venice I had set the passage for voice and chamber orchestra and also embarked upon a series of musical caricatures—sound-portraits of Carpentier, Charlie Chaplin, Freud and Mussolini which fairly bubbled over with wit. I was particularly hysterical about my treatment of Mussolini ; it was a march which featured " Giovinezza " in two keys at once while at the

G

same time there was a counter-melody (also in two different keys) provided by the march from *The Prophet*. The bitter cynicism of this satirical outburst fell rather flat when I realised that the tune I had chosen was not the march from *The Prophet* but the grand march from *Aïda*. The tune from *Aïda* would have been most appropriate some ten years later for in the opera, if you remember, it is used on Radames' triumphant return from victory over the Ethiopians. In 1924, however, the Duce's nine million bayonets could claim no more impressive battle-honours than the murder of Matteotti.

Matteotti may have been dead in September, 1924, but he would not lie down. Something which the *Corriere della Sera* said about him disturbed the Venetian Fascists no end and I was given my first opportunity of seeing a group of uniformed thugs at work when a gang of them went around Venice wrecking newspaper kiosks and burning all the copies of the *Corriere* they could find. I managed to refrain from any active demonstration against this behaviour by members of Italy's ruling class ; as a foreigner I could only sit back and reflect that, after all, Mussolini had made the trains run on time. The man was obviously a genius, for who ever else would have discovered the connection between castor oil, knuckle-dusters and the railways ? The backward democracies had to string along on coal.

I hadn't the faintest idea who Matteotti was, but if he had been the wickedest crook in Christendom I would have taken his side after witnessing the incident of the *Corriere*. I returned to my musical portrait of Mussolini with extra relish, adding a gone-off quotation from the music of John the Baptist in *Salome* to the other two tunes. The significance of this now eludes me, unless it was that I hoped the Duce would come to the same sticky end. Which he did ; more or less.

It must not be supposed that the second half of my holiday in Venice soured my outlook on life completely. On the contrary, I found the romantic surroundings of the place sufficiently irresistible to become sentimentally attached to a French girl with the most beautiful name I had ever heard. She was called Hélène Lefort des Ylouses and she and her brother, who were both painters, lived in the same pension as I did.

As love affairs go I didn't get very far with Hélène, mainly because I never had an opportunity of being alone with her ; her brother was always around and I came no nearer to holding her hand than helping her in and out of the ferry-boat between San Marco and the Salute.

However, the weeks spent with Hélène and her brother improved my French no end and it was largely in their company that I became better acquainted with the Venetian school of painters. I was perplexed at first to hear them speak of a painter whom they referred to in French as " Tintoret " though I quickly got used to " Botticelle." We did our Bellini and Veronese, our Canaletto, Tiepolo and Tintoretto pretty thoroughly ; we took steamers to Chioggia and a tram on the mainland to Strà to pick grapes at the roadside and see a Tiepolo ceiling in a palace. We swam on the Lido where, as a change from the attention of the homosexuals we had to suffer the loud, if complimentary, remarks passed by young Italians on Hélène's figure.

I was sorry when Hélène and her brother returned to Paris, and though I promised to write to her and visit her when next I was in Paris I never did either. One never does.

Meanwhile, my thoughts turned once more to Tilly Losch and I resolved that on my return to Vienna I would write her a full-length ballet. I had already received word from the London publisher that my two piano pieces and the dance suite had intrigued everybody so much that they were being extra carefully considered and I now had little doubt that I was on the threshhold of fame as a composer.

Considering that I was supposed to be having a holiday in Venice I seem to have composed music prolifically while I was there. In addition to the caricatures and the passport music, I had begun to write a set of piano pieces called *Notturno Veneziano*, consisting of a scherzo of mosquitoes, a serenade of drunks and an impression of the lagoon by moonlight. Further, I had started an unaccompanied violin sonata which I set down on paper in green ink and at Fever Heat after meeting Kreisler on the Piazza. It would hardly have suited Kreisler's somewhat conservative tastes in music, but I dedicated it to him nevertheless.

I discarded these projects, however, while my mother and I set to work evolving the plot of The Ballet. It concerned, I believe, some nondescript goddess and a human sacrifice which was put before her altar in a temple. The action opened quietly, with the goddess sitting motionless on a throne ; the sacrifice came to life ; the goddess made a pass or two at him ; there was a *pas de deux*, and from somewhere or other a lot of spirits appeared and there was an ensemble.

Finally, everything quietened down again, the sacrifice subsided, the goddess went back to her throne and the scene faded as the curtain fell on the same stage-picture that opened the proceedings. As a plan for an original ballet, it was hardly a world-beater, but to give the thing an air of authenticity I credited my mother's share in it to a fictitious Russian choreographer called "Tamara Kamarskaya." I fully understood the value of snob-appeal.

This sudden excursion into the pseudo-Russian

(previously I had been obstinately faithful to German and Italian for all title pages, credits, dramatis personæ, lighting plots and descriptions of make-up in my works) was a throw-back to a short season which had been given in Vienna during the summer by the Moscow Chamber Theatre. Tairoff's company had come to Vienna, taken a small out-of-the-way theatre for a few weeks and knocked the customers sideways with the sheer lunacy and gaiety of their productions.

All my life I have had the greatest difficulty with the Russian drama and the Russian film. I have difficulty, that is, if I set out to try and understand it. I have seen the film *Potemkin* six times in as many countries, and I still don't know what it's about except that somebody didn't like the meat they had in the Imperial Navy. In modern Russian plays and pictures there is always one character who is bound to call everybody else " Brother ! " at one stage in the proceedings ; whereon everything ends up happily and the counter-revolution is put down until the same story is dragged out by another author under another title and the whole confusion starts all over again.

The safest way to enjoy Russian plays and films is to see and hear them acted by Russians. You don't understand a word, with the result that it all looks very exciting and the politics don't get in your hair.

With Tairoff and his Kamerny Theatre, however, the ideological plug did not exist. The theatre had been formed as a purely artistic enterprise before the 1914 war and the policy of the organisation was largely to ensure that a good time was had by all. I saw the company playing on its home ground in Russia in the summer of 1934, but that is an experience I shall talk about later. In Vienna, ten years earlier, the repertoire consisted of *St. Joan, Salome, The Man Who Was Thursday* and Lecocq's operetta *Giroflé-Girofla*.

The productions were highly stylised (I think that is the right word) ; the actors' make-up was slapped on and was as grotesque as the exaggerated eye-shadow and corn-flour foundation of Italian movie actors. The scenery consisted mostly of ladders, scaffolding and upturned boxes. Everybody in the company could dance and usually did ; and those who did not dance were acrobats—which is where the ladders and scaffolding came in useful, for they swarmed up and down them on the slightest provocation.

And yet though the settings were somewhat " utility " and to the casual eye the performance of Shaw and Wilde appeared a little flippant, it was astonishing how sheer acting in a language one did not understand could hold one. The figure of the Dauphin, wearing tails and a top hat, was a music hall caricature, and yet in an odd way it was a strangely authentic characterisation. In the same way, the scene of the Inquisition (of which I understood not a single word) was uncannily moving. It helped, of course, to have read *St. Joan* in a Tauchnitz edition before, but even so there was something about the acting which was as universally intelligible as the music of a Verdi opera.

Tairoff's effort with *The Man Who Was Thursday* was a triumph of mechanics. The stage was filled with lifts, moving staircases, ramps and illuminated signs in Russian which lit up at the back from time to time. *Salome* was a comparatively sedate affair, though Wilde's words, even in Russian, cannot have lived up to the magnificence of the property moon dangling against the backcloth.

But of all the Kamerny performances my favourite was *Giroflé-Girofla*. This operetta, with its delicious music, was Commedia dell'Arte played by the Marx Brothers. The action was frequently interrupted, not just for songs on the usual cues, but by hordes of supers who climbed poles and squatted there, dressed as pirates. As if these diversions and distractions were not enough the company's leading comedian would leave the plot behind him, come down to the footlights and tell funny stories in broken German. He had a supremely comic face and a red wig which, by pulling a string, he could make to whirl round his head like a chimney-sweep's brush. His name was Sokoloff and it is not so long ago that I saw him in a Hollywood film (I believe it was *Ninotchka*).

For all that Tairoff's Moscow Chamber Theatre was my introduction to the Russian stage and what occurs thereon, my collaboration with " Tamara Kamarskaya " was deadly serious. When I returned to Vienna from my Venetian holiday I worked feverishly for three days and nights composing the music. When it was done I called the ballet *The Secret of the Goddess*.

Whatever may have been the Goddess' secret, the stage instructions did not suggest that she kept it from the audience. She was to appear entirely nude but for the conventional G-string round her middle.

CHAPTER XII

BRIEF ENCOUNTERS

To compose a 25-minute ballet in three days looks a rather big claim to make on paper; but the " composition " was no more than the roughest of rough sketches, full of all the abbreviations, cross-references, ciphers and bare outlines which only composers can invent and understand. The hard work began with the orchestration of these sketches; and, as usual, current experiences tended to creep in as the scoring proceeded and to change first thoughts.

The instrumentation took exactly a month ; except for inclusion of two gongs, a rattle, castagnettes, a piano and a choir to sing " Ah ! " from time to time, it was a reasonably conventional score.

The mis-en-scène, however, was not so straightforward. In the course of working on *The Secret of the Goddess* I went to see the dress-rehearsal of Schönberg's " Drama mit Musik," *Die glückliche Hand*. It was performed at the Volksoper as part of the festival celebrations in honour of the composer's fiftieth birthday and it was an oddly exhilarating event.

One of these days, when critics and public have grown used to Schönberg's idiom, they may discover that this forbidding and unlovable composer can make the most extraordinary noise with an orchestra. Because his music has (to put it mildly) no immediate appeal, his orchestral writing is virtually unknown to the general public. Which is a pity, because as long ago as 1909 Schönberg was just as much a Master of the Modern Orchestra as Strauss, Stravinsky, Debussy or Ravel ; indeed, he did things with an orchestra which none of these composers ever lived to do. But as it is likely to take several generations before the most cultivated ear is able to find half a bar of Schönberg's music that resembles a tune, the chances of getting to know this composer's work or taking to it with any affection are a little remote.

The fact remains, though, that the Five Orchestral Pieces written in 1909 are masterpieces of orchestral virtuosity ; the third, in particular, has no parallel in music as an example of a subtly changing wash of orchestral colour. (I'm sorry to fall into trade jargon, but there is no other way of describing the indescribable. You have to hear the third piece in this set to believe it, and then look at the score to discover the whole thing is improbable, if not impossible.)

I have heard the Five Orchestral Pieces once only—at a Promenade Concert under Sir Henry Wood (who else?) —and I am glad to have heard them. They were an unforgettable musical experience and I welcomed an opportunity of taking my bound copy of the full score to Queen's Hall for a change instead of using it at home as something to press on when I write in an armchair or on my stomach in the garden.

Die glückliche Hand, written a couple of years later than the Orchestral Pieces, was all that one might expect a " Drama mit Musik " by Schönberg to be. There were plenty of dramatic noises coming from the orchestra pit and precious little music in the conventional sense of the term ; the libretto was ever-so-literary and symbolic and the whole effect was that of a nightmare accompanied by a sound-track running in reverse.

If I was " influenced " by (i.e., copied anything from) this frolic of Schönberg's it was certainly not the music. One of the rules of plagiarism (conscious or unconscious) is that you should like the thing you are pinching, or if you don't like it, at least possess the technical facility to make a tolerably convincing counterfeit. With Schönberg it might have been comparatively easy to give a superficial impression of the joys of atonal music ; on the other hand, the effect might merely have been one of elaborate parody, which would be fatal because the average audience has its work cut out to keep a straight face when the scholars of the Schönberg Kollege of Musical Knowledge are being serious.

There was also one other danger in apeing the Schönberg method : I would never have been able to tell at rehearsal or performance when wrong notes were being played.

G*

It must not be imagined from this that I am anti-
Schönberg, in the way that one may be anti-Communist
or a pillar of the temperance movement ; being, as it
were, a musical grandchild of the Master, I was brought
up with a healthy, if somewhat mystified, respect for him.
Certainly few people in the history of music have suffered
more for their convictions; when he was not being attacked
for his musical principles, he was attacked for being a Jew.
Whatever one may think of his experiments in music, one
cannot but admire his courage, and feel greatly relieved
that now, a man of over seventy, Arnold Schönberg is
living a quiet life in America, teaching, composing and at
last being respected as the figure in music he obviously is.

I met Schönberg once only. I was in a tobacconist's in
Vienna with Wellesz when a little man in a blue serge
suit with a brown bald head and a nose that listed to
starboard came in to buy cigarettes. He presented an
unreal, grotesque figure rather like a gnome having trouble
in wearing an unaccustomed collar and tie. Wellesz
introduced us and I was left passing the time of day with
the tobacconist while the two composers went off
into a corner to speak in the busy conspiratorial
whispers always used by the Viennese intelligentsia in
those days.

It is unusual that a " revolutionary " composer should
still be considered a rebel when he is over seventy ; most
people by then have settled down to become respectable
elders. But Schönberg is rather in the position of somebody who has learnt to split the atom and hasn't yet
learnt quite what to do about it. He split the eight notes
of the conventional scale into twelve semitones and presented the musical world with the discovery that none of
these twelve tones was more important than the next.
With this discovery, of course, all the fun goes out of
music. When keys and the contrast of one key with

another cease to mean anything then the element of surprise in music, the unexpected modulation which has been exploited by composers from Mozart, Beethoven and Schubert to Verdi, Puccini and Sibelius, no longer exists. It may be very good communism, the idea that all notes are equal, but like good communism it makes for a very drab social set-up. Applied to painting " atonality " would mean a complete absence of colour-values, of perspective and a disregard of the fact that canvasses have limits. In music it leads to dull design and a remoteness with which the listener has no point of contact.

It is significant that since Schönberg's initial splitting of the musical atom composers have done their damnedest to put the bits together again. This is no mere reactionary gesture ; like the discovery of the atomic bomb Schönberg's twelve-tone system has scared the pants off musicians. To control the discovery may prove helpful in the end ; to accept it blindly can only lead to chaos and the destruction of the standards of some 400 years of musical tradition and effort.

Lenin's revolutionary maxim of " Two steps forward, one back " has been followed successfully by the most talented of the Schönberg school of composers. Schönberg himself took the two steps forward ; Alban Berg followed him, but took the step back. Berg in his early music shouted " Up the rebels ! " as loudly as any of them ; but in his opera *Wozzeck* he modified his manifesto and, allowing his natural lyrical and dramatic gifts to get a few words in edgeways, succeeded in keeping one foot on the ground the rest of us have to live on.

I feel, as a pupil of a Schönberg pupil, that I ought to appear a little more loyal to my old school ; on the other hand, the whole tradition of the Vienna atonalists is foreign to me. Schönberg is essentially a Wagnerian romantic ; his early works begin where *Tristan* left off.

The thick, wet-lipped sexual romanticism of Wagner with its orgastic doggerel and its general sanctimonious air of pornography masquerading as Art still remains the starting-point of all Schönberg's music, whether it is written in the conventionally romantic idiom of *Verklärte Nacht* (who but a German romantic would dream of writing a piece called " Transfigured Night " and what the hell does it mean ?), or reduced to the intense, concentrated capsule-form of *Pierrot Lunaire* and the last string-quartet.

Introversive art has its points, no doubt, but the deadly seriousness of the introvert composer, with his eternal search for the Higher Meaning of something the rest of us know as the enjoyable but rather commonplace pastime of fornication, tends to get one down after a while. Music, heaven knows, is a serious art ; but there was never yet a composer of genius who was unable to let his hair down and indulge in what are known as Lighter Moments.

Schönberg, however, is a composer who has never smiled in his music or once recalled the true meaning of the term "allegro." He writes waltzes, but they are ungay, unfriendly, uncharming ; the most endearing dance-rhythm ever invented leaves him unmoved, embittered that such things were devised for anyone's pleasure.

Alban Berg's sense of humour may be cynical, but at least it is a sense of humour. The dreadful millstone of the twelve-tone scale does not hang round his neck and threaten to drown him ; he knows how to escape from it and write such refreshingly near-conventional music as the dance, the military march and Maria's cradle song in *Wozzeck*. Posterity may take a different view of Schönberg's music from us and our contemporaries, but I doubt it. The old man has had his system on the market for nearly forty years and even a backward public like the present-day one would have bought it by now if it had supplied any kind of demand. The chances of

Schönberg's music becoming what Miss Doris Arnold so tenderly describes as " well-loved " are pretty slim.

If Berg's chances of a more lasting fame are better, then it is because in spite of his being an " atonal " composer, he had something to say which was connected with the main stream of Western music.

The morning after writing that last paragraph I got to talking about Schönberg and the atonalists with Constant Lambert. I often wish Constant could be allowed a completely free hand with music for he has the most deliciously impish outlook on things. It is his ambition, he says, to publish an album of Schönberg waltzes, gavottes, and other essays in what the composer is pleased to call "dance forms," put them on the market with a pretty 1890 cover on them and then sit back and watch the fun.

Lord Berners, on the other hand, has an even more mischievous scheme which is to include without warning a couple of Schönberg waltzes in a programme by Lanner, Gung'l, Waldteufel and the Strausses. And why not ? Schönberg was born and bred in Vienna and is qualified to be represented in any programme of Viennese waltzes ; indeed, he is far better qualified for inclusion than Richard Strauss, who is a Bavarian.

Until I talked to Constant Lambert I had forgotten that in his book, *Music Ho !* he had picked on exactly the same characteristic of atonalism as I have in writing of Schönberg : that it is impossible to be gay and atonal, for the emotional range of the twelve-tone system is ridiculously limited. So it happens that in *Wozzeck*, Berg is frequently having to desert the straight and narrow path of atonalism and get down to ordinary music in order to express ordinary human emotions. You cannot live for ever in the musical stratosphere ; a rarified atmosphere may present a novel experience at first, but it gets a little difficult to breathe after a while.

The atmosphere of *Die glückliche Hand* was rare enough ; if you can imagine an over-heated stuffy nineteenth-century German drawing-room suspended in the stratosphere, you may have some idea of the nature of the work. The music came from the stratosphere, the action from the drawing-room.

The stage was people with characters known simply as The This or The That, some of whom sang, some of whom mimed and all of whom were intensely Significant. There was a chorus who moaned away making the hybrid vocal sounds which Schönberg calls *Sprechgesang* and from time to time poked their heads through curtains and peered at the audience in semi-darkness.

The complicated lighting plot evolved by Schönberg for this drama was carefully marked in the score and was also intensely Significant. The true meaning of all this attention to detail tended to be rather lost on the audience, to whom the sudden switching on of front-of-house ambers suggested no more than the switching on of coloured lights. Schönberg, however, has never been one to underestimate the ability of his audience to take in all that goes on in his scores. The peppering of his pages with mirror-fugues, inverted crabwise fugues and numberless other ingenuities which appeal only to the eye of a student and not to the ear of the listener, had its counterpart in the careful instructions that this light should symbolise Death, that one Love-Transfiguration, and the other a Yearning for Alcohol Towards Opening-time.

The only lighting which made any obvious sense was the use of hand-torches (with No. 8 batteries) carried by members of the chorus to light up their green faces whenever they peeked through the curtains in the gloaming.

A few days before my sixteenth birthday, however, all the pretentiousness and mumbo-jumbo of Schönberg's stage action made a deep impression on me. I included a lighting scheme in the score of my ballet which, if it had ever been put into practice, would have made the dancers appear to be successively in the last stages of carotinæmia, sea-sickness, frost-bite and cyanosis. Further, I was sufficiently taken by Schönberg's desperately solemn symbolism to decide that my *corps de ballet* should be made up to appear as sinister as anything in *Die glückliche Hand*. Where Schönberg had one figure with bats' wings I had thirteen. (There was no particular significance in the number 13 ; it just struck me that 13 was about the maximum number of people with bats' wings who could conveniently find room on a normal stage.)

Nor did I stop at bats' wings. The instructions in my score demanded that the Thirteen Wild Spirits should have " hiddeously (*sic*) distorted features (masks), bats' wings torn and ragged ; hair like the Medusa's." Whether the Thirteen Wild Spirits were meant to be male or female dancers was never explained ; in view of their appearance it can hardly have mattered.

The dress rehearsal of *Die glückliche Hand* was, as you may have gathered, something of an Artistic Event in my life. As a spectacle it got into my ballet ; as music it has since got into my hair. At the time, however, that morning performance in October at the Volksoper was notable in another respect. I found myself sitting next to Tilly Losch in the stalls.

It says a great deal for my ability to concentrate on the artistic business in hand that the physical proximity of the *ferne Geliebte* did not entirely wipe out all memory of what was obviously the high spot of the Schönberg festival. When the curtain fell I waited patiently until composer, cast, conductor, producer, designer and a regiment of unidentifiable hangers-on had taken their calls and then nervously introduced myself to Tilly Losch as that Irishman who had been inspired to write all that music for her. (I made a point of correcting any impression in Vienna that I was English ; to say I was Irish made me a countryman of " Georg Bearnart Shaow " and a citizen of a poor oppressed little state which had at last gained its freedom from the tyranny of the wicked English).

Tilly was sweetness itself. She was even lovelier to look at close to than she was on the stage, and I was delighted when she remarked that she considered my Dance Suite to be " sehr interessant." It did not occur to me that she could hardly have admitted it bored the hell out of her, so I mistook her natural graciousness and tact for a most encouraging unsolicited testimonial. I parted from her feeling the happiest of all mortals, though my head was not too high in the clouds to notice that she glanced curiously at the grey suede shoes I was wearing. I was very proud of those shoes, which had been custom-built by a Venetian cobbler for 6s. ; but when I reached home I took them off and blacked them all over. I thought Tilly would prefer them that way.

Though I took Tilly Losch's reproving look to heart I have never been really able to present a respectable figure in any kind of clothes. I present a more or less conventional appearance in tails and on the cricket field, but otherwise I am the despair of my intimates who hesitate to be seen around with me. Battle-dress is probably the only solution to my sartorial problems, for only in this functional costume are pockets numerous and spacious enough to carry all the scraps of paper with telephone numbers on them to which I never possibly refer. (Barbara is apprehensive of the end of clothes-rationing. She fears she will no longer be able to go around excusing my raggedness on the grounds that I have no coupons.)

The somewhat startling eccentricity of those grey suede

shoes and the noticeable absence of an elegant, or even normally tidy note in my appearance away from Covent Garden Opera House or the village cricket pitch at Great Missenden are not things to have disturbed my relationship with Tilly Losch. That first casual meeting led to a friendship which has lasted more than twenty years ; we have met spasmodically in circumstances ranging from Tilly's arrival at my bedside with a parcel of grapes and marrons glacés when I had been injured in a motor accident to unexpected encounters in Salzburg and the New York Yacht Club.

At sixteen, however, having actually met her in person, my phantasy build-up of Tilly Losch grew more passionately romantic than ever. I saw her as the Beloved of All Beloveds ; I was in love as I had never been in love before.

For an infatuated adolescent, on the other hand, I did remarkably little about it. I didn't pester her with letters or hang around the stage door of the Opera in the hope of catching a glimpse of her. On reflection, indeed, I appear to have taken a strangely realistic view of things ; my dream-world and Real Life were quite distinct from each other, for I knew that I had not the faintest chance even of being allowed to kiss Tilly's hand, let alone make love to her. (If I had been Viennese, of course, I could have kissed her hand and no questions asked, but I was a foreigner.)

I took the fact that Tilly was not for me so philosophically that I am almost afraid to admit it lest it should seem I was indifferent and unloyal to an exceptionally beautiful and charming woman.

But when I got back to the silence of my lonely room, it was a different story. Cole Porter's " Night and Day " told a tale of part-time devotion by comparison. One of the first things I did was to re-write the dedication of my ballet. I could now give my flowery inscription an added authenticity ; *The Secret of the Goddess* was dedicated " in deepest admiration and sincere friendship " to Tilly Losch together with the date, time and place of our memorable meeting.

As an afterthought I revised some of the music and rescored the whole piece, had it handsomely bound and embossed with its new title, *Phantasmagoria*. The score eventually began a series of journeys round the opera houses of Germany to be examined by one Intendant after another until it was eventually lost. Which is probably just as well.

At one stage of its grand tour the score of *Phantasmagoria* was sent to Edwin Evans, in the faint hope that it might appeal to Diaghileff, whose British representative he was. The score reached Edwin through Hubert Foss, then head of the music department of the Oxford University Press, and on its return it was accompanied by the following note from Edwin to Hubert.

" I am afraid Diaghileff must be ruled out. In the first place the modern ballet has done with veiled goddesses and their like, which belong to an earlier period. Pavlova still does things of this type and you have probably seen what she gets for it. I believe they are also to be seen in Central Europe, where the modern idea of ballet has not yet prevailed. As for the music, you may take it as a mathematical impossibility for a composition to please at the same time Wellesz and Diaghileff, whose ideas are diametrically opposite.

" Now for the music, viewed objectively . . . It is a background only, for the few patterns that emerge into the foreground are lacking in definition. They are just the vague expressions of orchestral music.

" That, of course, militates against it more on this side of the map than beyond the Rhine, where the making of such music is still a flourishing industry. I fancy that what his music suffers from is due to germs absorbed in an infected area. When he has rid himself of the illusion that bricks can be made without straw, I should think that with his natural facility he ought to go ahead very rapidly. Apart from his ability to knead a satisfactory orchestral paste, there are, in the details of the score, many encouraging signs. In fact, it was the rich promise that it showed that prompted me to get another opinion before telling you what I thought of the substance. But there is no getting away from it. Pick out any theme yourself, and ask yourself whether it *really* is a theme. That is the trouble. There is so much that is good, that I should feel very nervous about discouraging him."

I have reproduced Edwin Evans' criticism at length for it shows how wrong a composer can be about his own music. I was quite convinced that what I had written was neo-Stravinsky and therefore right up Diaghileff's street. Edwin's comments not only show that I was wildly off the mark, but also describe the kind of music I was turning out far more lucidly than I can, in spite of a certain objectivity I have acquired in the years between towards the work of my adolescence.

The autumn and winter of 1924 in Vienna seem to have been oddly bare of any outstanding musical experiences comparable to those I had had earlier in the year ; for, apart from the Schönberg festival, only the death of Puccini made much difference to the ordinary day-to-day repertoire.

Puccini's death was characteristically taken by the Viennese as a personal bereavement. The newspapers carried heavy black borders round his obituary and the news columns were filled with minute-by-minute accounts of his last days in Brussels. Although the façade of the Konzerthaus was inscribed with Wagner's lines from *Die Meistersinger* about " Ehrt Eure deutschen Meister " the public of Vienna refused to interpret the idea too literally. It honoured masters whether they were German or not, and particularly if they were Italian.

On one occasion, when Mascagni was in town to conduct a drivelling new operetta he had written, the composer came into a café for a quiet drink after the show. He was recognised at once and the place was in an uproar until he rose and conducted the five-piece café band in a performance (repeated four times) of the Intermezzo from *Cavalleria*. This typical Viennese demonstration annoyed the local intellectuals no end, of course, but what had they to offer by way of competition ? As a counter-attraction Schönberg conducting café performances of his waltzes would hardly have had much of a future.

The death of Puccini was commemorated on a handsome scale by the Opera and led to the revival of the three one-act operas of the *Trittico*. I didn't take greatly to *Suor Angelica* ; I preferred my Puccini with all the blood and thunder of *verismo* and had little patience with tinsel miracles and souls being wafted to Heaven. I would like to hear *Suor Angelica* again, however, for study of the score leads me to believe that it is by no means as uninteresting as I thought.

Il Tabarro and *Gianni Schicchi*, on the other hand, I took to at once and can never have too much of either. The appeal of *Gianni Schicchi* is an immediate one, of course, but just as Verdi's *Falstaff* overshadows *Otello* because it is so startlingly gay, whereas *Otello* is the greater music, so *Gianni Schicchi* by its unexpected light-heartedness tends to dazzle the ear at the expense of *Il Tabarro*.

This little one-act tragedy is the epitome of Puccini's genius, for in it we find a concentration of the composer's greatest gifts ; there is tenderness in the duets, gentle comedy and characterisation in the *genre* painting of the ballad-monger and the other riverside types, and a consistent inevitability about the music and the atmosphere it creates. In its lighter moments it harks back to the fun and caricature of *La Bohème* and in the dramatic scenes it anticipates on a small scale the majestic conception of *Turandot*.

After hearing the *Trittico* I began to listen to Puccini's music more carefully. Hitherto I had treated it rather casually, accepting the more familiar operas with no outstanding enthusiasm, perhaps even with a certain condescension owing to " germs absorbed in an infected area." This newly acquired respect for Puccini, however, had no immediate influence on my own musical outlook ; it was many years later that I seriously began to study Puccini's manners and methods and write deliberately " in the style of " the Master.

I have no shame about my sub-plagiarism of Puccini, though I get a little impatient with people who trace a phrase or an orchestral effect to *Butterfly* when in fact it comes from *Turandot*. I know well enough where I get things from, without having to be told. If I have to justify my method and the absence of any originality in my music then it is because it is more fun to write the kind of music I do like (such as Puccini's) than to write the kind of music I don't (such as my own).

The deliberate filching of other people's ideas, tricks and technique may sound a rather shabby pastime to the pure in artistic heart ; but it is not only rather fun : it is unusually instructive. If I were a teacher of orchestration, particularly, I would encourage the counterfeiting of music by Mozart, Rossini, Donizetti, Verdi and Puccini, each of whom has very definite personal characteristics in his scoring, but which, because we are so familiar with their music, we tend to take for granted.

I don't clearly recollect how I learnt to orchestrate ; it was mainly something I picked up as I went along, with Wellesz pointing out that this passage would be inaudible or that one impossible. It was not until I was nearly thirty and engaged in composing incidental music in the Mozartian manner for a radio version of Molnar's *The Swan* that I learnt to write music that not only looked like Mozart on paper, but sounded like it on the orchestra. And I did this by working with the full score of *Figaro* beside me, learning how Mozart spaced out his chords in the woodwind and achieved his peculiar orchestral colour. In this way I came to know the value of individual instruments and to give the music clarity, for Mozart was never one to fill up his score with a lot of superfluous instruments merely because they happened to be in the orchestra and not working office-hours unless they had something to do.

In the same way, when it came to writing music for a radio operetta, I worked with the scores of Puccini on the table, learning how to score effectively for an orchestra accompanying singers in a more modern idiom, how Puccini makes it an almost invariable rule to have his strings in one register for the soprano and in another when the tenor is singing the same tune. Such tricks pass unnoticed in the opera house, of course, for there the voice plays the leading role ; but if Puccini did not resort to these tricks the voice would play no sort of a role at all, for it would be swamped.

As a teacher, then, in addition to teaching my pupils orchestration by the more obvious examples of Berlioz, Wagner, Strauss, Debussy and Elgar, I would make them concentrate on the *style* of individual orchestral scores, study the characteristics of Mozart, Rossini, Donizetti, Verdi and Puccini until they could take a piano score of *Figaro*, *Il Barbiere*, *Don Pasquale*, *Rigoletto* and *Bohème* and score certain passages to tally with the composers' own orchestration.

There may not seem much point in this suggested method, for composers mostly learn to orchestrate in order to express their own thoughts in as an original manner as possible ; but it is surprising how in practice the art of deliberate counterfeit adds to one's technical facility. And for that reason alone I pass on the idea to anybody who wants it, for I am too lazy to open a correspondence course myself.

The effect of hearing the *Trittico* in November, 1924, was delayed in its action ; other, non-musical influences made a more immediate impression. For one thing, I went through a sudden and violent Oriental phase. I cannot think what started it, but my room began to smell of joss-sticks and I fixed the lighting to an exotic dimness ; I read Tagore and Lafcadio Hearn and the veil of secrecy that already surrounded the Goddess in my ballet became even heavier and more symbolic of whatever-it-was.

This phase was short-lived and gave way after a few weeks to an enthusiasm for Expressionism, the result of a large dose of the new German silent films which were just beginning to be shown in Vienna.

I have always been extremely catholic in my taste in films, which is just as well, for in Vienna one never had the slightest idea what kind of a picture one was going to see. The titles conveyed nothing and the stills provided few clues. On one occasion I went to see what I thought was going to be a good who-dunnit which turned out to be a film version of *If Winter Comes*. The catholicity of my taste did not quite run to this, I must confess, but the general repertoire was pleasantly varied by a generous amount of Larry Semon and Buster Keaton shorts, westerns with Tom Mix and William S. Hart, comedies with Charles Ray and Constance Talmadge, and the usual quota of dramas with Norma Talmadge, Mary Pickford, Rudolph Valentino, Wallace Reid and a feature player called Adolphe Menjou who always got the worst of things in his pictures, but cheerfully shrugged his well-dressed shoulders and went on to more villainies next week.

The German captions were not without a certain quizzical charm of their own. In one Hollywood picture a character called " the Duke of Middlesex " was introduced on the screen as " the Duke of Middle Sex "

("Herzog von Mittelgeschlecht"), a description which fitted the part admirably.

Among the more remarkable German pictures shown about that time were *Dr. Caligari*, *Waxworks*, *Vaudeville*, Jannings in *The Last Laugh*, Conrad Veidt in *The Hands of Orlac* (which provided the theme for the English play, *Duet for Two Hands*) and in an excellent make-up in a film about Paganini. There was also a film called *Nju* superbly acted by Jannings, Veidt and Elisabeth Bergner which, apart from being a very fine picture, was also one of the few silent pictures I ever saw of Miss Bergner in which she did not dress up as a little boy. The Vienna cinema provided unique experiences all right.

I suppose it is inevitable as one grows older to think that things are never so good as they were, but in more than thirty years of film-going I am certain there has been nothing to equal the impact of those early German films. Until then the movies had shown little ambition to be more than the product of a successful entertainment industry ; since then the Russians and the French have had a considerable artistic success. But when the Germans arrived nothing of the kind had ever been attempted before ; they presented the audience with something entirely new which seemed to have evolved on its own and had no apparent roots in the past of the cinema.

The cock-eyed sets and unusual lighting of *Waxworks* and *Dr. Caligari* got well under my skin, and it wasn't long before I started out on an " expressionistic " ballet called *The Bridge* (it was later retitled *Choros* when I thought it would be smart to write " Χόρος " on the title-page).

The Bridge symbolised the gap between Life and Death and what went on in the course of twenty minutes on that bridge was nobody's business. It was crossed by prostitutes, unborn children and down-trodden workers, and there were enough murders and suicides committed on it to have lasted a Grand Guignol company for a month.

As I never did first things first I designed numerous stage sets for the ballet in oils and covered the walls of my room with them—an eccentric array of jagged roofs and drunken skyscrapers which startled an already gloomy Frau Schlesinger every time she brought in my breakfast.

Meanwhile, my everyday social life underwent a considerable change. My mother had left Vienna to join her husband in Egypt and, while I was quite content to be left alone in Vienna, I found myself increasingly seeking the company of my English friends and developing a first-rate nostalgia for England.

Exactly what it was I pined for in England I never quite knew ; perhaps, as Adrian had said, it was because the simple things of life were always so much better in England than anywhere else—things like blotting paper, telegraph forms, lavatory paper and matches. While I did not yearn to spend an abnormal amount of time drying ink, sending telegrams, sitting in the W.C. or lighting fires, I began to take an inexplicable dislike to Vienna and the Viennese.

I made no active demonstration of my feelings ; I merely spent a lot of time and money trying to escape from my surroundings and searching for High Life—a High Life which was a mixture of what I had read in P. G. Wodehouse and what I admired in the worldly elegance of Adrian.

Though I do not want to depict him as a corruptor of youth or anything like it, Adrian proved an admirable and sympathetic guide in my curious quest for Glamour. He was so obviously at home in the smartest surroundings and I wished to be so too. Looking back on it all I cannot imagine what it was I hoped to derive from all this ; for the search resulted in nothing more rewarding than an acquaintanceship with the more respectable bars and night clubs in and around the Kärntnerstrasse.

Certainly, in the course of my education in the ways of High Life, I encountered one or two odd people. There was an elderly son of a knight who was always having his pocket picked by the young men he seduced ; and there was an American diplomat who sneezed continually when he was drunk, attributing his catarrhal explosions, even in mid-winter, to hay fever. Neither of these, however, can reasonably be said to have satisfied my nostalgia for England and I did not consider them necessarily typical of High Life, although at intervals between his *amours* the one provided Adrian and me with a great deal of Tokay and the other shared his brandy and soda with us until he started sneezing ; then the rest of the evening would be spent in trying to prevent him breaking up furniture and fighting taxi-drivers.

One small thing came of all this : my first experience of a jazz band. Back at school I had shown a fondness for a record of " Ain't we got Fun ? " and during my last Christmas holiday in England I had been enchanted by Jerome Kern's music to *The Cabaret Girl* ; otherwise I knew no more of the popular music of the 1920s than I heard whistled by errand boys or sung at unexpected moments by Adrian.

Adrian had a considerable repertoire of words and music which he burst into without warning. There was one particular song which delighted us all, especially Lionel Penrose who recognised it as a superb example of narcissism. It was called " I Love Me " and it was a ditty to end all June-Moon lyrics. It started something like this :

" I love me, I love me, I'm wild about myself . . ."

and went on to a climax with the words :

" I take me to a quiet place,
" I put my arm around my waist,
" If I get fresh I slap my face,
" I'm wild about myself."

Ten years later " I Love Me " might have had some effect on song-writers, in the same way that the Marx Brothers put an end to Hollywood's cycle of college films with *Horse Feathers*, and to opera films with *A Night at the Opera*. But the satire was premature, and in 1945 we had quite a seriously offered masterpiece which ran : " I love you, I love you, I love you (sweetheart of all my Dreams)."

Adrian's songs were inevitably associated in my mind with High Life. They were tunes which people danced to in smart places, they were played by musicians who made a lot of money and they were written by composers who made even more. I was a little disconcerted to find that one apparently needed to be black to be a successful merchant of popular music, for my first experience of this new and mysterious world was an American Negro drummer in Vienna who sang and was called Bo-Bo ; but it turned out that one of Bo-Bo's most requested numbers was written by a white man called George Gershwin, and if Gershwin could do it then so could I.

I cultivated Bo-Bo assiduously, and long after Adrian was in bed I would go off to Bo-Bo's night club by myself, making a cherry-brandy last me all night and listen to this unfamiliar music produced by five coloured musicians.

Even by the narrow standards of jazz I do not think Bo-Bo was particularly outstanding. He hit his drums very hard and sang raucously through a megaphone the words of Gershwin's " Somebody Loves Me " to a roomful of people who hadn't the faintest idea what he was supposed to be singing. If he had substituted a dirty limerick for the lyrics of Ira Gershwin nobody would have been any the wiser. Bo-Bo's performance, however, was enough to make me curious about jazz. It was the era of music known (quite incorrectly) as " the blues."

At this point perhaps I had better explain that " the

blues " is not—as was generally thought in 1924—any tune in a slow 4-4 time. The blues proper is a traditional sequence of harmonies, 12 bars long, which serves the American Negro as the basis of a narrative song. The tune varies according to the whim and fancy of the singer who improvises ; but the twelve bars and their harmonic pattern are always the same, though the tempo may vary according to the mood of singer or instrumentalist.

In 1924, however, " the blues " came to mean anything slow with the word " blues " in the title, and teachers of ballroom dancing—never slow to exploit any peculiarly Negro idea or expression they do not understand— actually invented a dance known as " the blues." It was as though having heard of something called Sonata Form they had evolved a dance to fit that. (Exactly how ignorant dancing teachers are may be judged from the fact that there is something known today as " Jive dancing." In Harlem, where the expression originated, " jive " is a line of talk comparable to the R.A.F. " shooting a line," neither more nor less.)

When I first heard Bo-Bo I knew nothing of the technical distinctions between one form of Negro secular music and another. What appealed to me was the marked and heavy rhythm of the 1924 " blues " songs with their faintly novel harmonies (novel, that is, for popular songs) and the possibilities of the unusual instrumentation of jazz.

As it became a little expensive to gain experience of this kind of music at first hand, by listening to Bo-Bo in his night club, I began to collect sheet-music of current tunes. I went to the music store where I had bought my full-scores of *Die Meistersinger* and *Tristan* and shocked the assistants by coming away with song copies of popular classics called " Chili Bom-Bom " and " Broadway

Blues." It struck me that if I used these American *Lieder* as models I might eventually make a great deal of money, for I had only recently read of the romantic rise to fame of Irving Berlin who apparently couldn't read or write a note of music.

Within a few days I produced my first popular song. It was called " Daisy, You're Driving Me Crazy " (I wrote lyrics as well). I showed it to Adrian, who said it was very neat and why not write a sequel called " Gertie, You're Nice, but You're Dirty." Thereafter I neglected lyric-writing for some years ; not that I was discouraged ; it was just that I thought maybe I had more talent for the instrumental side of jazz.

But I did not discard the tune of " Daisy " ; I kept it in a bottom drawer to form the nucleus of what I was sure would be a vast output of the same kind of thing. " Daisy," in short, was to be the first step on a golden road to universal fame and fabulous fortune. I would continue to write operas and ballets, of course, for my ambition was still to be a great composer of dramatic music ; but I would make money by dashing off foxtrots and " blues," with tongue in cheek and a big balance in the bank.

At sixteen I had not yet discovered what I learned in later years : that no composer can write a popular tune with his tongue in his cheek and get away with it. That curious quality of " sincerity " is an indispensable ingredient of even the trashiest ballad. Popular " slush " music is written by people who believe profoundly in every note they create ; they must do, for how else can we explain the banality of " It's My Mother's Birthday Today " or " When the Mighty Organ Played ' O Promise Me ' " ? Nobody would dare to sell such music who did not mean it seriously.

Music may be a universal art but it is chock full of

class distinctions. A composer in Class 1 may write music which falls below his own standard, but he would be foolish to try and compete with a composer in Class 2, for each class has its own distinctive manners and way of life. The Class 1 composer may imitate what he *thinks* is the music of Class 2, but as he is by nature a superior artist the effect is one of musical slumming and no more. He doesn't really know his way around.

Thus you find that the successful composers of popular music, such as Jerome Kern, Richard Rodgers, Cole Porter and Harold Arlen, succeed because they keep to their own class ; they write the music they understand and believe in. Wisely they refrain from slumming with the still lower musical classes, and, less wisely, they occasionally confirm their *métier* by trying to go up a class and failing dismally in the attempt. Their hobnobbings with the aristocracy are as embarrassing as the antics of any *parvenu* in " Society."

The only instance I know of a " legitimate " composer successfully slumming and making a definite hit among the lower classes is Vladimir Dukelsky, a talented but not outstanding composer who wrote *Zephir and Flora* for Diaghileff. As " Vernon Dukes," Dukelsky wrote a quite charming foxtrot called " April in Paris " which has lasted from 1933 to the present day, and is still frequently played both here and in America.

Technically there is no reason why your " legitimate " composer should not do well as a writer of " pops " ; he will have learnt all there is to know about the harmonic construction of a foxtrot when he was a child, and (I hope) had his knuckles rapped for being so primitively unenterprising into the bargain. But when it comes to it, he must either automatically avoid the commonplaces of Tin Pan Alley, in which case the public will have no time for him ; or adopt an accent which goes against his artistic grain and fail to be convincing because the result will be little more than the parody of an idiom.

To the casual listener all modern dance tunes may sound alike ; closer study, however, will show him that the four composers I mentioned just now all have very definite and personal characteristics. I have learnt from experience to be able to distinguish each of these composers' work from that of others. That each has a peculiar style will be realised if I cite the following well-known tunes : Kern's " Long Ago and Far Away," Rodgers' " With a Song in My Heart," Porter's " Begin the Beguine " and Arlen's " Stormy Weather." Those four songs are typical of everything their respective composers have ever produced.

Not that the public cares a damn one way or the other. The only names that will attract the public on sight are those of George Gershwin and Irving Berlin, both of whom changed their style in every new tune they invented. But if you are looking for the needle of musical personality in the haystack of Tin Pan Alley it can be found in the music of Kern, Rodgers, Porter and Arlen. And personally, because I have very catholic tastes and am willing to listen to composers in Class 1 or Class 101, I have found the search most rewarding. Moreover, my admiration for these four composers' tunes long ago proved to me that I had no gift for writing popular songs. I have facility, but I lack faith.

CHAPTER XIII

VIVE LE SPORT !

My yearning for High Life and my growing nostalgia for England were further increased by spending the

Christmas of 1924 with my Meacham grandparents in Bordighera. I arrived there with a copy of *St. Joan* which I gave my grandmother as a Christmas present (hardly a fortunate choice, for she and her husband considered Shaw a dreadful anarchist), and a collection of Ibsen plays in German. I read *Ghosts*, *A Doll's House* and *The Wild Duck*, and they made sufficient impression for me to write to my mother that " they give one rather a lot to think about but they're very good, I think."

Bordighera I found most sympathetic. It was Italian enough to enable me to make the most of the climate, the sea and the smell of the shops full of cheese and salami ; and it provided me with a healthy sniff of what I imagined was the atmosphere of England. I had forgotten so much about England in just under two years that I was deeply moved by signs which announced " English Tea," " English Library " and " Gentlemens' W.C." (The only other place I have seen that misplaced apostrophe was in the bar of the Savoy. It was corrected during the war, I believe, by a purist American.)

The centre of Bordighera's social life, I discovered, was the Tennis Club. Here I really came into contact with the English, for its members were all jolly fine retired military chaps who read the Continental *Daily Mail* and discussed the latest Test Match scores from Australia. I entered into the conversation with the greatest of ease, for I knew the life history and batting averages of every member of the England side. Though I was fascinated by the English way of life as I found it in Bordighera, with its whiskies and sodas and straight-faced references to " tiffin," I don't think I was a great social success myself.

To begin with I was obviously rather a queer kind of fellow. I lived in Vienna (wherever that was) and I spoke Italian, I preferred Cinzano to Guinness and though

I was very keen on tennis I'd never (goodness me) been to Wimbledon ; and above all I didn't appear to have a dinner jacket.

I didn't have a dinner jacket for the simple reason that my mother had never dreamed I should ever need one. Tails, perhaps, when I conducted in an opera house, but not a dinner jacket. However, I made fulsome excuses and explained that I'd really only come to Bordighera for a week and all that. But in spite of my bit-of-a-bohemian way of dressing I did not miss my share of High Life. I sneaked timidly into gala dances at the Casino and the largest hotel and by wearing a funny paper hat like everybody else succeeded in making myself inconspicuous in conspicuously festive company.

At tea dances, on the other hand, I passed muster—as far as my dress was concerned. My dancing rather cancelled things out, for I was a learner and had my own views on the movements of my own and my partner's feet. As a dancer I have always been a flop. If I get sufficiently drunk I still try it occasionally ; but when I get as drunk as that it is an effort to stand up, and I don't frankly think the effort is worth it. So the rest of the time I sit still, maintaining that if a band is worth listening to there's no point in dancing, and if it's not worth listening to then there's no point in dancing either, and one might just as well go on drinking and talking.

Amidst all the jolly good fellowship of the English in Bordighera I had one slight retch of homesickness for Vienna. As a cabaret turn at a tea-dance a young lady was announced as " Anna, from the Vienna Opera Ballet." I could not recall ever having seen anybody of that name, but when she had finished running around on her points to the tune of the Pizzicato from *Sylvia*, I went and spoke to her. I started a long story in German all about Tilly Losch, only to find that Miss

H

Anna did not speak a word of German and had obviously never heard of Tilly in any language.

Perhaps it was a little unfair to challenge the poor girl like this ; she could hardly have reckoned on meeting somebody in a place like Bordighera who was on the free list of the Vienna Opera. But I must confess I take a malicious, if boring, delight in checking up in cases like this. I once knew a famous jazz-pianist who advertised himself as a pupil of Ravel—the sort of *cachet* which greatly impresses the ingenuous enthusiasts of the jazz world. When I eventually met Ravel in London I asked him whether he knew Mr. F., the jazz pianist. The name meant nothing at all to Ravel, and so a promising topic of conversation went for nothing.

This same jazz-pianist, however, was a little bit too much of a line-shooter. He once handed me a copy of the full score of *Rosenkavalier*, saying that it was a privately printed edition given to him by the composer—one of half a dozen copies. Unfortunately, he didn't known that I read German ; on the title-page were the words : Students' Edition, No. 785.

One wonders whom people like this aim to impress. There is one man I know who makes a habit of boasting that he was at the world-première in Italy of Puccini's *Trittico* and that he sat with the composer in a box. A very plausible statement ; except that the *Trittico* was first performed in New York. But then this same gentleman claims, according to his mood, to have been at both Balliol and B.N.C. I don't know about B.N.C., but out of idle curiosity I looked for his name in a Balliol College Register which Barbara, for no known reason, has by her bedside. There is nobody of his name in the Register at all—at least, not since 1832.

However, I suppose I am being unnecessarily particular. I have just airily talked about meeting Ravel, so who am

I to speak of these things ? Ravel is dead, so there is no way of checking up on whether my claim is true or not. But I will say one thing : by the end of the evening I met him Ravel still hadn't the faintest idea who the hell I was.

When I returned, a little reluctantly, to Vienna after my holiday in Bordighera I was more strongly convinced than ever that England was the only country in the world worth living in. I even wrote to my mother to tell her of my newly-awakened enthusiasm for everything English— English food, English people, English dinner-jackets. I must have felt very strongly about it all, for I rarely wrote to my mother to tell her very much beyond the fact that I wanted some more money. My mother was always a very close confidante, but there is little suggestion in my letters to her that she was anything very much more than a means of supplying an inexhaustible financial demand. I imagine she must have dreaded the arrival of my letters, for it had long been understood that I wrote only if I wanted something. My silences always reassured her, for she knew then that I was happy and busy.

Though I did not neglect my work with Wellesz or fail to send frequent titbits of news about Schönberg to the *Musical News and Herald*, the greater part of my energies in the early months of 1925 went into the pursuit of High Life.* I discovered a new jazz band, a group of coloured musicians led by an American Negro trumpet player called Arthur Briggs. The band played in one of the smarter night clubs and I became as regular a patron there as I was at the Opera ; indeed, I went quite happily on to the Weihburg Bar after listening to Mozart and Verdi and suffered no noticeable æsthetic shock from the

---

* Wellesz wrote to my mother that he was sorry " Paddy should become an habitué of the Moulin Rouge and such places, but in consequence he has written a good ' Blues.' " Egon is the only person who has ever called me Paddy, and I have always been as puzzled by this idiosyncracy as by the affection which prompted it.

sudden change of surroundings and musical standards.

I have been cursed, up to a point, with what is loosely termed " versatility," but much as I would prefer to keep my interests in separate compartments, I have never been able to do so completely. I might discuss jazz band orchestration at length with Arthur Briggs during his moments off the stand in the Weihburg Bar, but the next moment I found myself picking the brains of his flute player, a fine " legitimate " performer from Haiti who produced that lovely silvery tone from his instrument which is peculiar to French flautists. In short, I didn't waste my time ; though I doubt if I could have convinced anybody else of this.

It was Arthur Briggs' band which had the doubtful distinction of performing my first experiment in popular dance music. Everything that Edwin Evans said of my score of *The Secret of the Goddess* applied to my early essays in the jazz idiom. The form was there, the instrumental writing was effective, but there wasn't a tune in a carload. I produced on an average one new " blues " every week, copied the parts out myself and was as mystified by the result as Arthur Briggs was. I was still a very " modern " composer, and though I have no conception now what any of this must have sounded like, I can well believe that the pained looks on the faces of the Viennese dancers as they trooped around the floor to my music were not due entirely to tight corsets and bad ventilation.

My experience of Vienna's night life did not lead only to my learning how to score for a dance band ; it led also to the fulfilment of a cherished boyhood ambition.

In the course of my rounds of the night clubs one Saturday evening I finished up playing the piano very badly with an Hawaiian band at the Moulin Rouge. (These tours never cost me very much money ; I just drifted in and out, talked to the musicians and scrounged drinks at staff prices.) While I was playing, a young Englishman came over and asked for some tune I didn't know.

" Well, come over and have a drink, anyway," he said.

I went to find myself in the company of a number of South African and English medical students and one or two young men from the British Legation whom I'd already met with Adrian.

After some general conversation one of the South Africans turned to me and asked :

" Would you like to play tomorrow ? "

I replied that I should probably be playing at home ; I had a contrapuntal exercise to finish for Wellesz, and in any case I knew my limitations as a pianist.

" I don't mean the piano—I mean football," said the South African.

" Football ? Who for ? "

" For us—against Rumania."

It was explained that a Rumanian XV—no, *the* Rumanian XV—had arrived from Bucharest to play against Austria. Since it was a considerable journey from Bucharest to Vienna it hadn't been thought worth while to play just one international Rugby match ; there had to be three. Two games had already been played on the Friday and Saturday ; there was to be a third and final one on the Sunday. It was for this game that I was invited.

I accepted with enthusiasm ; it would be wonderful, I thought, to be playing a real English game again. It was just what I had been waiting for. I insisted that I " hadn't played for years," but when we got down to it we discovered that it was really only two years since I had played rugger, whereas my team-mates for the most part had not seen the shape of a ball for at least five.

My first—and last—Rugby international was a little

different from what I had dreamt about as a child. As I kicked the ball and swerved between imaginary opponents in the meadow during my holidays at Ditchling I played before cheering mobs at Twickenham or Lansdowne Road. In Vienna the cream of Austrian and Rumanian exponents of The Handling Code (I worked for the sports desk of *The Daily Herald* once during the war) appeared before a gate of one spectator—the son of the groundsman of the large soccer stadium in which we played. The boy was not only our sole supporter, but as he had a bicycle he was very useful for returning the ball whenever it went in touch. As a retriever of the ball he lacked any highly-developed sense of position ; but the delays resulting from his mounting his machine and riding it across the ground to fetch the ball from the back of an empty stand were very welcome to the majority of us who were in shockingly poor training.

As a Rugby match, Austria v. Rumania was a curious affair. I played outside-half for some time but retired finally to full-back where life was a little quieter and I didn't get so out of breath. There were moments of fairly heated discussion with the referee when the Rumanian forwards decided to head the ball from the line-out ; we protested that this manœuvre was a little unconventional, but as nobody could think up any specific rule which forbade it the matter was forgotten—especially as we scored two tries as a direct result of it.

The final score was Rumania 15 points, Austria 9 points. The following day's papers referred briefly to the result under the heading " Ruggby Fussball." I read the papers in bed where I had to remain for several days because I was too stiff to get up.

With the exception of a somewhat eccentric game at Cambridge some years later which finished at half-time with the arrival of a barrel of beer delivered by a man on horseback, I gave up any active participation in Rugby after my appearance as an international. Today I am content to be a member of the committee of the London Irish R.F.C.—a cheerful body of several hundred fellow-countrymen who sing and drink a great deal on Saturday afternoons while fifteen younger members rush up and down the field.

Rugby football is almost the only sport I am content to watch. Cricket I would always rather play than see, and if I had the choice of watching a Test Match on one side of the road or playing in a village cricket match on the other, I would choose to play every time. In normal times I contrive to play about four days' cricket a week throughout the summer, and I enjoy it whether I have any personal success or not. At any rate, one is always given a chance to succeed, and if one does not bat or bowl a catch comes no more or less difficult in the gulley at Lord's than it does on the brewery's ground at Marlow. But with football physical strength is all-important, and whereas I might be able to catch Bradman out at Lord's if the occasion arose, I could never hope to bring down Wilfred Wooller at Cardiff. So I am happy to remain a spectator of Rugby and make the most of the social side of its big occasions.

Rugby, unlike soccer, has a very highly-developed social side to it. The difference between the bar at Twickenham or Richmond and the bar at Wembley or Highbury is characteristic of the atmosphere of the two games. In the one game the players are merely members of the crowd who play better than the crowd does and return to drink with the crowd after the match; in the other, the players are a race apart and as unlikely to mingle in the bar after a match as racehorses are to dine with the Stewards at Newmarket.

The possible reason for this distinction between the social aspects of the two games may be that Rugby is a comparatively intimate game ; it is played by members of clubs in front of other members. The general public is in a minority. In soccer it is the general public which forms the greater part of the crowd ; the " members " of Chelsea or Arsenal are a small and exclusive group known by sight to few but the attendants at the gates.

But at an international at Twickenham ninety per cent. of the spectators are members of clubs affiliated to the Rugby Union. Rather than miss the social occasion of the big match, clubs in and around London will play their matches on the morning of an international ; which is something unthinkable in the Football League.

Compared with soccer, Rugby is an unglamorous sport. It does not attract small boys with autograph books and it never supplies pretty headlines all about transfer fees for the Press. To the casual observer, indeed, it might appear to be an unimportant little backwater of a game ; but it has an atmosphere of its own and, in Wales particularly, can assume the importance of a religion.

My doctor, who came to Britain from Frankfurt some years before the war to work as G.P. in a Welsh mining village, tells me of one incident which could only happen in Wales. Paul was called to the pithead one Saturday afternoon to treat a youngster who had had an accident in the mine. He arrived to find the boy seriously injured but conscious ; it was an amputation job and it had to be done on the spot. The patient had been brought up on a stretcher and was being entertained by a portable wireless switched on to a running commentary by H. T. B. Wakelam of an international at Cardiff. Paul suggested that the wireless should be turned off, but the boy refused ; it was a close game and beginning to be exciting.

Hacking off the miner's leg was no easy operation, but Paul did it ; and he maintains that the broadcasting of that Rugby international was a better anæsthetic than anything invented by medicine. It kept the patient's mind off a very unpleasant and difficult business, and to this day Paul believes he could have done the amputation " cold," for the young miner took no notice of anything until the final whistle blew and he began to pay attention to less important things.

An international played at Cardiff or Swansea is an unforgettable experience for the visiting foreigner. Of the two towns, Cardiff is the more convenient. The journey from Paddington is not too long and one arrives at a station only a few minutes' walk from the centre of the town and the ground. Indeed, I would always rather make the journey from London to Cardiff than from London to Twickenham.

Cardiff on the day of an international is unique. The local papers are filled with pages of details and photographs of the two teams, and the entire population talks of nothing else but the game. The horrors of an overcrowded town are alleviated by the charm and good manners of its citizens (especially the barmaids, whose good humour is exemplary) and the admirable sense and psychological understanding of its Chief Constable.

Jim Wilson is the only Chief Constable I have ever met who sets out to try and make things easy. He trains his police force carefully to be patient with the public and understand the *reasons* for crime as well recognising its commission. On an international day, Jim Wilson makes the Welsh Rugby Union open the gates of the Cardiff Arms Park ground five hours before the match is due to start. His object, he says, is to give the crowds somewhere to go when they are tired of walking around the streets. The plan works admirably, for given an adequate supply of saucepans and frying-pans from Woolworth's on which it can bang quite happily a Welsh Rugby crowd will keep itself amused for hours at a time.

H*

I first heard Welsh football-singing in a bus going from Richmond to Twickenham, when somebody at the front began to sing quietly and the tune was taken up in four parts or more by the rest of the passengers. It was at the height of the 1931 depression and I was most deeply moved by the sound that came from the voices of men whom I knew to be mainly unemployed, but who had saved up a few pence every week from the dole in order to make the trip to London. I was glad when we arrived at the ground, for I was unpleasantly near to tears.

By the time I first went to Cardiff for an international I had come to know my Welsh fairly well. Apart from having come to blows with a Welsh roundsman over an overdue milk bill on one occasion, I had made friends with London Welsh colonists like Parry Jones and a host of others whom I know very well but whose surnames I can never remember for the simple reason that they are always either Jones, Evans or Thomas. For a nation of so much character the Welsh strike me as showing little imagination in their choice of family names. Among my Welsh friends, the names of Vivian Jenkins and Arthur Rees always stick in my memory—not only because they were both members of the great Welsh team which beat the All Blacks in 1935, but also because of a charming story about a motor car they bought. The machine cost them £5 and was very old ; eventually it broke down altogether on a cliff road in South Wales ; it refused to start and was obviously done for. So, instead of abandoning it (which would have been untidy), they pushed it over the cliff on to the rocks below. They were rather puzzled to read some days later that the police had not yet finally given up hope of finding the bodies.

I thought I knew all there was to be known about Welsh singing after my experience of 1931, but on my first Cardiff visit I had the same trouble with my emotions as before. This time there was none of the intimacy of the singing I had heard in a bus ; it was the rich concerted depth of a few thousand voices in the cheap stand at the Arms Park and their performance of " Cwm Rhondda " sung with the dignity worthy of a hymn by Haydn which got me.. (And why not ? Haydn is a common enough Welsh name.)

At all Rugby internationals I am strictly partisan ; I root for any side that plays against England. The only game in which I am neutral is the one between Wales and Scotland and then, if I think of it, I take Scotland's side because I had a grandmother called McKay. This anti-English sentiment is not easily explained, but it is common to nearly all Rugby enthusiasts from the Celtic countries.* The Welsh and the Irish will disgrace themselves in their support of Scotland at a Calcutta Cup match at Twicken-ham ; indeed, when Scotland beat England there in 1938 Arthur Rees was furious because a gang of British Fascists caused a disturbance in Piccadilly and spoiled " his " Calcutta Cup night.

Perhaps the best-tempered of all international matches are those between Ireland and Wales. It may be because there are almost as many people called Hughes and Morgan in Ireland as there are in Glamorgan (wasn't one of our greatest actors called Sidney Morgan and our last pre-war rugger captain called George Morgan ?) ; or it may be that in addition to considering ourselves oppressed races, we both sing a lot of songs. But whatever the reason, it was characteristic of our relationship that when war came in 1939 the London Welsh and the London Irish Rugby clubs should have amalgamated almost instinctively.

An Irish match at Cardiff is always the highlight of the

* Jack Finlay, who led the New Zealand " Kiwi " forwards against England in November, 1945, showed me a stack of telegrams he had received from Ireland before the game. They all wished him luck against what one of the senders described as " the common enemy."

international tournament. The day that a player called Arigo scored the winning try there against Wales he was carried off the field on the shoulders of a Welsh crowd and the evening papers brought out special bills reading "Arigo bragh!"

The last time Ireland played at Cardiff before the war nearly 300 Irishmen spent the Saturday night in gaol. They had missed the boat back to Ireland and rather than have them wandering about the streets and sleeping in doorways, Jim Wilson opened the cells, where they slept as guests of the Cardiff City Police.

An international at Dublin, on the other hand, is much more of a local festival. The Irish capital is too far for the average Scottish and English supporter to travel to, and because Wales plays Ireland only in Belfast the red beret is not the familiar sight in Grafton Street that it is in Princes Street, Piccadilly or Royal Avenue. A Rugby outing to Dublin is a Friday to Sunday affair for those of us who live in England, and a Thursday to Monday blind for those who live in Ireland.

Again, the football match itself is the least important part of the proceedings ; which is understandable, for the game takes up no more than two hours of one's time during the week end. But even so the Irish are not completely able to keep their wretched politics out of it. Mr. de Valera, a considerable Rugby three-quarter in his youth, has never been allowed to visit an international at Lansdowne Road since he became Holy Ireland's Führer ; his presence there would offend the Gaelic Athletic League who do not hold with a foreign game originally invented by an Irish boy at Rugby school. And then there is the regular instance of bad manners which leads to the exclusion of the British National Anthem before the start of the game with England at Lansdowne Road. Apparently a simple gesture like the performance of " God Save

the King " is considered prejudicial to the self-respect of
the New Irish. The fact that " The Soldier's Song " is
played as a matter of natural courtesy whenever Ireland
visits Twickenham doesn't seem to count ; on that
occasion the Irish team show admirable manners, for the
Ulster members will stand to attention for " The Soldier's
Song " and the Southerners for " The King."

Much as I love the Irish, I feel they still have a long
way to go before they become an adult nation, not merely
because they seem to lack a sense of international responsibility, but because they tend to believe that their own
piddling backyard grievances are of universal importance. Their behaviour during the war—pardon,
" the Emergency " of 1939-45—was undoubtedly their
own affair, but it was nonetheless shaming to those
Irishmen who believed that Fascism was a little more than
an extra-parochial " trouble." For a nation renowned
for its wit, Ireland is singularly lacking in a sense of
humour ; the stupidities which the Eire censorship
thought up during the war surpassed anything ever
imagined by the Russians. For instance, while the B.B.C.'s
daily programmes were printed in the Irish Press no
reference was ever allowed to the B.B.C.'s news bulletins.
The times six o'clock, nine o'clock and midnight were
not ever mentioned in the schedules, so that to all intents
and purposes dance music and variety were broadcast
without interruption. Nor was the General Forces
Programme permitted to be mentioned. There was the
B.B.C.'s Home Service and something vaguely called the
" Alternative Programme." To mention the word
" Forces " would have been a breach of Eire's precious
neutrality. As a nation Ireland has little to be proud of
since 1939 ; as a race the Irish gave the Allies a liberal
share of V.C.s, Field Marshals, Admirals and Air Marshals.
In this respect, at least, we have nothing to be ashamed

of ; it is only a pity that the boys that beat the Black-and-Tans couldn't have been allowed to play their part a little more openly, instead of as conspirators in a foreign Emergency.

Mind you, I am not particularly devoted to " God Save the King " as a tune, unless it is played in Arne's original arrangement, but I find the regular discrimination against its performance at Lansdowne Road unnecessary and irritating. If the English can be grown up, then so, surely, can the Irish ; you never hear of the English not playing the Marseillaise when France plays at Twickenham merely because the French were enemies for nearly 800 years. And yet Anglo-Irish relations have been no more than the bickerings of a family argument compared with the international dust-up started by William the Conqueror.

I suppose, however, that the Irish take the political significance of music more seriously than anybody with the possible exception of the Nazis (for sheer musical inanity " The Soldier's Song " is excelled only by the Horst-Wessel-Lied). But at times the musical Irish show a remarkable ignorance of the very political tunes about which they are so touchy.

One day, on the way back from Lansdowne Road, a crowd of us visiting exiles stopped off for a drink at a shebeen, one of those places peculiar to Ireland where the publican carries on his business as a grocer and general stores as well as licensed victualler. While we were there a fiddler began to play outside ; we brought him in, gave him several drinks and he continued to play his reels and jigs on a cracked violin which he scraped at in the crook of his arm until he was so drunk he could scarcely stand.

When his repertoire was exhausted and he was in danger of falling flat on his face, he passed me his fiddle

and asked me if I could play something.   Rather labori-
ously I managed to pick out the tune of " Lullibullero."
The fiddler was delighted and made me repeat it until he
had learnt the tune ; he then took his fiddle back,
played this new addition to his repertoire once through
perfectly and staggered out into the street.   I hope he
came to no harm, for I had purposely omitted to tell him
that " Lullibullero " is the same air as that stirring
Orange ballad, " The Protestant Boys."   I would have
liked to have witnessed the reaction to his next public
recital.

My desire to return to England was further increased
during the early Spring months of 1925 by the visit to
Vienna of the Corinthians football team.   I met the
players in the Moulin Rouge the night before their match
with one of the crack Viennese sides ; I recognised them
as being English, for they all wore immaculate dinner
jackets, and I tacked myself on to them as a guide to the
night life of the city.   They were a restless body, these
young men from Oxford and Cambridge, but their
restlessness was caused less by a desire to change the wallpaper than by their eagerness to find a band which could
play " Tea for Two."

This song by Vincent Youmans had just become the
rage of London, but it had not yet reached Vienna so our
search was fruitless and no amount of humming and
whistling of the tune to the bandleaders of the night
clubs we visited had any effect.   In the end, a young
Corinthian called E. R. T. Holmes, who later played
cricket for Surrey and England, picked the melody out
with one finger on a piano ; but without its harmonies
" Tea for Two " was a pretty bare kind of affair and
didn't make much sense, so the matter was dropped.

What remained of the night was passed in wandering
through the streets of Vienna singing the bawdier verses

of " It Ain't Gonna Rain No Mo'," a tune of the moment which lent itself admirably to late-night community singing in the open. The Viennese police did not take very kindly to this form of music-making and a serious situation was only just averted when I mentioned the word " Fussball." It worked like magic, for the Viennese were great soccer fans ; the police were delighted by the opportunity of meeting a whole team from England and forgave us our trespass. Remembering my experience in Salzburg I assured them that our song had no political significance, but was merely the music of American " yetz-bents " and therefore more or less harmless.

I am sorry to say the Corinthians lost their match ; but since none of them had gone to bed much before 5 a.m. perhaps it was hardly surprising. In any case, it was a holiday tour so nobody cared very much.

The comparatively unimportant incident of an evening spent with the Corinthians, and its faint suggestions of Boat Race Night high-spirits, did more than anything to determine me to return to England. Not only had they given me a picture of High Life with their elegant dinner-jackets and Errol Holmes' casual references to *No, No, Nanette*, but I brooded resentfully on the characteristic but not unreasonable attitude of the Viennese which had led to the suppression of our caterwauling. Vienna began to irritate me ; the fountains, the lime trees in the Ring, the rich warmth and *Gemütlichkeit* of Viennese life in the early summer, the afternoons spent picking cherries in the garden of Wellesz's villa—all this lost its charm and attraction with the finality of an outworn love-affair. I would return in the autumn, but meanwhile I would spend my summer at home. The fact that I had no home in England was immaterial ; my first object was to get back there, and then worry about finding a roof over my head.

I packed the score of my ballet, a camera-size portable gramophone and set off on a journey that was one long crescendo of excitement and anticipation. I travelled with an uncharacteristic determination and could not be deterred from my objective even by a remarkably pretty young Polish dancer I picked up on the train and who invited me to spend the night with her in Brussels.

It was a Sunday when the boat docked at Dover, and my first action on disembarkation was to buy a copy of *The News of the World*. I turned to the sports pages and for the first time for nearly three years was able to read the previous day's cricket scores in full. I knew then that I really was home.

CHAPTER XIV

EXILE'S END

I SPENT a couple of blissful days in London, stuffing myself full of marmalade and cold lamb (the two foods I had apparently missed most during my exile), and set out in search of my youth in Cambridge where I stayed with Lionel Penrose. Lionel had returned to England some months previously and was now busy studying medicine during the Long Vacation.

Cambridge at this time was at its most beautiful and I revelled in the possession of complete freedom of movement in surroundings which had formerly been associated only with the grim proscriptions of life at school. I lay about in Lionel's canoe on the river, I swam at Grantchester, I rode a motor bicycle where and when I pleased ; it was a *Wunschtraum* come deliciously true.

The summer passed pleasantly and too rapidly, leaving behind it mingled memories of afternoons spent in King's with that charming, brilliant old man G. Lowes Dickinson (I'll never forgive the louse who stole my autographed copy of " Letters from John Chinaman "), of a slightly cock-eyed motor tour of Norfolk with Lionel and E. M. Forster where roads had a distresssing habit of ending inconsequently in fords ; of a spontaneous motor-cycle ride with Francis Baker-Smith (still at school) to the East Coast in order to visit a girl called Zillah who lived in a beach hut with a mother who never forgave me for liking fish and chips.

My mother turned up from Egypt for a brief visit, during which she had driving lessons, bought a very old Ford and took it back with her to drive it dangerously about the desert.

By the time the autumn came it was generally thought it might be a good thing if I stayed in Cambridge. Wellesz wrote to say that a University education would be no drawback to my career as a critic, and he recommended that I should try for a Modern Languages scholarship ; as far as my musical welfare was concerned he had no fears, for the reputation of Cambridge stood high in his estimation. (Wellesz's regard for Cambridge was largely based on his admiration for Edward Dent, who did not, however, become Professor of Music until 1926 ; but Dent's famous production of *The Magic Flute* in 1911 had made his name irrevocably synonymous with Cambridge to all Central European musicians.)

I sent to Vienna for my books and scores, took rooms in Cambridge and began a sub-undergraduate existence which lasted for the next two years. With the characteristic indifference of the adolescent to the elements, I was content to brave the raw damp of a Cambridge winter wearing a scarf instead of an overcoat, and generally look and behave as I imagined an undergraduate should. Evidently my make-up was successful, for to my constant delight I was frequently accosted by the Proctors when I appeared in the town after dark without a gown.

I did not go so far as to buy tobacco jars with college crests on them, for I had no claim to membership of any college ; but I joined in many of the more superficial incidents of University life without arousing comment. I was quite at home, for instance, in the atmosphere of " the Vic," a cinema on Market Hill where the ribald remarks of the audience and its gift for making a treble entendre out of the most innocent caption of the silent films were not without a certain rough wit. I learned, too, the peculiar joy of winter afternoon teas of crumpets in front of a raging fire ; I wore the brilliant monochrome ties which distinguished the " æsthete " from the " hearty," but neutralised the whole effect by regularly visiting the Grange Road ground to watch the University Rugby XV. In effect, I succumbed to the cosy atmosphere of Cambridge in a way that convinced me that here was the ideal existence. At seventeen, in fact, I was already looking forward to the time when I could retire—as a young Don of 28, maybe, with a comfortably secure future ahead of me which would enable me to compose my masterpieces in carefree surroundings.

The dream was harmless enough, and unlike most of my dreams I went quite a long way in my efforts to make it a reality. Having finished my regular schooling before I was fifteen, I now had to sit down and start all over again to learn algebra and the rest of the unfamiliar subjects I would have to pass in examinations entitling me to become an undergraduate, let alone a Don, at King's.

In order to succeed in the Previous Examination (what is the origin of the colloquial form, " Little-Go " ?) I set to work with a crammer, a busy, mousy little man who was a Methodist organist with the admirably occupational name of Mr. Humm. I divided my time learning mathematics with Mr. Humm and re-learning Latin with a master at the Perse, whose handwriting was so primitive that when I sent his bills to my mother she thought I was trying to disguise my own writing and swindle her out of the money in some way.

By the time the October Term of 1925 was in full swing Lionel Penrose had gone to London to work at St. Thomas' Hospital, but he left me with a number of Good Social Contacts in Cambridge. These were largely Dons, but through them I met an increasing number of people of my own age and I began to find myself with most of the advantages and few of the disadvantages of being *in stat. pup.*

As a musician I was considered a " bit of a Bolshie," for I was an anti-academic and over-inclined to argue in support of Schönberg and my Viennese background, not because I honestly believed in half the things I said, but because I could not resist disturbing the complacency of the academic mind. I was a regular attendant at the Sunday free-for-all tea-parties given by Dr. Cyril Rootham, a charming, hard-working and disarmingly conceited musician who was organist of St. John's College and the conductor of that enthusiastic, if somewhat inaccurate, body, the orchestra of the Cambridge University Musical Society.

Rootham's conceit was disarming inasmuch as his egotism was most inoffensively naïve. There is a typical (though perhaps apocryphal) story told concerning the pronunciation of his name. On being asked whether the " th " was hard, or soft as in " Booth," he replied : " It's Rootham—Beethoven, you know." If it was only a legend at least it was strong enough for him to be known to several generations of undergraduates as " Dr. Roothoven."

I was never a pupil of Rootham's ; which is just as
well, for our temperaments would hardly have blended.
I took a mischievous delight in bating him with arguments
in favour of modern music, our favourite topic of discussion being whether or not Ravel could write a tune.
Rootham insisted that he couldn't, whereon I would
whistle a large chunk of *Daphnis and Chloë* and throw in
a couple of phrases from *Petroushka* to prove that Stravinsky was whistleable too.   I fear I was rather a disappointment to Rootham, for I disagreed with him most
obstinately.

On the other hand, I had a great admiration for the
man and his enthusiasms.   Provided it didn't undermine
his morale too badly he was always willing to try anything
once, and as conductor of the C.U.M.S. he was almost
entirely responsible for the healthy and active life of
Cambridge music.   He conducted with a cork-handled
baton as thick as a quarterstaff and goaded his orchestra
into performances of modern works unknown to audiences
in other parts of the country.   (Some of the music tended
to sound a little more " modern " than the scores suggested, but if there was any doubt as to the intonation of
the C.U.M.S. there was never any as to its good intentions.)

My active musical contact with Rootham was limited
to my appearances in his orchestra as a percussion player.
As I have never been able to count bars' rests properly,
I played the cymbal part in the overture to *Die Meistersinger*
from a full-score instead of from the orchestral part.
Actually, this was largely over-cautiousness on my part ;
we rehearsed the piece so often that I could have written
the whole score down from memory long before we came
to the concert, but I feared I might dry up on the night.
I was less successful with Berlioz' Hungarian March, in
which I banged my bass drum prematurely and began the

cannonade a bar too early, though I did so with such conviction that the Guildhall has since had to be rebuilt.

The C.U.M.S. orchestra consisted of undergraduates (one of whom, Alan Hyde, is now the brilliant first horn of the L.S.O.), local teachers and amateurs, and a sprinkling of professional wind-players from London. The harpist was a young Cambridge lady with the most delightfully appropriate name any player of this instrument could have. She was called Miss Shillington Scales.

In addition to the large orchestra, the C.U.M.S. also ran a thing known as the Junior Orchestra. This was a kind of musical guinea pig which met once a week in private (and very rightly), and was an organisation on which budding conductors could practise music played by performers who were either totally inexpert at their instruments or experimenting on instruments which they did not usually play. Thus on Wednesday afternoons, Haydn and Mozart symphonies were stretched out on a musical chopping block and shredded by cellists who wanted a go at the oboe, by tuba-players bringing their unwieldy instruments to bear on the delicate filigree of a classical double bass part. The whole affair was under the direction of inexperienced conductors like myself who were too busy trying to beat a solid four to notice the appalling din which filled the Masonic Hall on these occasions.

These rehearsals by the Junior Orchestra were no place for the purist. On one occasion, having nothing to do, I tuned a harp to the key of a Haydn symphony and interpolated improvised glissandi and harmonics at what I considered appropriate points in the work. It was a novel effect.

I had no great ambition to be a conductor, and even when I settled down some years later to learn the job of Kapellmeister the idea was never more than a practical

means to an economic end. I have not the good conductor's temperament, let alone his technique, for I lack the
ability to concentrate and attend to detail ; an orchestra,
to me, is like an unfamiliar four-in-hand driven by an
inexperienced driver. We hope to finish the journey
together—a rough and erratic journey undertaken by a
driver who knows neither the road nor the horses—but
en route the experience is usually too alarming to all
concerned to be really worth it. Only when I have
written the music that is to be played do I become confident ; unlike many composers who conduct their own
works, I do manage to give a better performance of my
own music than other people give of it. But even a
begetter's familiarity with my score does not necessarily
result in an entirely authoritative and impeccable performance. On the last occasion when I conducted a
broadcast of my opera *Cinderella* (composed in 1937) I
suddenly became so fascinated with something I had
written that I turned back to look at the passage again
instead of beating the change of tempo which followed on
the next page. In this case, fortunately, the horses knew
the road and kept everybody from falling in the ditch ;
the lapse is one that has always puzzled me, for I had
already conducted broadcasts of the opera four times
before—twice from the B.B.C.'s St. George's Hall and
twice for Television. I may be a bad conductor, but this
incident had nothing to do with conducting ; it was just
a damnfool example of misplaced concentration.

Though I spent many hours a day at Cambridge in the
unattractive pursuit of enough knowledge to get me
through the Little-Go, I did not imagine that even if I
finished up with a fellowship I should ever be anything but
a musical Don. I even had visions of winning a musical
scholarship (after, of course, having gained one in Modern
Languages), and with this in mind I decided I had

better become proficient in counterpoint and learn the piano properly. Accordingly I went to work with Bob Broome, still music master at the Perse but now an equal who no longer had to be addressed as " Sir." (One of the first things that struck me on my return to Cambridge was the extraordinary stature assumed by masters. Men who had appeared as monsters of omnipotence less than three years previously now seemed what they really were—rather pathetic little creatures, pompous and insignificant, leading a sad and monotonous life.)

Bob Broome I had always liked, for his functions were restricted to conducting the school orchestra and the Saturday morning community singing. His individual tuition was private and appeared on the bill as Extra. He was not a form-master and therefore did not become involved in one's perpetual war against Authority. He was also one of several masters who never called me by my surname, and when I had sent a little suite for strings from Vienna for the school orchestra to play, he put my name on the programme as " Pat Hughes."

(Looking back I seem to have been oddly privileged in this way at school. Nicknames and surnames abounded among us, of course, but there were very few children so generally addressed by their Christian names by masters and schoolfellows as I was. I imagine it was largely due to my having been around so long. I had arrived at the School House when I was six, obviously an unsuitable age at which to address a child by his bare surname, and the thing had become a custom.)

Apart from his natural good temper, Bob Broome's friendliness may well have been due to his having been at school at the Perse himself and not having forgotten his own boyhood days there. He was quiet, unnecessarily modest and worked harder than he was ever given credit for ; it is not until this moment that I realised Bob

Broome must have sat up for hours at night copying the instrumental parts for his orchestra to play from.

Although Bob's charm and patience as a piano teacher did much to remove the memory of the blonde cow of Vienna, I still made no progress as a pianist. I managed to fake my way through the first two movements of Ravel's Sonatina, and he encouraged my newly developing enthusiasm for the sonatas of Mozart ; he even undid all the harm that had been done at Wickersdorf and succeeded in making me play some of the easier Bach fugues for pleasure. But he could not get me to practise ; the elementary technique I possess on the piano comes entirely from Bob's gentle encouragement of the Mozart sonatas. By playing these works I did at last acquire enough dexterity to be able to finger some, but not all, scales correctly in the right hand. With the left hand I am less well-equipped and I can't play an arpeggio for nuts.

As things have turned out, I have not lived to regret greatly that I am only a sub-normal pianist, except possibly once. This was when there was talk of my composing music for a film—a picture which, according to the modern fashion, inevitably included a pseudo-concerto for piano. I was not over keen on the proposition, for I believe the piano is the one instrument a composer must be able to play if he is going to write properly for it. One need have no more than A Feeling for the violin (and, of course, an elementary knowledge of its technical limitations) to be able to compose passable violin music, for violin-concertos have been written by non-violinists ; but no piano concerto has ever been written by a non-pianist. I do not know why this should be so, but I think it will be found to be a fact.

A much more regrettable result of my lessons with Bob Broome than my failure to become a pianist was my failure to develop any facility in counterpoint. I was lazy about it and would not concentrate because, through no fault of Bob's, I found the subject a dull one. I knew it to be an essential part of a composer's equipment, but it did not have the attraction for me of form and orchestration and today I find it a laborious business to write even the simplest fugue. I *can* write a fugue, if need be, but I have to work it all out very slowly ; even the light-hearted pseudo-fugues of mine which find their way into the ITMA arrangements take me far longer than they should. However, as these little pieces are not meant for the professional musician I am content to fool the ordinary listener by making a noise like a fugue to begin with and being pretty sure he won't notice that after a little while the whole idea has been forgotten.

If I had happened to be a conscientious practiser of the piano, at least it would not have disturbed my landlady at Cambridge. She took a great interest in all she heard coming from the instrument and was particularly devoted to something I played which she said was " ever so pretty—just like the variations." As far as I remember the music in question was a French folk-song, but what " the variations " were, which it was supposed to resemble, I never discovered. " The Prelude " I knew well enough and recently I have come to recognise " The Concerto," but " The Variations " are still unidentified.

Mrs. Webber, however, was a most encouraging patroness of the arts. She came in one day to report that the neighbours had complained of my playing the piano at four o'clock in the morning. She was most resentful of this unwarranted, Philistine attitude towards the freedom of the artist and remarked indignantly : " Some people are ever so narrow-minded, aren't they ? " Mrs. Webber herself slept at the back of the house, out of earshot. Or was she ? It suddenly occurs to me that perhaps she was just being tactful after all.

With no real home to call my own I began to get a little restless at the end of term ; for though I was unconnected with the University I found that life divided itself inevitably into periods of term-time and vacation-time. I had no plans of where to spend my first Christmas in England, but thinking that solitude among Bright Lights was preferable to solitude in an out-of-term Cambridge I descended on Lionel in Bloomsbury where I knew I could always have a bed, even though he might be away at Christmas-time himself.

Lionel's flat looked over the Foundling Hospital and the antics of the " Fondlings " in their playground afforded an interesting study of child-behaviour. The Fondlings (they were never known locally as anything else) played games which bore little relation to those played by other children—strange variants of tig and hop-scotch, games with stick and ball which, like the uniform they wore, can only have had their origin in the eighteenth century. They also presented first-rate instances of the spontaneity of motion peculiar to children, who stand still one moment and dart off to some distant point at full speed the next. Exactly what it is that suddenly prompts a child to move like this I have never discovered. The reason is obviously something which is forgotten when childhood is left behind. I thought I remembered quite a lot about being a child, but even watching my own three daughters in action has brought me no nearer to an explanation.

While I was staying with Lionel, Adrian Bishop turned up again and took me off to spend Christmas at his home in Dublin. Adrian's affection for me was sorely tested when he called round for me in the early morning to catch the boat train, to find that I had overslept and was only half dressed. We went by the night boat, an

alternative for which Adrian didn't thank me particularly ; the crossing was filthy and Adrian was very sick,
which annoyed him, for he was normally a good sailor.
As usual, I ate a disgusting amount and was quite happy ;
the Holyhead boats used to have peculiarly appetising
and bloody cold beef in the saloon which I found
irresistible.

I had not been to Ireland since 1914 and had never
been to Dublin. I took to our capital city enthusiastically
and at once. I knew from the moment when the guard
at Kingstown accepted our third-class tickets as we sat
in a first-class carriage that southern Ireland was going to
be very much my kind of a country. I am only sorry that
I have never spent more time playing with the Irish
railways, for from all accounts the Irish manage to get as
much fun out of trains as Mr. Rowland Emett does in his
Punch drawings. Not that the Irish do not take their
railways seriously ; they do. Lionel told me of one of his
experiences in the south of Ireland when he made a
detour which took him about 140 miles further than his
ticket permitted. On reaching his final destination Lionel
gave up his ticket and was told by the collector that there
was something to pay.

" How much ? " asked Lionel.

" Wait till I see now," replied the collector, " we'll have
to go to the station-master."

The station-master scratched his head ; it was an
unusual situation and would need considerable thought.
He rang up the station-master at Waterford, but could
get no answer to the problem. He next telephoned the
station-master at Wexford but without result. Finally,
refusing to be defeated in his determination to enforce the
railway's regulations, he decided to get on to Dublin ;
the station-master there was an old friend with many
years' experience of just this kind of puzzle. Unfortunately,

Dublin could offer no solution. The station-master replaced the receiver and turned to Lionel saying : " These suburban stations never know a thing. Anybody could have told them the excess fare would be one and twopence. . . ."

I had not been in Dublin more than a few hours before I was overwhelmed by a feeling of being " home." I do not really attach much importance to this feeling, for I get it in Cardiff and Glasgow ; on the other hand I do not catch the accents of Wales and Scotland, whereas within a few days of arriving in Dublin I had a brogue you could cut with a knife. It was not so much an affectation as a semi-conscious attempt to speak the same language as the people around me and make certain that I was understood. In my adolescence I was as imitative as a parrot, and when in England my natural accent was closely modelled on Adrian's ; in Ireland every scrap of Irishness I had ever inherited from my father came out in me only to go back under the surface as soon as I left the country. Today I speak a nondescript English which gives way to a faint suggestion of Irish when I am excited or consciously covering up some indiscretion with a lot of synthetic charm. (I have never been slow to trade on the Sassenach's romantic and lenient attitude towards the Irish, and in America I exploited the Irish in a disgraceful way. When I was asked what part of Ireland I came from I would reply that I was born near Barnet. Let me think, they'd say, that's Co. Down, isn't it ? I never disillusioned them, for Barnet is a very Irish-sounding name. The only thing that puzzled the New Yorker was the fact that I didn't speak with the same accent as the local cops. But then I never spoke better English in my life than I did in New York ; it was a natural reaction.)

Dublin inspired a number of mixed feelings. On the one hand I was deeply moved to see the scenes of The

Troubles ; the damaged Post Office, and the street corners which had been strong points in the battle roused me to a fury of indignation and anti-English resentment. On the other hand, I was delighted by the solemn patriotism of the Irish which put up street names in Gaelic but had to add English translations because otherwise nobody would know where they were ; by the deliberate use of green paint in place of " England's cruel red " on pillar-boxes which still bore the monogram " V.R.", and by the transliteration of homely phrases like " telephone " into " an telefon " in Gaelic characters.

If I derived a certain excitement and pride from the historical associations of Dublin with the National Struggle for Freedom my sympathy took no more practical form than a subscription to the *Irish Statesman*, an admirable threepenn'orth of weekly political and literary review edited by A.E. I have never understood Irish politics and I fear it is too late now to take up the subject seriously ; but I bought myself a bright green tie and took an ardent and outraged interest in the fate of the Lane pictures. It seemed that Sir Hugh Lane, by virtue of an unwitnessed codicil to his will (he was drowned in the *Lusitania*) had changed his mind and left his collection to the Irish National Gallery ; but the wicked English had ignored his dying wish and hung on to the pictures. A.E. wrote innumerable leaders in the *Irish Statesman* demanding the return of the collection, and he had every moral right on his side. The only thing that was never explained was why the hell the pictures should come to Ireland, where nobody would ever see them, while thousands could appreciate them at the Tate Gallery. The Dublin Art Gallery is one of the finest in Europe, but few people know it for the simple reason that reproductions of the pictures at Merrion Square are forbidden. You cannot go into the Gallery and buy a postcard to send home to suggest that you have seen some of the best Dutch, Flemish and Italian paintings in the world. It may be, of course, that the paintings are unphotographable ; they are certainly worse hung there than in any other national collection. But even so one feels a little publicity would do no harm, even if it meant moving the pictures away from positions where they reflect the light and are virtually invisible to the casual visitor, in order to give the rest of the world some idea of their worth.

A Government which introduced the world's most fatuous censorship at one time had a mind to introduce Progress in Merrion Square—by building a motor road diagonally across it. Fortunately, roads cost money so the project had to be abandoned ; but the scheme is no less frightening for having proved impracticable. One of Ireland's greatest attractions is the sparsity of her traffic, so the idea had not even a purely functional argument to commend it. In any case, the Irish are most reassuringly untraffic-minded. We drove one day the wrong way down a one-way street. A policeman hailed us, explained our error, but instead of sending us back where we'd come from, made us continue our journey against the on-coming traffic, on the grounds that it would have been far more trouble for us to turn round and go back. Parking too, unless things have changed, has never been too much of a problem in Dublin. Cars are strewn around St. Stephen's Green at night with their lights turned off. The Irish argue that any driver who is so blind that he can't see the parked cars in the street lighting must be drunk and should be arrested.

It is the same logic which is at the bottom of one of my favourite Irish football stories. In a Cup-tie Rugby match between a Limerick and a Tipperary team, a fight developed from time to time between two of the forwards, with the Tipperary man setting about the player from

Limerick. At last the referee began to get impatient, blew his whistle and separated the two players. He turned to the man from Limerick and in a stern voice warned him : " If I see you struck again, I'll send you off the field ! " That may appear a " typically Irish " story, but it is founded on good sense. Nobody gets a sock on the jaw in a Rugby game unless he is the provoking party.

Apart from the unsatisfactorily hung pictures in a gallery which has already done enough to spoil the architectural glory of Merrion Square, even without the motor road, the artistic life of Dublin seemed reasonably alive.. There was music at the Royal Dublin Society, where in addition to the regular visits of the " international celebrity " virtuosi, I am told they used to pay the highest fees in Europe for chamber music programmes. The concert hall there is hideous, but its stark appearance and profusion of thin steel girders remind one that, after all, the greatest attraction at Ballsbridge is the Horse Show. Why the R.D.S. should still officially be a Royal society nobody ever explained ; it seemed an inconsistent attitude to maintain after the trouble taken to paint all those pillar-boxes green.

Finally, there was the Abbey Theatre which was busy celebrating its 21st birthday. The stars of this little theatre, the cradle of so much that has been good in modern Irish drama, had long left the company ; but if there was no longer any Arthur Sinclair or Sydney Morgan, no Sally Allgood or Maire O'Neill, there was still a rising young actor called Barry Fitzgerald and a company of Irish players who showed that the Abbey's reputation for acting was not a pure fiction. The Irish, indeed, with the possible exception of the Russians, seem to take to acting more naturally than any other race in the world. A poor performance at the Abbey Theatre is a very rare thing.

The Abbey did its birthday on a grand scale, with speeches by Yeats, Lady Gregory and Lennox Robinson ; there was also a speech in Irish by a politician of some kind, which, as it was made in the nation's language, had to be translated by him into English afterwards that the audience might know what to applaud. I don't know how the out-and-out nationalists took this, for I never heard English spoken with such an acidly unmistakable Belfast accent.

Following a triple bill of Synge's *Shadow of the Glen*, Lady Gregory's *The Workhouse Ward* and Yeats' *The Hour Glass* I came away from the Abbey gala bursting with pride in our national theatre, a feeling which did a great deal to overcome the sensation of nausea caused by the smell of burning peat which pervaded the auditorium. The *foyer* of the Abbey is translated a little too literally for my taste as " hearth " ; I am all for a turf fire in the house, but it becomes a little oppressive in a theatre, especially as in the case of the Abbey it contributes smell without heat once you're in the auditorium.

For the rest, my stay in Dublin provided a refreshing experience of family life, for Adrian and his parents proved charming hosts with numerous relations called O'Connor and O'Reilly spread all over Co. Dublin and Co. Wicklow with a lavishness exceeded only by these relations' own hospitality. Family visiting in Ireland is a most rewarding pastime which is apparently limited by neither distance nor time of day. A relation living seventy miles away across the Wicklow Mountains is just as likely to be dropped in on for tea as an uncle who lives a couple of streets distant. This disregard of distance is largely dictated by the fact that the Irish roads, although not particularly good, are sufficiently free of traffic to make motoring a pleasure instead of a nightmare.

One may encounter certain eccentricities of behaviour

I

on the road in Ireland, but one never meets with the appalling bad manners shown by most motorists in England. It is a strange thing that the average English driver should consider himself within his rights to behave in a car, pushing and shoving his neighbours all over the place, in a manner he would never dream of as a pedestrian on the pavement. On the pavement, of course, bad behaviour can end in the offender getting his ears boxed ; on the road, his unfortunate victims are too busy saving their skins to be able to do much about it.

Our most frequent excursion from the Bishops' house at Ballsbridge was to play golf on the Island course at Malahide. The club house was a quarter mile journey in a rowing boat from the mainland, frequently a choppy fifteen minutes which landed one on the Island drenched to the skin.

Once on the Island one's troubles began in earnest. Though I am right-handed in the ordinary way, for some reason I hold a cricket bat left-handed, and this same inability to hold a bat, a hoe, a hockey stick, a scythe, a broom or any normally two-handed implement with the left hand over the right also applies to a golf-club. Now the chances of the casual golfer being able to borrow a set of left-handed clubs are pretty slim ; so I had to do the best I could with a bagful of right-handed clubs which, owing to my natural cack-handedness, I had to grip with the right hand over the left—an unusual stance at any time and a considerable handicap to one who had only ever been round a golf-course as an infant caddie.

It wasn't the clubs which worried me, however, so much as the course. The Island was so formed that a sliced drive from the first tee landed the ball in the sea, while a pulled drive landed the ball in the sea on the other side. A drive straight down the fairway certainly avoided the sea, but landed the ball in a river. It became a somewhat extravagant pursuit after a while, and in the end I began to start the game from the second tee. Here one had to drive over a small hill and though one rarely had any idea where the ball would land the chances of retrieving it were slightly better.

I did not become bitten with golf and played only once after leaving Dublin when four of us went over to Newmarket from Cambridge to play a four-ball match. Though the weather was fine it was a rather lonely day for us. We assembled at the first tee but drove off in such widely differing directions that we never met again until the last straggler, fearing he would be lost in the falling darkness, abandoned the course at the sixth hole and returned to the club-house. After that experience I decided that golf (the way I played it) was not a very sociable game.

CHAPTER XV

THE PERFECT BLACKLEG

From Dublin I returned to Cambridge and Mr. Humm, passed one instalment of Little-Go and failed in the other two parts. A later examination (which I passed) was postponed nearly a month by the General Strike of 1926.

To this day I have little idea of what the General Strike was about ; I was too young at the time to take much interest in its political causes and now I am twice as old the whole thing is rather stale. As one who has since joined a Trade Union I am usually rather reticent in referring to my activities during the Strike ; I fear they might be misunderstood and my principles questioned.

The truth is, of course, that I and some 2,000 other young men at Cambridge went to work in the General Strike with no thought of strike-breaking, of being "patriotic," saving the country from Bolshevism or anything like it. We saw in the whole business nothing more or less than a heaven-sent opportunity to run a railway.

To begin with I reported at six o'clock every morning dressed in a blazer and plus-fours and worked as a porter ; my picture was taken and appeared as the personification of " The Lighter Side " in the local Press. I had a bottle of beer in my hand at the time, for we were generously supplied with quantities of free drink and food. I did not greatly relish moving boxes of ageing fish, so I ceased to be a porter after a day or so and became a guard.

I was lectured on a guard's duties and responsibilities by an old retired railwayman, given a whistle, red and green flags, a handful of fog detonators and told to report for the 6.30 a.m. to Ely the following morning.

When I arrived at the train I found that I was by no means the only guard in the van. There were sixteen others, each of whom had been instructed to report at the same time and place. Our train consisted of two or three coaches and was driven by an engine-driver and a stoker who were rowing Blues. During our maiden voyage the stoker unwisely stood up on the tender as we went under a bridge ; but he came back next day, with his head bandaged and helped us to keep our record of having the only engine on the line that didn't go off the boil.

Our main job on a round trip to Ely and back was to collect the milk. At the first stop I understood why seventeen guards were considered necessary. I approached a churn on the platform and prepared to roll it in the casual manner I had seen porters employ. We needed every one of seventeen guards to collect the milk ; the churns which are rolled so easily are the empties. Full churns weigh like lead.

The Ely milk train carried no passengers even though accommodation was provided for them and the train's schedule was advertised in the Press. We used our flags and whistles, even the fog signals were exploded on the line to hear what kind of noise they made ; but none of us ever punched a ticket.

At last, one morning as we drew into a country station we saw two elderly women standing on the platform waiting for the train. Our engine driver overshot the station by fifty yards in his excitement and if a public-spirited small boy had not previously opened them we would have shattered the level-crossing gates ahead of us. When the train had been manœuvred into position, seventeen guards scrambled out with ticket-punches in hand to show our first passengers into the best first-class seats (nobody had provided us with forms for excess fares, so we couldn't have taken any extra money if we'd wanted to).

All our invitations were refused. Imagining that perhaps the two women had been unable to buy tickets and were shy of boarding a train without paying, we assured them that they could pay the other end. We were still anxious to have passengers even if they had no tickets for us to punch.

We asked the women where they wanted to get to.

" Oh," replied one of them sweetly, " we're not travelling anywhere. We've just come to say how *wonderful* we think you boys are ! "

It was a dejected whistle which gave the right-away to the driver, and on the return journey our van echoed to coarse and bitter words on the subject of public ingratitude. On my return to Cambridge I gave up being a guard, and became a signalman, though not until I had worked as guard behind 52 trucks of rotting cabbages which had to be taken to Tottenham.

To the layman the guard of a goods train appears to have an easy life spent in brewing tea or toasting kippers over the stove in his van. In reality it is an energetic existence. British goods trains do not as a rule have Westinghouse brakes, so that when the train goes down hill you hear the clanking of buffers getting near you as the engine puts on its brakes. The guard then turns his own brake-wheel furiously and holds on for dear life as the full force of 52 trucks hits the brake-van a tremendous crack.

A signalman's life provides more opportunity for tea and kippers, though my first spell in a signal box during the Strike offered a little too much leisure. I had the misfortune to be posted to a box just outside Cambridge station, where I found a young viscount (now a Tory M.P.) already installed and resentful of the idea that he needed an assistant. He refused to allow anybody but himself to touch the signals, and after a few hours of inactivity, my mates and I (the authorities considered every job on the railway should be done in triplicate at least) bade his lordship a good day and left.

We were then sent to another box at the junction near Shelford, where one line goes from Cambridge to Liverpool Street, another to King's Cross and a third to some small market town in Suffolk.

We were much happier in this box. Every day at one o'clock the only passenger train of the day passed, bound for Liverpool Street, and the guard would throw our lunch and a bottle of beer on to the grass verge as the train went by.

One day, though, the guard was careless; our lunch landed on the grass, but the beer bottle hit the side of the signal box and was broken.

The next day the 1 p.m. Up never got to Liverpool Street at all ; or if it did, it wasn't the fault of anybody in our box, for we set the points so that the train went along the line to some unknown destination in Suffolk. And for all we know or care, that train is still there.

Shortly afterwards the General Strike ended ; we were all paid handsomely for many hours of overtime and I was a little disappointed when, drawing my money at the Labour Exchange, I was not allowed to have a card entitling me to draw the dole as an out-of-work railway-man. I have been told by strikers who were " out " during the General Strike that they felt they had lost something when it was all over. They were not the only ones ; those few days in May, 1926, were, for thousands of us, pure, ecstatic wish-fulfilment.

During this May term I fell in love with a girl called Marion. She played the violin in the C.U.M.S. orchestra and I thought seriously enough of the affair to become what I gaily described as " engaged "—a popular state for young couples in any May Term. We spent hours together in a canoe on the river (Lionel had lent me a beautiful Canadian canoe called " Trunkles ") discussing the kind of rose-covered cottage we would live in ; and when the weather was wet we spent the time murdering the César Franck sonata—Marion with her intonation and I with fistfuls of wrong notes on the piano. Marion was rather addicted to country dancing, but I was opti-mistic enough to think she might grow out of it ; in any case, I thought she was very sweetly " English " with her pink-and-white complexion and would fit nicely into the surroundings I visualised for our married life together. She had some interesting friends, among them a family which I understood to pretend to the throne of France. I was less interested in this family's claim to royal blood than in the fact that their suburban villa was crammed full of remarkable pictures, including two Rembrandts, a tiny Leonardo and a Perugino or two. The paintings were not generally considered in Cambridge to be genuine.

Marion, almost alone of all the young women with whom I have ever fallen in love, did not inspire me to write any music. I did not even dedicate anything to her, mainly, I suppose, because I wasn't composing anything just then. A couple of songs, here and there, maybe ; but they were too unimportant for me to remember even whose verses I set. Apart from playing trains during the Strike, indeed, the early summer months of 1926 seem to have been passed principally in playing cricket. " Playing cricket " is a misleading phrase, for all I did was to spend three afternoons a week in the nets at the Perse ground, bowling for hours on end and in the late afternoon being allowed to have a knock.

Unlike the time when I had been at school there, the Perse now boasted a whole-time cricket coach—a square, stout little man with a wrinkled brown face and a faded blue cap over one eye. His name was O'Connor, but his brogue was pure Cambridgeshire, though even this gave no clear clue to his origin ; he had been known to play for Derbyshire in his time, while his son was Jack O'Connor of Essex. On looking back, O'Connor, Senior, was nothing more or less than the typical school cricket coach ; he was ageless, untiring, patient, genuinely interested in every moment of his work and as sincerely intrigued to see whether or not you improved when he said " A little bit quicker, sir ! " for the 500th time as he had been when he said it the first time.

When, at the end of the day, it was my turn to bat he would introduce every trick he knew, clean-bowling me four times out of five and then, by way of consolation, announce that the next one would be a half-volley to be hit out of the ground. If I failed there was an unmistakable note of disappointment in his voice when he said : " Oh *no*, sir ! That was nearly two yards *this* side of the hedge, sir. Now hit this one properly. . . ."

O'Connor was never a coach to try and alter a player's natural game, and I feel he would have been delighted to have seen me play the innings which, years later, I played in Sussex. It was an innings of such perfection that I despair of ever being able to repeat it. It lasted precisely three balls, and I played the same stroke to each. The first ball I missed, the second I hit clean over an oak tree for six, and the third bowled me all ends up. I have occasionally totalled more runs in an innings (I once made 39 against the band from the Hammersmith Palais de Danse), but I have never batted more satisfyingly nor more characteristically.

Through the good offices of old O'Connor I came to find myself practising in the nets on Parker's Piece at Cambridge, a huge square of grass where Jack Hobbs played his first games of cricket. I bowled in the Cambridgeshire County net and in due course received a printed postcard from the secretary of the Club which read : " You have been selected to play for the County against Huntingdonshire on June 23, at 11.30 a.m."

Unfortunately, the words " You have been selected " were crossed out and over them was written " Would you care to play . . . ? " This meant either that they were hard up for players, or else I was too grand to be " selected " and had to be asked nicely instead. I have my suspicions as to which it was.

When the postcard arrived I was staying with Lionel in London. I caught a train by the dawn's early light from Liverpool Street ; at Cambridge there was no connection for Huntingdon, so I hired a Daimler and went on by road. I was out first ball (caught near the

I*

sight screen), didn't bowl at all and misfielded in a shameful manner. My fielding lapses were largely due to the ground being beside the L.N.E.R. main line and I found the Flying Scotsman and the rest of the Scottish expresses more interesting than our opponents' batting. I returned to London a proud, if penniless county cricketer.

I am sorry to say there is no record of this Cambs. v. Hunts. match in Wisden's because it was not a championship game ; in any case, perhaps my name is best kept out of it. I do feel, however, that they might have let me have a bowl for my money, for that's what I was played for, after all.

With the years I have abandoned all my early cricketing ambitions and my natural preference is now for what I call " Coarse Cricket," which is not quite so fierce as village cricket proper, and for quasi-country house games played in pleasant surroundings with (usually) the kind of luncheon which undoes all the good one may have done in the morning's cricket.

" Coarse Cricket " is notable more for the enthusiasm than the skill of its players and it is best played against breweries. Archie Macdonell's famous chapter on cricket in *England, Their England*, which so delights the serious cricketer, is nothing more than the normal way of life to the player of Coarse Cricket. My own teams have included brilliant batsmen who prefer to play in sandals, Irish peers who disappear from the long field to answer the call of nature behind a hedge just as one is bowling a slow one for them to catch ; wicket-keepers who "keep" wearing a monocle, publicans, Rugby internationals, policemen, tenors, golf Blues, schoolboys, bystanders in wellingtons, almost anybody who cares to make up an eleven but doesn't mind being out first ball or having innumerable catches dropped off their bowling. If any of them should play cricket well, it helps ; but on no account must they take the game too seriously, expect sight-screens or hope to have them moved if there are any at all. Extra cover is at liberty to gather mushrooms if he is lucky enough to find any (I picked a pound and a half in the slips at Great Missenden one afternoon), and the umpires shall at all times be permitted to suspend play in order to replenish the beer mugs they have brought out with them.

Occasionally I have made the mistake of including a good class club player in the side, and I have regretted it. For he dislikes my kind of cricket as much as I dislike his ; we have no time for wicket-keepers who protest that a leg-bye is signalled as a bye, nor for batsmen who kick at what was obviously an outrageous l.b.w. decision. I have played one or two games against " business houses " but I have done so without knowing the class of cricket I was in for. I can bear the neat suburban sports ground, but only if I am bowling to the studious left-handed caution of Chesney Allen or batting against the unceasing monologue of Bud Flanagan standing at what he considers is cover-point but which is in reality square leg because he has forgotten to cross over after the over. (One of my proudest cricketing memories is of capturing the wickets of both Flanagan and Allen in one innings. This is undoubtedly a record.)

In these circumstances cricket is tolerable and worth four days a week of anybody's time ; it is mainly tolerable because it is not the sort of cricket to lead to boring post-mortem discussion or serious conference on a Plan of Attack. Indeed, so unimportant a figure is the captain that there are times when his authority is openly flouted. On one occasion, for instance, I was captaining my team against a brewery and—as always when captain—bowling over after over right from the beginning of the innings. When I had bowled about fifteen overs without a break,

the entire fielding side lay down and refused to get up.
I pleaded with them to stand up but without effect. In
the end, I took my run and bowled ; the strike broke up
immediately, for no fielder feels himself safe lying down
where he cannot move out of the way of a ball hit in his
direction or protect himself if he cannot avoid it. It was
a simple psychological remedy.

Another, rather more dignified type of cricket, but no
less enjoyable, is what I call " Monastic Cricket." This
I have played with a Catholic team known as the Emeriti,
a wandering side which plays against Catholic schools.
The game is interrupted from time to time for the Angelus,
but I noticed that it was I, the lapsed convert, who as
a rule first recognised the bell's ringing and stood still
while looking for a lost ball or preparing to bowl.

I am not sure that I would choose schoolboys to play
against in the ordinary way ; they tend to be far too
good. There was one child at Douai who was a particular
little pest. He was only sixteen, but imperturbable ; he
would stop my best yorker and then congratulate me on
it. He had a bat which appeared to be the size of a house
and his final insult was to retire when he had made a
hundred. I learned afterwards that he played for
Yorkshire 2nd XI.

There was some consolation in this game, however, for
I made the sporting columns of two Catholic papers
with the parenthetic mention of (Hughes 5 for 45).
Otherwise I rarely find my way into the Press as a cricketer.
Apart from appearing in the score-sheet details of some
of the Sussex papers when I played for Ifield I can recall
only one instance of featuring in a report of a game. This
was at East Grinstead when the local paper remarked that
" Hughes did not appear happy."

Now, this was a gross libel, for I made 9 not out ;
and I have only to make 1 not out with my batting

to be in a seventh heaven of happiness at any time.

Finally, there was a startling action photograph of me fielding in the gully which appeared in *The Sporting and Dramatic*. The occasion was the first game ever played by the British Empire XI in 1940. I was included in the Empire team as " S. Hughes (London Irish) "—a form of description which always infuriates me. " Spike Hughes," yes ; or " P. Hughes " ; but never just " S. Hughes," which might stand for Samuel or Stanley.

The British Empire game was against Rosslyn Park, the match being played for a barrel of beer. I took one wicket—by bowling a full-toss on the leg which was hit to be caught by Hugh Bartlett on the boundary. I was then taken off. In other respects, that game was enjoyable enough, except that having won the barrel of beer we found some fool photographer had rolled it out of the pavilion, taken its picture and left it out in the sun for the rest of the day so that it was quite undrinkable.

One game I played which I do feel should have been noticed by the Press was against a team raised by Maurice Tate to play *The Daily Herald* in 1938. We played this on a ground we had found in Surrey ; the ground was very conveniently owned by the pub which meant one did not go thirsty for long at any time on a hot day. I bowled unchanged and helped to dismiss Maurice's XI for 17 (Hughes 6 for 9), but the greatest satisfaction came from square-cutting my beloved boyhood idol for four. I know Maurice was playing in carpet slippers, for he had a septic foot, but even so a dream came no less true for all that.

In between running trains in the Strike and watching them from the Huntingdon cricket ground, I found time in the summer of 1926 to compose my first successful piece of music. I call it successful inasmuch as it was eventually performed in public and published.

Played over on Lionel's early nineteenth century piano it sounded a little odd ; but that didn't discourage me, for I have never composed *at* the piano, though I have often composed with a piano. Since the work was an unaccompanied sonata for cello it is perhaps hardly surprising that the piano version tinkled out on Lionel's instrument should have been rather bizarre.

I do not know what prompted me to write for solo cello unless it was a final determination to write practical music ; in two years, after all, I had come down from the gigantic idealism of the *Agamemnon* orchestra to the stark modesty of a sonata for a solo string instrument. As cello writing pure and simple I believe it was quite successful. I have never played the cello ; on the other hand, I have always had a pretty good notion of how an instrument should *sound* and only when a cello is unaccompanied can one make the most of its full range of tone and colour. The accompanied cello nearly always tries to sound like a violin and the poor player finds himself stretching along his finger-board as though he were trying to touch his toes.

With the unaccompanied cello, however, there is an occasional chance of exploiting the rich depth of the low register so that it can be heard, thereby reviving public confidence in the idea that the cello was invented to be something more than a shadow of the double bass part in a symphony orchestra.

CHAPTER XVI

SALZBURG REVISITED

In August, 1926, I packed the first sketches of my cello
sonata into a folder and set off for Salzburg. I travelled
with two friends from Cambridge ; one of them was
Romilly Roget, a quiet, sensitive fair-haired boy from
Trinity whose timid manner disguised a charming nature
and a generous heart. Romilly, who by now is probably
editing his grandfather's *Thesaurus* (it was a family
affair), was typical of a minority of young men who
managed to enjoy University life, although they did not
conform to the accepted pattern of the English public-
school boy. One of the most heartening features of both
Oxford and Cambridge is the determination of the two
universities to undo all the harm done to a boy at the average
public school. Where the public school system seems to aim
at a stereotype the universities provide every opportunity
for the young man to develop his individuality and reassure
him that artistic and other " unmanly " pursuits are
nothing to be ashamed of.

My other companion, also from Trinity, was a dark,
temperamental young man called Walter Meyjes, the son
of a Dutch art dealer. Walter later became an actor and
finally went into the Roman Church and distinguished
himself by some incredibly courageous behaviour as a
padre during the war in a minesweeper.

The Salzburg Festival of 1926 had not begun to attract
Society as it did in later years. The audiences were
cosmopolitan enough in all conscience, but the place had
not yet acquired that air of *chi-chi* which inevitably led to
high prices and pictures in the shiny weeklies. In 1926
Tyrolean costume was worn only by the natives, whereas

by the time Toscanini became the Festival's main attraction and meal-ticket any foreigner was instantly recognisable by the gaily coloured dirndl frock or bright new leather shorts, affording a striking contrast to the sombre occidental clothes obviously adopted in mute protest by the Salzburgers themselves.

I have never returned to Vienna, but on this visit to Salzburg it was almost as though Vienna had come to meet me half way ; for the opera performances given in the small Stadttheater brought back all the familiar voices on the stage and the familiar faces in the orchestra pit. Marie Gutheil-Schoder had now retired, but she it was who produced the Salzburg *Don Giovanni ;* there was Richard Mayr as Leporello, and an astonishingly beautiful performance of Don Ottavio by Richard Tauber. There was Bruno Walter conducting *Seraglio,* and Tilly Losch in *Les Petits Riens* and Gluck's *Don Juan* ballet. There was Richard Strauss conducting *Ariadne auf Naxos,* there was the Vienna Philharmonic, and there was Richard Mayr giving a recital to show what an exquisite Lieder singer he was.

In addition to the music there was the usual Reinhardt circus of plays produced in cathedral squares, riding schools and the vast barn called the Festspielhaus— anywhere, it seemed, except in a normal theatre unless it happened to rain.

A month or two later, when I got back to England, I wrote a couple of articles about the Festival in *The New Age*—the third member of my family to become a contributor, for my father had started his career as a critic in its pages and my mother had also written for it in her time. I was only sorry that when it came to my turn it had not been the original *New Age* which A. R. Orage had edited from 1907 to 1922. A little of Orage's tradition had been carried on when he gave up, but with the best will in the world it was no longer *The New Age* of G.B.S. and Max Beerbohm, Sickert and Will Dyson, G. K. and Cecil Chesterton, Arnold Bennett and the young writer with the unpronounceable Armenian name which was later changed to " Michael Arlen."*

Most people of my generation probably do not remember *The New Age* at all, which is a pity. I remember it myself only because one of the first words I ever learned as a child was " Orage." My mother had known Alfred Richard Orage (his surname was significantly pronounced as in the French for " storm ") since she had been a girl ; it was he, in fact, who gave her the nickname " Meena " because she wore her hair in plaits like the Queen of the Netherlands. But neither my mother nor anybody else (except myself who called him " Mr." when I was very young) had ever called him anything but plain " Orage."

When Orage died in 1934 I had to write his obituary in *The Daily Herald*; I was glad to be able to do it in the freedom of my own gossip column, for I realised, when it came to writing about him, that I had known him all my life.

As I grew older and went to school, Orage was associated with an occasion in my life which became almost a ritual : a visit to his flat in Chancery Lane on the last day of the holidays when I was on my way to catch a train back to Cambridge from Liverpool Street. It was a long climb up the stairs, past offices and lawyers' chambers, until the black and white tiled floor gave way to bare boards and at the end of a dark corridor near the very top of the building we reached Orage's flat. There was no bell or knocker on the door, so we had to rap with our

* Michael Arlen told me once how Orage picked on this pseudonym for him. In one of the short stories by Dikran Kouyoumdjian which appeared in *The New Age* one of the characters was called " Michael Arlen." Orage was intrigued by the smooth sound of the name and suggested to the author that he should adopt it as his own pen-name—one of the few instances, I imagine, of an author adopting the name of one of his own creations.

knuckles. The top half of the door was made of glass with three huge and crudely painted figures on it—257, I think they were—and some minutes after we had banged on it Orage would appear—always in his slippers.

Inside the air was blue with pipe smoke and the walls were covered from floor to ceiling with bookshelves. As Orage and my mother talked together I was allowed to wander round and look at the books, though the only ones that made any sense to me were old bound volumes of *The New Age*.

It was in this atmosphere that Orage worked, writing his brilliant, anonymous political commentary called " Notes of the Week," in a small, backward-sloping hand in which only the " t's " and " g's " and " d's " ever seemed at all decipherable. I am ashamed to say that the reason for my regular end-of-holidays visit was largely mercenary ; Orage, with no children of his own, understood perfectly that small boys needed " tips " in order to face the ordeal of going back to school. (Now I think of it, it was largely through Orage that I ever went to the Perse in the first place, so perhaps his generosity was a form of conscience money.)

Orage died when he was 61. He left very little behind him that he had written under his own name ; his greatest monument was the devotion of a score of writers who first got their chance in *The New Age*. He picked his writers young, and when they became famous they never deserted him. None of them was ever paid a penny ; there was just about a living wage for the staff who worked in Cursitor Street (known familiarly as " Cursitordammit Street "), and no more.

In 1922 Orage threw up *The New Age* and became a disciple of Gurdieff at Fontainebleau. Lionel spent a day or two at this strange institute and reported that the system of spiritual salvation was largely based on being made to do the things you most loathed. A clever inmate, said Lionel, would tell Gurdieff that he hated eating cream buns and drinking Burgundy above all other things ; it was the only way to ensure a pleasant life, for Gurdieff always believed you, and would provide unlimited quantities of food and drink if he thought you hated it.

Around 1932 Orage packed it up, came back to England and founded *The New English Weekly* ; and it was a stimulating thing to see this charming, quiet-spoken man with the large ears and the sweetest nature of any grown-up I ever remember, back in the familiar surroundings of the Café Royal, his personality a magnet whose attraction was irresistible. After Orage died, my mother and twenty of his friends used to meet for a memorial dinner from time to time. It was a moving gesture, but it was a sad occasion ; it was perhaps as well that the war put an end to it, for Orage left a gap in his followers' lives which grew wider and less tolerable as the years passed.

I passed down Chancery Lane a week or so ago. The building Orage lived in has gone completely, and I couldn't help feeling glad of it. There was something providential about his death as there was about Will Dyson's ; they could neither of them have contained themselves in the New Age which began in September, 1939.

In one respect at least the post-Orage *New Age* carried on the tradition of its founder : contributors were not paid. Orage's successor as editor was Philip Mairet, another old friend of my mother's and known generally as " Pam." He was an actor as well as a writer and while he had a stammer which seemed unending and insuperable in conversation all trace of the impediment vanished when he appeared on the stage. As an actor Pam used the name " Henry Cohen." He maintained that a name like that attracted much more attention than an obviously made-up one of the Louseborough-Goodby type.

Pam duly published my two articles about the Salzburg Festival, and on re-reading them I appear to have taken an unnecessarily gloomy view of everything. At this date, it seems to me that it was a particularly good Festival, though I am willing to believe that the revision of my first thoughts may largely be due to a certain hankering after the good old days. In print I did not think at all highly of the wholesale importation of the Vienna Opera's Mozart productions ; apparently I had expected to hear an all-star cast collected from all over Germany and had little time for the obviously first-class teamwork of the Vienna company.

Though I may have been misguided in my opinion of the opera performances, I was by no means so hyper-critical of Reinhardt's contributions as I would undoubtedly be if I saw them today. Reinhardt, never one for using simple methods of production if he could possibly include the kitchen sink, was always at his least restrained in Salzburg. In Hugo von Hofmannsthal's version of *Everyman* he had at his disposal not only an auditorium provided by the cathedral square but the cathedral itself and several neighbouring church towers as scenery from which voices were heard and actors appeared. Nor, of course, was the audience itself spared as a springboard ; the voice of God came from the cathedral (interrupted frequently by trombones), but the Devil was in and out of the audience behaving and dressed like a restless pantomime cat.

If Reinhardt aimed to achieve simplicity by the most elaborate methods his *Everyman* certainly came off. Hofmannsthal's play succeeded, as the author hoped it would, in bringing the morality out of the scholar's study back into the theatre again—well, in front of an audience at any rate. And the actors were first-class. Two of the chief players, one of them a great tragedian (Alexander Moissi) and the other a great comedian (Max Pallenberg) are now dead ; but a third actor, Oskar Homolka, is still alive and well-known to English and American audiences. He played the part of Mammon under a thick coating of gold paint, but as he had previously earned his living as a professional footballer no doubt he was in sufficiently good training to withstand the rigours of a Reinhardt Festival season.

I use the word " rigours " advisedly. With Reinhardt's predilection for highly sophisticated primitiveness it was hardly surprising that his two other productions at the Festival should have been plays by Goldoni and Carlo Gozzi. For a man of the theatre Reinhardt put a tremendous amount of energy into working out ways to avoid using even the elementary mechanical devices and conventions of the modern theatre. He staged Goldoni's *Servant of Two Masters* in the Riding School, a square courtyard which had been cut out of the rock. It was all elaborately Commedia dell'Arte, with the actors shifting their own scenery and a lot of intimate gagging from the Thimig family of father, son and daughter (Helene Thimig later became Mrs. Reinhardt, to nobody's surprise).

In Gozzi's *Turandot*, which had been dolled up by Karl Vollmoeller, there was scarcely any peace for the audience at all. It was performed in the Festspielhaus, which had been designed on the lines of a huge barn with a stage at one end, from which—for this production, at least—a long platform had been constructed to run up the centre stalls-gangway. (Anybody familiar with the construction of American strip-tease theatres will recognise the kind of contraption I mean.)

The production of *Turandot* was a peculiar mixture of excellent entertainment and hideous chocolate-box vulgarity. When Reinhardt set his mind to it he could outstrip even the New York revue-producer in his efforts to over-light and over-dress. There were moments in

Turandot of almost unbelievable banality, dream-sequences worthy of an English pantomime (though not as long) and a pseudo-oriental atmosphere at times which reminded me of those suede-leather bound copies of *Omar Khayyam* found in vicarage drawing rooms.

When Reinhardt could forget about Art and allow interruptions which had nothing to do with Gozzi's fairy tale, *Turandot* became tolerable once more. The quartet of traditional Commedia dell'Arte figures—Pantalone, Tartaglia, Brighella and Truffaldino—were let loose to improvise and run in and out of the audience in a way which leaves no doubt as to the ancestry of our own Crazy Gang. Reinhardt's Crazy Gang consisted of Max Pallenberg, the versatile Oskar Homolka, and two comedians well-known in Berlin cabaret, Roman Romanowsky and Hans Moser. The amusement these four actors provided at least justified Reinhardt's self-conscious obsession with " folk-drama," or whatever it was he used to explain his repertoire that August in Salzburg.

As with the Contemporary Music Festival of a couple of years earlier, the social side of Salzburg in 1926 kept one as busy as the official reason for one's visit. There seemed to be few English visitors, but many American ; and as I always find it easiest to make friends with Americans abroad, it wasn't long before I had attached myself to a particularly charming party. (I saw relatively little of Walter except at the theatre, for he was up to some private mischief that occupied him during the day ; and, now I think of it, I didn't meet Romilly until I got to Venice early in September.)

The dominant figures of this particular American party were a professor of history from Columbia University, his wife, a pianist called Oskar Ziegler and a cellist called Rozsi Varady. Rozsi Varady was a New York Hungarian, fair, plump and with a squint that made you dizzy to look at it. She was a very fine cellist and died before she was thirty.

Officially, Rozsi Varady was at Salzburg to play the Haydn concerto ; as far as I was concerned she had made the journey across the Atlantic solely to help me with my sonata. In the end she certainly spent more time with Hughes than with Haydn ; in the cramped space of her hotel bedroom, Rozsi played through my pencilled manu-script (which was propped up on a commode) ; she altered some of the phrasing, made the more ambitious passages practicable and decided that, while the sonata was not easy, it was by no means impossible. I took all Miss Varady's criticism to heart and was overjoyed to hear—for the first time in my life some of my own music being played by a first-class performer.

Rozsi Varady's interest in my cello sonata had one most stimulating effect : it gave me a certain confidence in my ability to stand on my own feet as a composer. Hitherto, I had written as a student, taking my music off to Wellesz for correction and encouragement. Now I had become independent and grown sure enough of myself to sit down and write music I was not too ashamed to show to strangers. I knew that the sonata was neatly formed on paper ; and by hearing it I was reassured that I under-stood the tonal capabilities of the instrument.

This new-found confidence was largely superficial, for even today—after nearly twenty years of earning a living by writing music—I still anxiously look round for a second opinion to convince me that what I have written will pass muster. I know I am a very third-rate composer; on the other hand, I am not such a fool that I do not know the standards of the third-rate. I am only terrified that I may fall below even these low standards. With the result that I will spend many hours over the orchestration of a couple of bars of music, though I know perfectly well that if I scored them in the most obvious, unoriginal way nobody would notice. Nobody would notice? Yes, I would notice; and I would also suspect that the orchestral musicians who played them would notice. But most of all I would be letting myself down technically; for, lacking inspiration and originality, the only satisfaction I ever get from writing music is the purely private one of knowing that I have learnt the technique of instrumental music. In a world where clumsy modulations and slovenly scoring pass unnoticed (and are handsomely rewarded) I have always tried to keep to my own standards of workmanship. I lose sleep and money in the effort to maintain these standards; but at least I have never lost face in the attempt—at any rate, in my own opinion. Where music is concerned I have a highly developed gift of self-criticism; but occasionally I reserve myself the right to self-praise, though I do not expect others to agree with me.

I was sufficiently pleased by the private success of my cello sonata with Rozsi Varady to exploit the work as personal propaganda at Salzburg. It was talked about enough in the Café Bazaar to attract the attention of a French woman journalist. Madame Peyrbère was one of those typical bi-lingual figures who abounded in the Central Europe of the 1920's. She seemed to live in Wiesbaden, to contribute industriously and enthusiastically to a hundred cosmopolitan journals and had the peculiarly *mitteleuropäische* knack of convincing any editor that the most trivial item of gossip was a world-shattering news story.

Madame Peyrbère became a fan of mine. She had never heard a note of any music I had ever written, but she was convinced that I had A Future. We corresponded regularly in the years that followed—she to describe how interested the Intendant of this or that provincial German opera house was in my latest project, I to ask how she was progressing with her schemes for what (if her plans had ever come to anything) was obviously destined to be an International Hughes Festival.

I took a great liking to Madame Peyrbère, for she did me good. She had a great gift of dangling the carrot of fame and fortune in front of my eager assinine nose, and I was never so happy as when she started me off on my pipe-dreams of a sensational career as a composer. By a curious and contrary streak in my psychological make-up I have never yet been disappointed by the non-materialisation of even my most modest ambitions. Indeed, I have become superstitious in my belief that nothing good ever comes of anything I ask for or plan. I have a riotous time thinking how nice it would all be if everything came true ; but when it doesn't, I shrug my shoulders and reflect that it is all undoubtedly for the good.

This being so, it is hardly surprising that I am lazy. I have had too much experience of not getting what I ask for ever to set any store by planning work or asking anybody if I might be allowed to do this or that. On the other hand, I sometimes grow so superstitious about the whole thing that I will deliberately embark on a wildly improbable scheme with the unshakable knowledge that something quite unexpected and much more profitable will turn up while I'm at it. I have to spend a lot of time touching wood, leading a life like this, of course ; but on the whole it works out to my own satisfaction, though it scares the life out of my dependents. To be what is commonly called " versatile " (but which I prefer to regard as the lucky chance of being able to earn one's living in as many amusing ways as possible) may have its points ; but it is no life for the naturally lazy person like myself. It is reassuring to know that if one line of business should fail, there is another to fall back on. But the time

comes when all one's talents are in demand at the same
moment, and there is no peace. Being " versatile "—and
therefore having no ambitions in any one direction—
means that one takes a purely professional interest in the
whole affair, and is determined (for the sake of *amour
propre*) to do everything as well as possible. Furthermore,
because one is master of no trade, one tends to grab at
everything greedily while the grabbing is good rather
than, by turning a job down, allow anybody to suspect
one is incapable of doing it.

With a bookful of addresses of American professors,
pianists, cellists, Madame Peyrbère and the memory of a
reunion with Tilly Losch, I left Salzburg for Venice. My
cello sonata was now in its final form and I had no doubt
that it was only a matter of time before its public performance. Walter Meyjes travelled with me but spent no
more than a day in Venice before deciding to return to
Salzburg and continue the pursuit of happiness he had
found there. Walter never pined for anything if he could
go and get it.

In any case, much as I loved Walter, Romilly was a far
more restful companion to have in Venice ; our temperaments were better suited—provided, of course, I always
had my own way.

It would be ungenerous of me not to recall that I fell
very seriously in love in Venice this time, for Sanchia
dominated my thoughts for many months afterwards.
She was extremely beautiful, the grand-niece of a famous
Shakespearean actor, and though she was only fifteen, our
boy-and-girl affair developed to quite serious proportions
under the sympathetic, but watchful eye of her mother.
Our love-affair could not have started in more appropriate
surroundings, for not to fall in love in Venice is as much
a waste of time as going to the Derby and not backing
a horse ; it is part of the fixtures and fittings of the place,

an essential experience. The romance, however, not only survived a month in Venice, but a raw English winter and most of the following spring. I was quite determined that I would marry Sanchia when we were both older, and I wrote a most heartlessly cruel letter to Marion to announce as much.

I cherish no souvenirs of this love-affair, for I eventually burned all Sanchia's letters ; it was a voluminous correspondence and a rather high-class one, if I may say so. We both glamourised our relationship beyond all reasonable belief and indulged in an orgy of self-dramatisation. Our deadly earnestness was tolerated with remarkable sympathy by our friends, though I fear Sanchia tried her mother's patience a little when she returned home one day having bought an enormous Alsatian. With her fair hair blowing in the wind and leading this monstrous animal, Sanchia looked the image of Diana the Huntress. Unfortunately for the dog, Sanchia was no huntress ; it had not occurred to her that the creature needed food and it was in danger of starvation in a household which was already having to cope with mother, Sanchia and a pair of ravenous twin-sisters. So mother said : " Yes, Sanchia, you look very pretty. Now take it away and ask for your money back."

And that was the end of the incident of Ivan the Alsatian. If a *Vogue* photographer could have seen the dog with Sanchia, it might have been another story, but it all happened in a tiny Hampshire village. A picturesque episode, but a little impracticable.

When my cello sonata was eventually published it was dedicated to Sanchia, although I wrote it before I had met her. Dedications to the Beloved are tricky things and it did not occur to me that my love for Sanchia could be anything but immortal ; but, as it turned out, I have never regretted what might have been a rash act. The dedication is still to be seen by any who care to go and look for the sonata in the British Museum—where the work reposes to conform with the Copyright Laws. Perhaps if the music had been " inspired " by Sanchia, I would now feel embarrassed by the dedication ; as it is, the inscription acts as a pleasant reminder of a Very Serious Romance.

While meeting Sanchia in Venice had important emotional results, I must confess that my month there provided me with another, more lasting experience. This was the first performance in Venice of Puccini's *Turandot*, an opera which captivated me at once and which still remains my favourite Puccini music.

CHAPTER XVII

PREMIÈRES PUBLIC AND PERSONAL

I HAVE a deep affection for *Bohème*, *Manon Lescaut* and *Gianni Schicchi*, an immense enthusiasm for *Il Tabarro* and the first act of *Tosca ;* I am sympathetic towards much of *Madam Butterfly* and curious to know more of *The Girl of the Golden West* which I have heard only once. But to *Turandot* I give my whole-hearted devotion and admiration ; it is the one work of Puccini's to which I return repeatedly to discover new beauties and unexpected strokes of genius.

In the twenty years that have nearly passed since that evening in the Fenice, I have heard *Turandot* many times. I have heard it not only in the opera house, but I live with the work in the sense that the complete Parlophone recording played on my automatic gramophone affords me music while I work. I had better admit at once that I am a shameless addict to the habit of " background " listening. If I am engaged in writing music, then I keep the radio switched on while I am composing or scoring ; but it has to be switched on to the broadcasting of *words* only. Music naturally distracts from the writing of music. Similarly, if I am writing an article or reading, I can bear the radio only if music is coming from the loudspeaker ; the broadcasting of words tends to get mixed up with the words I am reading or writing. I cannot manage to keep similar mediums apart.

So it happens that when there is nothing even faintly worth hearing on the air (which is frequently) I sit down to write my more regular articles and broadcasting scripts to a background provided by my gramophone records ; and of the seventeen complete opera recordings I possess, *Turandot* is the one which most frequently serves to entertain me while I am earning my living.

The Hughes household, I might say, is no place for those in search of order or a quiet life. Both Barbara and I have at present to provide more than two hours of gramophone record broadcasts every week, so that in addition to my own collection of some 3,000 records (more or less tidily arranged on shelves) our home is littered with a hundred loose records from the B.B.C.'s library—records for the next programme, records from the last programme, records in process of being timed with a stop-watch, records being tried out, records we just happen to like to play, records that lie about because there is not yet any room for them on the shelves, records in cardboard boxes, on sofas and on the floor under tables. Occasionally, above the din of the gramophone playing one of these records there can be heard the sinister crack of shellac being crumpled under foot as one or other of us treads carelessly across the room in search of some scrap of paper on which is written a precious timing of a Verdi aria or the catalogue number of a Mozart overture. And yet, what we may lack in method we make up for by an uncanny instinct for finding almost any record we need within a few moments. If our search for a missing record takes longer than five minutes then it is given up ; for then we know that what we want is in a chest out in the corridor, and to open the chest means lifting a cricket bag, the laundry basket and half a dozen volumes of privately printed music sent to me by a soldier I have never met who found it in an empty house in Italy.

The records of *Turandot*, however, are kept within easy reach of the gramophone ; so close, in fact, that their music has become an everyday experience and I no longer have the faintest idea of how the opera must have sounded to me when I first heard it.

Thinking back to that September première in Venice in an attempt to remember the impression Puccini's music made on me, I find the memory is an indistinct one of sound and colour. And on reflection, I don't think this is at all a bad memory to have ; in *Turandot*, more than anywhere else, Puccini's genius for the translation of stage action and colour into terms of music is at its most inspired.

Like Verdi before him, Puccini could create a dramatic atmosphere in the space of a bar, sometimes by no more elaborate means than a single chord. It is characteristically Italian to presume intelligence in the listener, so that neither in Verdi nor Puccini do you encounter that reiterated sign-posting which takes up so much of everybody's time with Wagner. Nowhere is Puccini's ability to get on with the job more marked than in two typical passages of *Turandot* : the sudden change to the *piano* chord of D major which introduces the " Invocation to the Moon " in Act I, and the opening bars of the nocturne mood of Act III.

Turandot is a great problem. It is not popular ; and yet it does not lack performances. It is unfinished ; and still it is in many ways the most finished of all Puccini's operas. It is " typical " Puccini, inasmuch as there is a tenor with an aria and a soprano who dies ; but it does not attract the rank and file of the Puccini fans. If it has a fault, then it is perhaps that it is too musicianly to have the immediate appeal of the earlier works. There comes a time in all composers' lives when they sit down and write entirely to please themselves. Puccini's moment of musical self-indulgence came with *Turandot*. He was a successful composer, but he was never too successful to notice what was going on around him or to learn from his contemporaries.

Giacomo Puccini was what the Germans call " fesch." It is a difficult word to translate, for it implies a more lasting elegance than is suggested by " fashionable " and it is more virile than " chic " or " dapper." Puccini was *fesch* in the tilt of his trilby hat, in the cut of his moustache, in the efficient driving of his cars and motor-boats, and above all in his insatiable curiosity about modern music. He didn't necessarily like what his juniors composed ; but he listened to what they had to say, and when it came to the point he knew as much about it as they did themselves. Thus, when he came to *Turandot*, Puccini was no back-number, no elder statesman to be revered for the sake of his past reputation. There is nothing more embarrassing in music than to see the elderly, " established " composer embarking upon a composition obviously designed to " show up all these youngsters." Vaughan Williams did it in his Fourth Symphony, and it was a great relief to all when he reverted to his natural behaviour and wrote his more conventional, less alarming No. 5. In *Turandot* we find a concentration of all Puccini's great dramatic and lyrical gifts, sustained by a tremendous technical strength surpassing anything hitherto shown by a composer by no means lacking in theatrical and orchestral sense. But whereas in Puccini's earlier works the technical facility has to be *looked for*, in *Turandot* it sticks out a mile.

There is no bar in all Puccini's operas about which one can honestly say that it would have been better scored in this or that way. But the Puccini who orchestrated *Bohème* or *Tosca* could never have orchestrated *Turandot*, for in his last opera the composer drew on the experience of a lifetime. I was rather surprised, while writing these last few paragraphs, to discover that Puccini was actually 66 when he died ; I thought he was younger, for that is the impression I have always had from his music. His style and manner were fixed early in life and the music which accompanied the death of Manon Lescaut is unmistakably by the same composer who wrote the death of Liu in *Turandot ;* but even so the late Puccini was no mere repetition of the earlier. He died as full of promise for the future as ever any young composer half his age.

I hope I have not suggested, by emphasising the technical brilliance of *Turandot*, that Puccini was using his great craftsmanship to cover up any shortcomings of inspiration. There are no tricks in the score of *Turandot* as there are in the later scores of Richard Strauss. When Strauss' invention gives out he resorts to an orchestral sleight-of-hand designed to deceive the ear ; and it fools a very few of the people a very little of the time. The score of *Turandot* abounds in novel orchestral effects, but each of them is there to clarify an original musical thought, not to camouflage a poor one.

The greatest problem raised by *Turandot* was the composer's own, and he never lived to grapple with it. Of all forms of speculation the most fruitless is that on what a composer might have done if he'd lived longer.

It is too late to shed any tears over Schubert not finishing his symphony or Puccini not living to complete the last act of *Turandot ;* on the other hand, while we haven't the faintest idea what Schubert's finale would have been about, we do know the libretto Puccini intended to set to music.   Personally, I incline to believe that *Turandot* was saved, not spoiled, by Puccini's death.   The last scene could hardly have escaped being a dramatic and musical anti-climax.   The " story " of the opera is unimportant after the death of Liu, and there was nothing more to be said beyond that the Prince and Princess lived happily ever after, though considering that Turandot is a first-class bitch this seems a little unlikely.

Unfortunately, nobody has yet had the courage in an opera with a happy ending to ring down the curtain before the final duet, so *Turandot* could not end with Liu's death and a few well-chosen words to confirm what the audience suspected would be the outcome of the opera all along. If the last scene of *Pagliacci* were followed by an inquest and the arrest of Canio for murder, the sequel would lack drama.   The finale of *Turandot* lacks drama precisely because an attempt has been made to sustain interest in a situation which no longer contains any.

Puccini wrote some lovely music for Turandot's scenes, because he couldn't help it ; but even in the magnificence of " In questa reggia " there is a strong suspicion that he didn't like the woman, and I do not believe that whatever music he had composed for the finale could ever have made her more attractive.

The unsympathetic character of Turandot may well help to explain the ordinary Puccini public's difficulty with this opera ; also, it is a little unconventional for a composer to reserve his finest music for three subsidiary characters like Ping, Pang and Pong.   But experience suggests that the average member of the musical public

K

always prefers its favourites' less good music to their best. Thus we find *Rigoletto* and *Traviata* more popular than *Otello* and *Falstaff*, the " Unfinished " than the *Winterreise*, Beethoven's Fifth Symphony than the late quartets, *Figaro* than *The Magic Flute*, and *Bohème* than *Turandot*.

I have always considered it a great pity that while " they " do not hesitate to cut one or two passages from Puccini's own score of *Turandot*, it should be considered essential to retain intact those which he did not write at all.*
The really astonishing thing about this finale is the almost unbelievable bungle made by Alfano and the other disciples who " completed " the scene after Puccini's death.

Nobody is going to ask those who undertake such a task to write *music* worthy of the dead composer ; but at least they might have a stab at reproducing the kind of orchestral noise he made. The last pages of *Turandot* might have been scored from a vocal score by somebody who had never actually heard a Puccini opera. There are long passages of mushy orchestration (incidentally of thoroughly inept music) which would disgrace a first-year student in my Class of Counterfeit Orchestration.

When *Turandot* was first performed the production ended with the death of Liu, and I believe that for some time after Alfano's finale had been added Italian audiences always stood up for a moment at Puccini's last bars. It is a pity the habit cannot be revived, for having got the audience on its feet there might be a chance of getting it out of the opera house and thus rendering a performance of the last scene unnecessary. I have heard the complete

---

* The cuts in *Turandot* are inexplicable ; they do not save more than a minute in time, all told, and are unjustifiable on artistic grounds. When Constant Lambert conducted the opera at Covent Garden he put back the missing passages, and one wondered more than ever why on earth they had been cut in the first place. The singers had to learn a few bars they hadn't known before, but admitted they could see no reason for their traditional omission.

Turandot only once ; on all other occasions I have managed
to escape before the non-Puccini part begins. At home
I can be flippant about music and will inconsequentially
listen to Benny Goodman after Haydn ; I adapt myself
to the change of mood and standards happily and immediately. But with " live " music I am not so adaptable
and Alfano's supplement shatters the mood created by
Puccini ; I am always deeply moved by the sad procession
carrying Liu's body and I prefer to leave the opera house
with the distant, fading sounds of that scene as my final
memory of *Turandot*.

My love of Puccini's music had no immediate effect on
anything I wrote for many years, though on my return
to England I embarked on a *Turandot* of my own, in the
sense that I began the composition of an opera which is
likely to remain unfinished at my death. This was a
version of the story of Orpheus and Eurydice which
occupied me off and on for the next couple of years. The
plot followed the Gluck pattern of the legend, but though
I proposed to have three scenes the whole action was
designed to be over and done with in the course of a single act.
I wrote the libretto as I went along, in German penta-
meters of no poetical merit but which seemed to me better
suited to the accent of my musical language at that time
than English. Knowing that there were already in
existence some forty or fifty operas on the subject of
Orpheus I didn't think one more would necessarily spoil
the market. I even went so far as to take over Gluck's
idea of introducing a ballet who danced gloomily while
the chorus lamented over Orpheus' sorrow in the first
scene and appeared as Furies in the second. It would
have been a reasonably effective dramatic work if I had
ever persevered with it, though I doubt if my idea of
having the voice of Zeus interpreted by four invisible

basses singing through megaphones would have come off. Nowadays, of course, one voice bellowing through a loud-speaker would do the trick, but I hadn't been to an English music-hall with a P.A. system then.

But even with Gluck's model before me, there was one problem raised by my *Orpheus* which I never solved. I proposed to stick to the original story and have Eurydice die at the end. It was obviously the right and logical ending and I did not anticipate any difficulty with the music to go with it. What did puzzle me was where to set this final scene. If I had had my way the scene in Hades would have been a pretty elaborate and sizeable set, and the question was how to strike this scene quickly enough to maintain the continuity of action between Orpheus and Eurydice leaving Hades and their being seen on their journey back to earth.

I have since found a simple enough solution, but at that time the only way out appeared to be the introduction of an interminable orchestral interlude telling the story of their ascent to earth. However, as I never got any further—even after two years—than the end of the first scene, I didn't lose much sleep over the affair. The first major interruption of the composition of *Orpheus* occurred when an institution known as the Festival Theatre opened at Cambridge.

The guiding spirit behind this venture was a bearded Irishman called Terence Gray. He had been an amateur Egyptologist, drove around in an electric motor-car, and was dead nuts on The Art of The Theatre.

Gray's theories as to what the Drama should be were well enough known in Cambridge, for he had written a couple of books to explain them. He was obsessed with the idea that scenery should consist of cubes and luminous screens, that the commercial theatre presented no worth-while plays, that the Lord Chamberlain was an ass and that in consequence of all this the Theatre was decadent and useless.

To put his ideas into practice, Terence Gray took an old theatre on the outskirts of Cambridge and converted it from its most recent form of a mission-hall into a place where he could do justice to The Drama. He had a built-in cyclorama constructed and dispensed with footlights altogether. There were steps leading down from the stage to the auditorium, and it wasn't long before actors were in and out of the stalls like ants. A great deal of fuss was made about the lighting, but since the seats were far more comfortable than any in the local cinemas the place had its points.

The Festival was full of *chi-chi*, with caviar sandwiches and mulled claret (" Festival Cup ") in the bars, and programmes printed in white ink on black paper bearing the typical Irish instruction " to read this in the dark hold it up to the light."

Terence Gray did not stop at programmes which told you only what you wanted to know about the play and its players ; they were part of a magazine known as the *Festival Theatre Review*, the official organ of the theatre and Terence's mouthpiece. Gray, in addition to his picturesque appearance, also had a very bad stutter ; he made up for his inability to speak easily by being one of the most verbose writers I have ever encountered. He filled the pages of his magazine with articles expounding his favourite theories, cursing the Lord Chamberlain and the local undergraduate critics and entering into endless controversies with all who wrote to disagree with him.

Terence could not have chosen a better place for his theatre than Cambridge, for he was the embodiment of the undergraduate spirit which rebels against the conventional and traditional ; an idea had only to be a success on the Continent and a flop in England for him to take it up at once.

As Director of the Festival Theatre, Terence Gray's position was that of dictator and ideas-man. He had under him Norman Marshall as a producer, Ninette de Valois as choreographic director and a company of repertory actors which included no women of either talent or remarkable looks, but several men possessed of both. There were no " stars," of course, but two actors stood apart from their fellows : one was T. G. Saville, who died during the run of *Ten Minute Alibi* at the Haymarket, the other was Maurice Evans.

Tommy Saville was the most experienced member of the company, and had acted in America, the Orient and in every kind of part that came his way. He had a beautiful voice and would have received the recognition he deserved as an actor if he had only had the luck to reach the West End earlier in life. As it was, his death robbed the theatre of a player who might have made a great name for himself—not as a star, but as one of those actors who go from play to play in a solid, unspectacular but highly-polished way.

Maurice Evans, on the other hand, was at the very start of his profession. He had previously been an accountant at Chappell's and had taken time off to make occasional appearances in some sort of workers' theatre in Bloomsbury ; the Festival season was his first full-time season of acting. Maurice, too, was gifted with a fine voice ; and the Festival repertoire being what it was, he had to sing as well as speak with it. I cannot truthfully remember whether Maurice was a good actor or not ; the week-by-week contrasts of the Festival productions have left only a jumbled impression on my mind, and there was no opportunity for Maurice to show that he was likely to become the extraordinarily successful Shakespearean actor he is in America today.

For some reason the Immortal Bard did not figure on Terence Gray's menu, except on one occasion when—for a single Sunday performance—a scene from *Twelfth Night* was played. But even so it was difficult to tell whether the company had any talent for Shakespeare ; the scene was played in the Elizabethan English of the original (transcribed by a famous phonetician) and nobody could understand a word. I don't think the company actually appeared in masks, but I wouldn't have been surprised. Terence Gray had a horror of being considered " old-fashioned " and to have played Shakespeare straight would have smacked too obviously of what he contempt-uously called in his weekly mouthpiece the *trade theatre* (the phrase was always printed in italics).

My own connection with the Festival Theatre began through Walter Meyjes joining the company when he came down from Trinity, and by the time the second season began (the seasons coincided with the University terms) I would have been on Terence's payroll—if there had been a payroll for me to be on. Much to the Direc-tor's disgust the need for music arose, and as I happened to be around and unattached I was rather reluctantly roped in.

My first assignment, through no fault of mine, was quite abortive. It had been decided to produce *The Immortal Hour* as a play and I was asked to provide music for the occasional songs which cropped up. I composed what was asked of me and Maurice prepared to sing them.

Now the Director, who had so whole-heartedly sunk his enthusiasm and his fortune in the Art of The Theatre (always in capitals), was quite unconvinced of the value or even existence of music as an Art. He was prepared to regard painting, sculpture, dancing, electric lighting and cooking as essential components of the Drama, but no provision had ever been made in his wildest plans for the inclusion of music. This was all the more puzzling as one of the four books by Gray regularly advertised in the *Festival Theatre Review* was called "Dance Drama." It may be, of course, that the "Dance Drama" was not intended to be accompanied by music ; I do not know, for I must confess I never read the book. But Gray tended to practise what he preached, even to the extent of putting on one of his own plays. This was a drama of Old Egypt called *And in the Tomb were Found*. . . . It was produced in the week immediately following *The Insect Play* and owing to the habits of the particular Egyptian dynasty it concerned, was inevitably known in Cambridge as "The Incest Play."

It seems likely, therefore, that Terence Gray had no time for music, because he invariably tried out everything in his theatre that he had mentioned in his books.

There was no question of an orchestra pit at the Festival, of course, for that would have spoilt the look of the place ; and since there was no pit, there could be no orchestra. So to accompany Maurice Evans in *The Immortal Hour* an instrument called a "Dulcitone" was scrounged from somewhere and duly delivered at the theatre. The Dulcitone is a keyboard instrument no bigger than a yacht piano ; it produces a sound not unlike a celeste, though not so penetrating, which comes from hammers striking a series of tuning-forks. It is a whimsy little noise.

In any other theatre, an instrument as small as a Dulcitone could have been placed in the wings and forgotten ; but the Festival was so constructed that there were no wings to talk of. The Dulcitone, which had begun by being A Good Idea, now became an embarrassment, until in the end the wretched instrument was lifted up by a rope and placed on the lighting bridge some fifteen feet above the stage, where it could scarcely be heard by Maurice and was quite inaudible to the audience.

It was not my immortal work which suffered, however, but Rutland Boughton's. The week before Fiona Macleod's play opened an injunction was granted to restrain any music but Mr. Boughton's being used, so *The Immortal Hour* was presented with the Faery Song and all its pentatonic familiarity.

Under the heading "The Place of Music in Drama," Terence Gray wrote in the *Immortal Hour* issue of his *Review* : " In the case of a play such as this, music is being introduced solely for its dramatic value, for music can have a supreme use in the heightening of dramatic effect. That indeed is the sole function of music in the dramatic art, and apart from it music has no business in the theatre at all."

I am afraid in the case of a production such as that, music failed to perform even the modest function Terence Gray considered it should. Music was an unwelcome guest at the Festival, though, as it turned out, a very difficult one to get rid of.

A few weeks later, Terence staged Congreve's *Love for Love*. Here was a play the Lord Chamberlain couldn't touch, so it was put on in all its bawdiness and almost uncut. On the opening Monday night, the last thirty minutes of *Love for Love* were played to an empty house, the audience having left not in disgust but in haste to get back into college by midnight. Generous cuts were made next morning and the play was a tremendous success. Word had gone round that it was full of dirty lines with the result that the production attracted all the " hearties " and the Festival acquired a reputation worthy of the Folies Bergères.

As usual, Terence Gray had overlooked the possible necessity of having music invade his sacred Theatre, and it wasn't until he came to read *Love for Love* carefully that he discovered the play called for three or four songs and

K*

several dances. The job was given to me and I embarked
on it with enthusiasm ; I liked the period and was already
fairly adept at faking period pieces.

But a Dulcitone would not do this time, and Terence
had to agree to our having an orchestra of a string quartet
and a harpsichord belonging to Edward Dent. A combination of this size, however, could not be slung up on
a lighting bridge in a light-hearted way, so it was put
under the stage. This, thought Terence, was what we
should have done all along. Unfortunately, when we
played under the stage nobody on the stage or anywhere
else could hear us and I, who was conducting, could
neither see the singer nor hear him.

Though he thought we were being unnecessarily
troublesome and temperamental, the Director eventually
had constructed a kind of trap-door through which singer
and conductor could occasionally see each other provided
the conductor did not expect to be able to see the orchestra. As far as I was concerned it was rather like conducting an orchestra hidden away under a dinner table and
hoping one's host wouldn't notice.

The trap-door should have been disguised and decorated like an opera prompt-box, but this did not occur to
anybody ; instead, when the cues came near, I had to
lift the trap, wedge it so that it stayed open and hope the
audience would not be too distracted. Knowing what
the audiences expected at the Festival I have no doubt
they were prepared to see the Director himself emerge.
All they got, however, was some rather faint music played
by a different set of amateurs at every performance, for
music at the Festival not only had no business in the
theatre, but no claim to share the box-office receipts.

However, a Handel hornpipe danced by Hedley Briggs
and Walter Meyjes had to be repeated nightly, and two of
the songs I composed (one of which is dedicated to

Maurice Evans) were eventually published, so the experience of *Love for Love* was not entirely wasted.

The following week I made my first and last appearance in public as a pianist. The Festival staged *Sweeny Todd*, and I was put at the side of the stage in a spotlight with a monstrously battered piano, a huge false moustache, a bowler hat on my head and as much beer as I wanted. The programme gave me credit for music " specially arranged and composed," but it was an over-generous acknowledgment, for I improvised completely different incidental music at each performance.

Since I had previously received a five-page, closely-typed letter from Terence Gray rejecting my suggestion that there should be a resident, salaried musical director at the Festival, I had no compunction in delegating the melodramatic accompaniment to *Sweeny Todd* to a member of the company for three days of the play's run.

I spent those three days in London preparing myself for the ordeal of the first performance of my cello sonata. I had submitted it to the English section of the International Society for Contemporary Music in the hope of having it accepted for the 1927 Festival to be held wherever it was. It hadn't qualified for the finals, but it had been drawn for one of the preliminary rounds inasmuch as it was selected for one of the monthly concerts of the London Contemporary Music Centre. These concerts were held at the old Court House, in Marylebone Lane ; smoking was permitted and it cost nothing to go in and nothing to get out, for even the programmes were free.

The sonata was played by an excellent Hungarian cellist called Paul Hermann, whom I had previously met and rehearsed with. At least, I heard him play the work through and made no comment ; I was much too terrified to say anything and in any case it seemed to me he knew the piece better than I did.

After the performance I grabbed the manuscript and tried to dash away quietly ; it was an unfestive occasion and there didn't seem to be any party or anything. The whole experience was a great anti-climax, indeed—so entirely different from what I had always imagined a première would be. I was cheered up a little, however, by a young man (obviously a critic) who asked to be allowed to study the sonata for a moment. He studied it carefully and from the detailed description of its form which appeared in *The Daily Telegraph* two mornings later, I deduced that was his name was Scott Goddard.

The performance of my sonata produced notices in *The Times*, *The Daily Telegraph*, the *Observer* and *The Christian Science Monitor* (I never understood why such an unremarkable concert should have interested Boston readers). There may have been other references in the Press, but if there were I did not read them. There are three stages in one's attitude toward Press cuttings. First, when one is too modest to subscribe to a cutting agency, because one doesn't expect to be written about. Second, when one does subscribe to an agency because one is hoping to be written about. And third, when one no longer subscribes at all because one does not care any more whether one is written about or not.

At my time of life I have already reached the third stage —the most advanced stage of conceit—though if this book is ever written and published I may well relapse into the second stage just out of uncontrollable curiosity.

The Press was extremely kind about the cello sonata. Scott Goddard, representing my father's paper, wrote that the work was " obviously written with a full knowledge of the potentialities of the instrument," and that while it demanded high efficiency from the player there was " nothing that a first-class executant should find impossible. . . . The work very properly, is short, for the finest writing and the most fertile inventive powers are hard put to it to make a length work for a bass solo instrument avoid an increasing dullness. But Patrick Hughes does not allow such a feeling a chance. We shall be pleased to hear this work again, and more from the same pen."*

The Times said : " Patrick Hughes is a very young composer, the son of the well-known critic, and he shows a sense of form in his solo sonata and a straight way of dealing with deliberately uncompromising material. Not an immediately ravishing work by any means, but promising."

The Observer thought it " an interesting work in a medium that is of the most austere. But for all that it sounds forbidding, the work is well built and the writing for the instrument is very capable."

The Christian Science Monitor was plainly a little bewildered by the form : " This sonata apparently presents three movements within the span of one continuous piece, i.e., a species of Prelude, in which double stopping is a feature, a Scherzo with ingeniously effective passages, and a melancholy Finale. Without being anything unusual as music, it is well planned for the cello : the work of a man who understands his job."

Reading those four notices I more or less understood what the critics thought, and they were obviously right ; at any rate, if I had ever set out to fulfil *The Times'* hopes I could have done worse than take these criticisms to heart. I was a little impatient, however, when the sonata was published a year later and the reviewer of the *Musical Times* referred to it in that hearty colloquial manner peculiar to his kind as " modern stuff." I wasn't

---

* Dear Scott ! He used almost the same kind final sentence writing of Michael Tippett's Symphony in November, 1945. I hope he is more fortunate with Tippett than he was with me.

even appeased by being described as "a young musician of lively imagination," for the writer went on to say that my work would be more interesting when I had "learnt the value of restraint and measure."

If ever I wrote anything restrained heaven knows it was that cello sonata, Opus 3. It was hardly the appropriate medium for a display of abandoned hilarity, let's face it.

With the sonata performed, noticed and published neither I nor anybody else ever took my music seriously again. Looking back on my five faded Press-cuttings I might be justified in regretting that I should have done so little to fulfil what promise I did show as a composer of seventeen. But I have no regrets ; and if ever I feel at all ambitious I go to my shelf and take down a volume of Grove's Dictionary. There I read the names of composers whose music is forgotten—quite good composers, some of them—and reflect that, after all, it takes two people to make music come really alive : the creator and the consumer. I prefer to be a consumer, because I think I have more talent for receiving music than for dishing it out.

The summer season of 1927 at the Festival Theatre provided fewer opportunities for incidental music than even before. It started off with *Androcles and the Lion*, a production mainly remarkable for the presence at the Saturday matinée of the author, who as usual insisted on paying for his seat knowing well that he would get some of the price back in royalties.

All efforts to get G.B.S. to make a curtain speech failed, though the familiar tweed-clad figure stood up in the stalls at the end of the performance and remarked that he wouldn't make a speech as there was not room for two lions on the stage.

The next distinguished author to visit a Festival production of his own work was W. B. Yeats, and it was for *The Player Queen* that I composed a couple of songs, unaccompanied fragments of which I have long since forgotten the tune.

Yeats held court in the foyer of the theatre, a colourful, flamboyant figure wearing an old Irish silver ring on his index finger the size of a saucer. He had just recovered from a bout of sciatica and affected to be disappointed at his recovery. He had looked forward, he said, to spending the rest of his life being pushed around in a bath-chair while he gave orders as to where he should be pushed and when.

As my father's son (the son, that is, of the man who found the best of all Irish tunes to fit " Down by the Sally Gardens ") I was able to make the most of Yeats' presence, and though he seemed rather vague as to exactly where he was, the fact that I had written music to *The Player Queen* registered with him. Or was he really so vague ? I base my assumption purely on his suddenly remarking : " There are a lot of pretty girls in Oxford, aren't there ? " I have never been quite sure whether in saying that he was being absent-minded or just mischievous.

Some months later, however, Yeats did remember having been at Cambridge, for I had some correspondence with him over the projected use of my music for the Abbey Theatre production of *The Player Queen*. For some reason the play was never put on in Dublin when it should have been and the whole scheme fell through. I lost Yeats' letters years ago, but they would have had little interest for autograph hunters as they were typewritten by his wife. So it happens that the only true relic I possess is a copy of *Deirdre* given to me by my mother for my last birthday. It is inscribed " To Mrs. Emery, from her friend W. B. Yeats." I cherish this, for Mrs. Emery was Florence Farr and but for her I might never have been born.

And so, with *The Player Queen*, my career as a composer of incidental music came to an end for the next nine years. I had little time during the summer term of 1927 to compose at all. I had exams to pass (which I passed) and I had also been commissioned by the Oxford University Press to translate a huge book from the German.

The assignment came from Hubert Foss, whom I had first met in Salzburg three years previously, and I undertook it rashly, but eagerly. The promise of £80 as a fee was almost more money than I had ever dreamt of and I believed its possession would enable me to be independent and be spared angry visits to Cambridge by my father, who found that he was still legally responsible for the modest bill I had incurred in at last procuring the long-desired dinner jacket.

The book was by Paul Bekker, a German musicologist who wrote as only a German musicologist knows how. His 580-page essay was entitled " Richard Wagner : His Life in his Work." I devoted many months to the job of translation and when I had finished it and the proofs began to come in neither I nor anybody else could understand a word of it. Reading Bekker in German I knew more or less what he was getting at ; the German author is a past-master of the art of inventing jargon and composite words as he goes along, but it is possible (with experience) to get the hang of it. In attempting to translate it all, however, one can succeed in approaching readable English only by the most drastic cutting and rewriting. At 18 I had not learnt this, and consequently my version of Bekker contained sentences like : ". . . . it acts stylistically as a tendency to the formation of sequences in all moments of gradation " and " . . . the small dimension of which is connected with this determination to expansive revelation."

In the end, the page proofs contained more corrections

in the margin than words in type ; Foss cut his losses, paid me £60 and sold the rights to another publisher. I was greatly relieved by Hubert's decision and was left to reflect that if telegrams were charged by the word in Germany then the German Post Office can hardly have shown a profit on anything sent by Paul Bekker—not the way he strung words together.

My nature being what it is, in spite of examinations, the Festival and Bekker, I still found time during the spring and summer of 1927 to revive an interest in the type of music commonly known as jazz.

There were two reasons for this renascence of a dormant enthusiasm, and one of them was the all-Negro revue at the London Pavilion, *Blackbirds*. In one respect I was rather disappointed by *Blackbirds* : I never really found that Florence Mills was my cup of tea. I thought she was charming and had an enormously strong personality, but in an inexplicable way I felt she was somehow too refined. I had made no great study of modern Negro music at that time, but I believe if I had shut my eyes while Florence Mills was singing I could not have told whether she was white or coloured ; in short, she was a song-and-dance artist who might have come from either side of the Atlantic.

All this happened so long ago that I am prepared to admit my judgment was completely wrong and that if I heard Florence Mills today I would think quite differently about her. On the other hand, recalling the people who raved about her at the time and reflecting since on these same people's tastes in Negro music and dancing I have a hunch that I was right ; for the people I have in mind were those who considered the Cotton Club to be " genuine " Harlem—as if any place were " genuine " Harlem that did not admit coloured guests.

Many years after Florence Mills had died, Paul

Robeson confirmed my original suspicion. He had admired her greatly, of course, but in his view the greatest of all genuinely Negro artists was Bessie Smith, a woman who never appeared except before audiences of her own people ; her down-to-earth singing of the blues was far too exotic and violent to appeal to Broadway and Piccadilly with their sentimental, patronising idea of what coloured art should be.

Bessie Smith, however, is a subject which I hope to discuss another time. As it was, that part of *Blackbirds* which appealed to me most was the singing of Edith Wilson, who came before the curtain and sang, "If you can't hold the man you love, don't cry when he's gone. . . ." This was a raucous, 12-bar song written and sung in the manner peculiar to the Bessie Smith school of blues-singing, a typical cautionary tale, brimful of cynical philosophy and good advice with its roots deep in the traditions of secular Negro song.

Edith Wilson was no Bessie Smith, but she had some of her attack and rough sincerity and I remember the song she sang while I can no longer hum more than the first bar of anything sung by Florence Mills. However, Edith Wilson's turn before the curtain was only one item in *Blackbirds ;* in addition there was the lugubrious panto-mime of a comic genius called Johnny Hudgins and there was the remarkable orchestra which played in the pit.

I saw *Blackbirds* several times and I returned to the London Pavilion mostly to hear what went on in the orchestra pit. I had already gained some idea of what Negro music was about from my experience of Arthur Briggs in Vienna ; but while Briggs' band was certainly all-coloured, it was by no means all-American Negro, for in addition to the flute-player from Haiti the drummer had been Senegalese and one of the saxophone players had come from the Belgian Congo.

The Pike Davies orchestra at the Pavilion, on the other hand, was purely American Negro and I was hearing for the first time Negro music played with all its characteristic colourfulness and vitality. The initial impact of this orchestra was rather strange ; here was a group of wind and percussion players using long-familiar instruments such as trumpets, trombones, saxophones, clarinets, piano and the rest, who played tunes with the most elementary harmonic scheme and of no great melodic originality, which yet succeeded in sounding entirely new.

Analysing the noise this band made (and I can only analyse it from memory), I believe the novelty lay in the unfamiliar use of familiar instruments. Whereas the Western European convention demands that brass instruments should be used in orchestras only for festive or solemn moments in music, here was a band which used them for gay, farcical and sentimental purposes so that the lions we knew could roar as gently as any sucking dove.

Above all things, though, I believe I learned from the *Blackbirds* orchestra that the music which cathedral organists and ill-informed writers of letters to newspapers described as " barbaric," " undisciplined," " crude " and " atavistic," was in fact based on a remarkable technical precision of execution in ensemble passages, and a strict, unalterable set of rules governing all improvised playing.

A more important factor in my growing interest in jazz than even the *Blackbirds* orchestra was the issue in the spring and summer of 1927 of some unusual gramophone records. Hitherto my gramophone record collection (played on a table model machine borrowed from Walter Meyjes) had consisted of oddments of Richard Strauss, the Debussy Quartet, a cut version of the Ravel Quartet, the Bach concerto for two violins, and a performance at breakneck speed of Ravel's Sonatina by Mark Hambourg. Dance music had virtually no place on my turn-table except for a record entitled " Did Tosti raise his bowler-hat when he said ' Goodbye ' ? "

One day, sitting in the private hotel which served as a home for Walter and Maurice Evans, a young actor named Guy Naylor turned up with a record of a tune called " Washboard Blues " played by a band with the novel name of Red Nichols and his Five Pennies. Guy was the son of E. W. Naylor, organist of Emmanuel College and authority on Shakespearean music, and the elder brother of Bernard Naylor who later became organist at Queen's College, Oxford ; as a music-lover Guy had been left untouched by the family tradition, and his tastes ran more to the choruses of musical comedy than the choirs of a college chapel.

" Washboard Blues " turned out to be a most ingenious little piece full of unique effects which were quite new to me. The scoring for this five-piece ensemble of a piano, trumpet, clarinet, guitar and chromatic timpani was remarkably restrained, the music itself was tuneful and well formed and the whole thing had an atmosphere of chamber-music about it which I had not hitherto encountered in jazz at all.

With all its vitality there was a certain roughness in the tone of the *Blackbirds* orchestra ; here, though, it seemed the rough edges had been smoothed down and in place of a rather primitive groping the sounds I heard showed signs of discipline and a sense of direction. " Washboard Blues " was the first of a series of records of this type issued during the summer at Cambridge and their success in the University town encouraged the gramophone companies to put many more on the market. After Red Nichols (who, we discovered, played the trumpet so neatly), we encountered a host of new names associated with this peculiar music. There was Fletcher Henderson, who composed music for his own coloured band to play and whose medium-tempo tunes had an odd, processional dignity about them. There was Bix Beiderbecke, a brilliant young cornettist who later died of drink ; there was Eddie Lang, an Italian-American, who played the guitar and with an old school-fellow called Joe Venuti performed the most delightful guitar and violin duets. There was Adrian Rollini who was reputed to play a dozen instruments, but who specialised in an extraordinary *legato* tone on that rare instrument the bass saxophone.

These players, all of them white except Henderson, brought a new charm to jazz, a technical dexterity which served an unusual inventiveness ; and they had the added attraction of being " uncommercial " and obviously playing to please themselves. It was this last quality which appealed most to us, for we were at a rebellious age, and while we were all prepared to hire a car and drive to London to hear Paul Whiteman at the Albert Hall, we were naturally proud to know that we appreciated the purely esoteric art of Real Jazz which was above the head of the rabble.

As things have turned out, I think we were right in our judgment ; those early recordings by Nichols, Beiderbecke, Lang, Venuti and the rest have survived the test of time—a very severe test in a form of music where fashions change from day to day. I do not want to embark on an elaborate analysis of jazz and its ramifications at this point, but if I were to try to define exactly what these early bands had which modern bands lack I would say that they had the gift of creating tunes. Your modern " swing " band makes a noise fit only for morons and obsessional adolescents, for the essence of " swing " is the repetition of an imbecile phrase starting *fortissimo* and getting louder from there. " Swing " is the musical extension of the maddening din made by a child fascinated by the dynamic possibilities of singing " I'm the king of the castle."

But the jazz of 1927 and the five or six fertile years which followed before the " swing " era began and genuine jazz fell into disrepute, produced music which could be remembered ; it was unambitious, it had charm, character, and for those who were prepared to understand the idiom, a very real fascination. It was a backwater of music, and its most violent critics were those who would not appreciate that a backwater can be a rewarding retreat so long as one does not expect to get anywhere in particular. The water may be stagnant, of course, but there may still be life in it of some kind.

The trouble I have always found with the more vociferous opponents of jazz is that they will insist on judging it by general standards. Musicians, on the whole, know what to look for, and whether they like it or not at least appreciate its finer points ; but the sombre, slobbering " music lover " will dismiss the whole thing as A Noise merely because it doesn't sound like Chopin.

Jazz, after all, is a very primitive form of music. It is based on the American Negro's traditional songs and their direct expression of fundamental emotions ; translated into terms of instrumental music this essential " vocal " quality is retained—in the note which starts flat but ends in tune, in the exaggerated *vibrato*, in the sudden contrasts between *legato* and *marcato*, between smooth and accented phrases. And just as the human voice is individual so each instrumentalist in jazz is individual ; the layman, listening to a ten-inch record by Red Nichols and his Five Pennies will not hear the music of one composer, but of five composers, for each player who improvises his own melody around a common theme must rank as a composer. I have had considerable difficulty when writing about jazz in explaining that improvisation is a form of

composition in the same way that composition is a form of improvisation. In the first case you hear the act of musical creation while it is happening, while in the other you hear the same act after it has happened ; in either case, the music is " made up."

Among those who take jazz seriously (and there are far too many) it is considered that the only True Jazz is that which is entirely improvised ; to write it down is to forego all claim to sincerity or spontaneity. This strikes me as absolute nonsense. As a thinker-upper of tunes which have more or less qualified as jazz, my own personal act of creation has taken the form of writing music down instead of playing it directly on an instrument. One reason for this is that I do not play any instrument well enough to be able to express myself on it. Must I then deny myself the fun of creating jazz merely because I can't play it ? Am I not " making up " music by putting dots and dashes on manuscript paper just as much as the man who prefers to express himself without warning on a trombone? Of course I am, and it seems to me as unreasonable to adopt this attitude towards jazz as to demand that a playwright should leave his actors to improvise their lines, or alternatively to play every character himself in his own play.

If, on the other hand, it is claimed that—so far—better jazz has been created by instrumentalists who improvise than by composers who write it down, then I have no quarrel. But this does not prove that one method is " better " than the other ; it means that there are more bright boys among the instrumentalists than among the composers. In practice it also probably means that those few musicians who can actually compose and write music prefer not to waste their talent on jazz but to do something a little more classy, while those musicians who can only improvise can find no outlet for their invention except in jazz.

If it is really so that True Jazz must be improvised, it seems a little odd that the greatest and most respected figure in jazz is Duke Ellington, who is a composer. Duke's improvised piano-playing is the constant despair of his admirers, and despised by the True Jazz purists.

I wish, for the sake of a sensational development of this story, I could honestly say that the summer of 1927 was a great turning point in my musical career, that having heard these first jazz recordings I had thrown all serious ambition to the wind, disgraced my poor old father's name and become a famous band leader with padded shoulders to my " dinner suit " and a Rolls-Royce to drive around in. In fact, this intriguing new music had a very delayed action ; I took no professional notice of what I heard, and treated the whole experience as something which, at worst, might develop into a harmless hobby if I ever had the energy to pursue it.

In any case, I was pretty well occupied with thoughts of my Future Career. I cannot remember how or when I decided it, but having finally passed all the necessary examinations to entitle me to go to Cambridge, I had made up my mind by the end of the summer that three years at a University would serve no useful purpose. For more than two years I had lived and made friends in Cambridge, enjoyed most of the social advantages of being an undergraduate without either their expense or restrictions and I became restless once again. I had no definite plans, but only a strong feeling that I ought to return to Vienna, or at any rate continue my studies somewhere outside England. I informed my mother of my decision and when she confirmed the wisdom of it, told the college authorities that I would not take up residence at the University in October after all. My decision seemed to be a relief to all parties concerned.

I gave up my rooms in Cambridge and removed myself

to London where I lived a somewhat nomadic existence in other people's houses. The first few weeks after the end of term I spent with Maurice Evans ; we shared a flat which had been lent to us in Bayswater by a rich and generous member of the Festival Theatre company. I spent my evenings at the Proms and my days visiting agents' offices with Maurice, tramping up and down brassbound staircases in St. Martin's Lane on fruitless visits, each of which was more discouraging to Maurice's career than the last. In the end Maurice found himself under contract to Leon M. Lion and made his first West End appearance at Wyndham's, playing the part of a policeman in a play called *The One-Eyed Herring*.

Maurice Evans' career in Leon Lion's company proceeded satisfactorily enough, and it was not long before he had been promoted from the part of a policeman to that of counsel for the defence in *Justice*. On the second night of the Galsworthy play Maurice distinguished himself by producing one of the record spoonerisms of all time. My neighbour, Michael Shepley (two floors up), made his own first London appearance in the same production, and still recalls with horror the state into which Maurice threw the whole company.

Maurice had had most pleasing notices after his first night and feeling on top of the world during his big speech in the court scene, thumped the table to address the judge with the menacing line : " I shall foire pint-blink in a mannet, me lud ! "

Since those days I have not heard of Maurice being anything but word-perfect. In America he sails through the complete *Hamlet* with the greatest of ease, compelling his audience to turn up at the theatre at the most eccentric times of day, and switching from Hamlet to Falstaff, Lear and Richard III with scarcely a breath between shows. *Hamlet*—not in Maurice Evans' production—once produced another good spoonerism, when the King in a South Coast repertory company announced : " Now the ham drinks to Kinglet. . . . " Which, the actor's colleagues aver, was reasonably fair self-criticism.

CHAPTER XVIII

WILLIAM WALTON

THE autumn and early winter of 1927 were spent in the pursuit of various musical activities. I began, dedicated to E. M. Forster, but never finished, a string quartet and developed a secret enthusiasm for Elgar's Second Symphony, an enthusiasm leading directly to a friendship with William Walton which began in the gallery of the Queen's Hall and still persists. As I sat listening to the Elgar with a score on my lap, a fair pale-faced young man moved to the next seat and asked if he might share the score. We went out together in the interval to find that we both knew Hubert Foss, who was in the bar, and introduced us formally. Though I may possibly have considered Willie a rival in those days, he has since become my favourite modern composer ; he speaks the same sort of musical language as I do and (at risk of appearing presumptuous) he saves me the trouble of composing by doing what I might do if I were not so lazy, and which he does so much better anyway. I feel more at home with any new Walton work than with the music of any other of my contemporaries ; it is not merely because I saw them growing that his symphony, *Belshazzar's Feast*, the viola and violin concertos sounded extraordinarily familiar to me when they were first performed

in public. They just happen to be my kind of music in
a very personal sense.

While William Walton makes his place in the history
of English music more certain with every new work, I feel
I can claim a tiny share of his success in one instance.
Some years ago Jascha Heifetz asked me if I knew a young
man by the name of Walton with whom he wanted to
discuss a violin concerto. I said I did. Why? Well,
could I bring him to lunch. I could and I did, and out of
that lunch at the Berkeley (smoked salmon and tournedos)
came Jascha's commission for the Walton violin concerto.
As a reward for my part in the affair I have a nicely
inscribed score presented, "To Spike from William" with
the letters written alternately in red and blue pencil.

Willie is also godfather to one of my daughters, but
so far he has done nothing very much about it. I think
one must have talent for godfatherhood and Willie has
talent for nothing on this earth but writing music ; even
to write a postcard causes him obvious pain and he
corresponds with the greatest reluctance. Though he is
unable to do anything but compose, Willie is surprisingly,
paradoxically unprolific ; his output is only a fraction of
that of some of his contemporaries with far less talent or
time for composition. But from this creative reticence
there emerges, every so often, a work bursting with
concentrated vitality and urgency.

British music at the present time is largely in the lily-
white hands of a clique of brilliant young men surrounded
by eloquent and sympathetic admirers ; they write lyrics
for each other, they sing each other's songs, they write
tracts about each other's music, they scratch each
other's backs with such enthusiasm and obvious satisfaction
that they have come to be known as the " Girls' Friendly
Society." They have their counterpart in the West
End theatre, which is as full of queens as the back of the

circle at the Russian ballet. For the moment they all seem to be getting away with it, for those who are not actively antagonistic to the idea tend to treat the whole set-up as a joke. Unfortunately, jokes too often repeated become wearisome ; nobody denies that these young exquisites have talent, but they do *not* possess as much talent as their camp-followers would have us believe, and it gets increasingly boring when, to qualify for employment, a normal actor or singer has to be as queer as a coot, or starve.

William Walton has mercifully been spared the adulation which results in the friends of some of our young composers proving to be those composers' worst enemies. Willie has fought for his reputation ; he has not sought cheap notoriety in Bloomsbury by writing " clever " little snippets of incidental music to dreary Left-wing satires full of capitalists in top-hats. He has not been above making a lot of money by writing film-music ; he has regarded movie assignments as good professional exercise, and those conductors who have played his film-scores tell me that a Walton sound-track is efficiently timed to the split second. If a director wants 90 feet of music from William Walton, he gets 90 feet—not 89 or 91. Willie's activity in British films was directly responsible for the attention which the Industry now pays to incidental music ; until *Escape Me Never* film-music had been provided by the studio's Musical Director, and was no more important in the scheme of things than the lighting and the make-up and the usual acknowledgements to Abdulla. Now producers fall over themselves to sign up Eminent Composers ; nine times out of ten they pick on the wrong one and the music ends up as an office job neatly done by a studio hack, but at least they've tried and had a little advance publicity out of the initial idea.

William Walton does not write music easily ; he thinks

hard about it, asks his friends for advice when he gets
stuck, and generally suffers prodigious labour pains. He
got thoroughly stuck with his symphony, with the result
that he goes down in history as the only composer who
deliberately wrote an unfinished symphony, heard it
performed, revised it and then completed it. Even when
the symphony had been performed in full, Willie still
mucked about with it ; for during the recording by
Decca with Sir Hamilton Harty conducting from the
photostat score, the composer came into the recording
room to remark that a couple of bars sounded wrong in the
finale. He turned to me and asked what he should do
about them. I said : " If you're not terribly devoted to
them, why not cut them altogether ? " Today, William
Walton's Symphony is two bars shorter than when it was
first performed in its entirety. As far as I'm concerned
my only trouble is that I cannot for the life of me remember where it was I suggested the cut should be. I have a
faint suspicion, but looking at the score that particular
spot seems to be one of the neatest in the whole work.
Which makes me think perhaps that is exactly the place
the cut was made. . . .

There was a time, during the past few years, when
William Walton worried his friends a little by appearing,
for such an aloof, slow motion composer, to be unnecessarily greedy about writing music ; if there was any
possibility of an aged musical knight being asked to write
something for the Scunthorpe Philharmonic Mixed Voice
Choir then Willie would move heaven and earth rather
than let the old dodderer get the job. Today, Dr.
Walton (*honoris causa*, Durham) turns down offers right
and left ; his agent cannot tempt him with a film, nor
Charles B. Cochran with the project of an A. P. Herbert
operetta. Instead, Willie—preoccupied with a string-
quartet or something— recommends his friends as stand-ins.

The A. P. Herbert operetta came my way on his recommendation, but I regret to say I let everybody down as neither Mr. Cochran nor A.P.H. considered me very suitable. However, I spent a pleasant evening with Alan Herbert at Hammersmith talking about it and drinking his Burgundy. As it happens I think I might have made a good job of a very difficult task ; unfortunately, when I am confronted with obvious problems my lack of outward enthusiasm suggests that I consider them insoluble. I am a poor salesman.

If I were to analyse exactly what it is about the music of William Walton which attracts me, I think I would say its virility. It is English music, but written by an Englishman who has something to say for himself in his own language, not in the olde-worlde droolery, folk-chantery of Somerset yokels. It is music by an Englishman who is aware of his nationality but is also aware that the world is a much smaller place than it used to be ; William Walton is a Lancashire lad who has lived in Italy, lain in its sunshine, breathed its clean air and absorbed its music. The Italian influence on Willie's music is strong ; it gives his music clarity, wit and colour and acts as a natural antidote to the English composer's national obsession with temperate half-tones and melancholy reflection on the mysteries of autumn and the holiday camp atmosphere of old Stonehenge. Willie can be gay ; thank God he is never " merry." He can be serious ; he can be aggressive. But he is serious and aggressive with all the guts of a man of strong convictions ; his seriousness and aggressiveness are never the self-pity and cantankerousness of the misunderstood Chelsea drunk.

One of William Walton's most endearing qualities is his ability to regard his own music with alarming irreverence, but it is the irreverence of a parodist who has a genuine affection for the thing he parodies. Thus it was

Willie himself who first announced that the main theme of the finale of his symphony should be sung to the soldier's immortal words " ——, and the same to you ! "

Once Willie had pointed out that the words fitted his music as well as they fitted " Colonel Bogey," there was no going back on it. Constant Lambert admits that whenever he conducts this movement he is compelled to sing the words to himself. When, in the autumn of 1945, Constant conducted the work in Cracow he found himself at last able to sing the words out loud. If the orchestra thought anything at all they probably imagined that the conductor was obviously moved to sing the words of an old English folk-song (which, indeed, he was) ; as it was, Constant's singing was broadcast the length and breadth of Poland and nobody was any the wiser. It seems that in Poland only some of the people speak some of the English some of the time.

In the autumn of 1927 I was given my first job. I worked in Tavistock Square as secretary to a psycho-analyst friend of my mother's. I opened doors, answered telephones, and made appointments for a woman called Miss Mary Chadwick, who had been a nurse and was now an expert in dealing with children. Miss Chadwick was a charming but rather perplexing creature ; she smoked a pipe, had a grandfather who designed the grand-stand at Epsom, and was most oddly unbalanced in her psycho-logical reactions to normal situations. Thus, when my mother called round to have lunch at Tavistock Square, Miss Chadwick would sulk in the most distressingly childish manner, obviously very conscious that my mother had some prior claim to my affection, though heaven knows I was the last person to show it.

For a psycho-analyst, indeed, Miss Chadwick's private life was scarcely a good advertisement for her profession.

Some years later I heard that she had made friends with
the Zoo's Curator of Reptiles, and that her flat was over-
run with borrowed African toads, small dragons, and
snakes of all sizes which she kept as pets. Miss Chadwick
was a Freudian and she should have known better, I feel.
    While I was working with her, however, " Chaddy "
seemed to have a lot of sense. Her patients were children
from all classes of society ; there were children from
working-class homes and children of the aristocracy who
arrived in Rolls-Royces. Of the two classes of patient
the " upper-class " children were the more alarming.
There was one little girl, youngest daughter of a peeress,
whose revelations of home life were appalling. The child
came for treatment with a stammer and a reputation for
" backwardness " ; after a week Miss Chadwick was so
distressed by what the child had told her that she stalked
out of her consulting room crying, " What's the use of
sending me the daughter ? It's that bitch of a mother
who wants treatment ! "
    The case book of Peggy, youngest daughter of a peeress,
was certainly a pretty frightening document. The child
had made her first mistake by being born a girl instead of
a boy ; in a last desperate effort the peeress had submitted
to the embraces of the peer (whom she loathed) in the
hopes of providing a son and heir. The peeress had failed,
and so took it out of the unwelcome youngest daughter.
Almost from the moment she could understand what was
being said, poor little Peggy had heard nothing but
" Oh, don't tell Peggy, she's so stupid she wouldn't
understand," or " Peggy's the fool of the family ; don't
bother with her." And so it had gone on—an endless
story of almost criminal victimisation of the child, of
sordid quarrels between mother and father each subconsciously blaming the other for failure to produce a son,
of a helpless little girl persecuted by elder sisters, despised

by servants and brought up to believe that she would never grow up to be as others were.

I have not seen the child since she grew up, but though Miss Chadwick cured her stammer, I fear the girl has the reputation of being a bit nuts. I am not surprised, for I doubt even if Peggy had been completely cured whether her mother would ever have allowed anybody to know it. Apart from anything else, Peggy is said to be by far the prettiest of the three daughters. Which, of course, is an unsurmountable handicap except in a fairy story.

Miss Chadwick's patient's mother, from all accounts, was rather like the one who is the subject of the following story of a man I know who found himself at a grand dinner party seated next to a young woman whose name he hadn't caught. In conversation my friend began to talk about The Aristocracy. " Now take that woman sitting over there," he said, " she's ill-mannered, boring, boorish, cruel to her children, hideous and beastly. And they call that aristocracy ! "

" She's my mother," remarked his neighbour.

" Your mother, is she ? Good. Then you know exactly what I mean ! "

Miss Chadwick had a nephew, Dan, who became an inseparable companion of mine for the next couple of years. Dan, recently down from Oxford where he had rowed bow in a Trial Eight, was a student at St. Thomas' Hospital and was in the Ukridge class of phantasist, inasmuch as he was the most prolific inventor of unique schemes for getting rich quick. He was also—in quite a nice way—something of a megalomaniac. He had an ear for music, but no technical dexterity, and his enthusiasm for music took the form of buying the largest instruments of their kind and learning to play them. In all honesty I cannot say that Dan ever got very far with his studies ; his ambition was only to play in a dance band (the *best*

L

kind of dance band in the Red Nichols class), but to this
end he made a habit of buying enormous instruments to
play on. There was a very expensive guitar with six
strings, for instance, on which Dan strummed for a time ;
but having had the satisfaction of knowing himself to be
two strings more modern than the rest of the country's
guitarists (who had progressed no further than instruments
with four strings), he sold it and imported from the United
States a gigantic bass saxophone. This monster machine,
which cost the earth, was the only one of its kind not only
in Britain but, Dan was proud to know, in the whole of
Europe. It looked most impressive, sparkled like the Crown
Jewels and as far as I know Dan was never able to get
more than an occasional, unexpected and very obscene
note out of it.

As time went by, Dan eventually gave up medicine.
He spent a period answering advertisements in *The Times*
for chauffeur-secretaries and then (on commission) went
around selling electric bell-transformers and lifts. The
bell-transformers were more or less saleable, but Dan had
no success with lifts. He found that most buildings had
lifts, and that those buildings which did not were liftless
for the very good reason that there was no room for one.
Eventually, Dan fell securely on his feet in the film
industry and became a first-rate film editor which occupation, I believe, he still pursues with every success.

Dan and I shared a common, beginner's curiosity in
what was now coming to be known as " hot music." He
had discovered Red Nichols at Oxford at the same time
as I had first heard Guy Naylor's records at Cambridge,
and it was not long after we first met that we went off in
search of this new music together. Our voyages of discovery took us miles down the Whitechapel Road, to
Levy's gramophone shop where we found all manner of
rare recordings imported from America and issued with

mud-coloured labels. It was at Levy's that we first encountered the music of Duke Ellington whose name was not yet known even to the expert collectors in this country.

Our enthusiasm for unlikely records, however, was not entirely inspired by our interest in the music we heard. In one of Miss Chadwick's psycho-analytic journals we had discovered an article on American Negro slang, and on reading it we learned that half the titles of the tunes we bought were very rude indeed. Thus we were delighted to be able to go into a gramophone shop and ask the unsuspecting girl assistant for something called " Virginia Creeper " or " Jelly Roll Blues " or even " Jazz Me Blues," knowing that each of these phrases had the most obscene significance in the coloured vernacular. (Many, many years later somebody at the B.B.C. heard that " Jelly Roll " was not quite nice, and it was ordered that the phrase should never be spoken over the air. It got a little difficult, however, when records by a Mr. Jelly Roll Morton had to be announced, and it was suggested that " J. R. Morton " might be enough. Quite solemnly Jelly Roll's records were announced therefore as being by J. R. Morton. Unfortunately, *The Radio Times* had never heard of this policy " stop," and gaily went on printing " Jelly Roll Morton " in bold face capitals. Today, as far as I know, nobody cares any more—perhaps it has been decided, wisely, that those who do know what it means won't mind, while those who don't know can't possibly come to any harm. And if anybody objects, —well, it serves them right for having a dirty mind, anyway.)

While Dan was not, in the strictest sense of the term, a musician he was nevertheless sensitive enough to take interest in music which was not jazz. Thus it was largely due to him that I found my way to Oxford to hear an opera by Monteverdi. Dan, to tell the truth, may well have been slightly bored by the whole affair, but there was a social side that went with it which more than repaid his efforts to understand primitive opera.

Monteverdi's *L'Incoronazione di Poppea* was the second annual offering of the Oxford University Opera Club, a body of remarkable enthusiasts who had made their début in 1926 with the same composer's *Orfeo*. And very well they did it, for the technical standards of the Opera Club were about on a par with those of the Mantuans and Venetians who had first performed these two early operas. Opera at Oxford was less successful when more modern works were tackled, for then the music was full of black notes, and though an orchestra and cast largely composed of amateurs could acquit themselves passably in the rather slow, declamatory music of Monteverdi, their intonation became just a little too carefree and enthusiastic in, for instance, Weber's *Freischütz*.

But *Poppea* was a moving experience and I regretted not having heard *Orfeo*. I am no antiquarian where music is concerned, though I will confess that occasionally I allow a sense of history to persuade me that some piece of very old music is more interesting than it really is. In the case of *Poppea*, however, there was no need to think back to 1642 and imagine how Monteverdi's music must have sounded to his contemporaries. I was far too busy coping with the impact of this opera on me, Patrick Cairns Hughes, in 1927 to worry whether the work was astonishing for its time or not. There are moments in *Poppea* which are astonishing at any time, moments of great dramatic power and lyrical invention which have remained firmly in my memory since that single evening spent in the old red plush New Theatre at Oxford.

CHAPTER XIX

BERLIN

AT some time during the first winter months of 1927 it was decided that I should go to Berlin early in the New Year. I was greatly encouraged in the idea by Walter Leigh, who was also due to go to Berlin. I had first met Walter at Cambridge during his last year at Christ's ; he had rooms near the college in which he had an upright piano and a harmonium. The walls were decorated with foils and photographs of Walter in fencing clothes, for he had gained a half-blue for fencing and distinguished himself by winning his contests against Oxford.

I never quite understood why Walter should have had a harmonium until one day I went into his rooms to find a most remarkable performance of *Le Sacre du Printemps* taking place. Walter was playing the piano, the wind-parts were being dealt with by Christian Darnton at the harmonium, while the incessant, but important percussion parts were being played by John Cheatle, who beat fire-tongs against the coal scuttle and the fender. Of that enterprising trio only Christian Darnton remains ; Walter was killed in Africa leading his tank into action against the Nazis, and Jack Cheatle committed suicide only a year after Walter's death, driven to gassing himself by a professional contretemps with the B.B.C., which proved the last straw to the endurance and pride of a gifted melancholic.

Walter Leigh was some three years older than I was, a rather portly figure for his age and one of the most truly gifted musicians I ever met. As a child he had acquired perfect pitch (always a source of great wonder and astonishment to me) by sitting under a piano and

learning to distinguish individual notes as other children
learn to distinguish colours or the letters of the alphabet.
He was a fine pianist, too, and music came naturally to
him as a medium of expression—perhaps too naturally, for
back of his decision to go and work in Berlin with Hindemith I suspected a desire to treat music as something
impersonal, to be composed, played and if not entirely
forgotten, at least to be remembered only on condition
that it was devoid of all personal emotion or preoccupation
with subjective problems. Walter was half German by
birth, and when he went to Berlin he lived with his
mother's sister and her husband in a typical German
household. He was bilingual, but I felt he was conscious
of a strong romantic German streak in him which made
him all the more anxious to study with a man like Hindemith whose whole nature was opposed to anything faintly
suggestive of romanticism. Hindemith's influence on
Walter was fortunately not a lasting one ; it led the
pupil to decry the music of Beethoven on the grounds that
such preoccupation with personal problems and musical
self-expression was " embarrassing " and to extol the
austere, machine-made, utility noises made by his master.
But in the end, the time spent with Hindemith paid a
handsome dividend to Walter Leigh ; he became a
thoroughly professional composer whose serious music was
never self-conscious and whose lighter music was never
flippant.

Whereas Walter Leigh can never be said to have been
an undisciplined musician (Hindemith could have taught
him nothing of discipline), Christian Darnton, who came
to Berlin at the same time, most certainly was. As an
undergraduate, Christian had put on a concert of his
chamber music at the old Grotrian Hall. The Press,
to say the least, had not taken kindly to an evening
of Darnton ; even Auntie *Times* had gone so far as

to describe the slow movement of Christian's string quartet as sounding like " a lament of snails in search of their shells."

I do not think Christian was in any way discouraged by the reception of his music ; the Grotrian Hall concert had given him what he most needed, which was an opportunity to hear what his music really sounded like. On leaving Cambridge, where he had been a familiar figure in the town with a particularly wicked and noisy sports car, Christian decided that he would start a new life and see what came of it. For his teacher in Berlin he picked on a man with remarkably little chin but a great deal of teaching ability called Max Butting.

With Walter Leigh studying composition with Hinde-mith and Christian Darnton with Butting, I found myself in Berlin for the unlikely purpose of learning to be a Kapellmeister. Egon Wellesz had decided that as a composer I would probably develop quite happily, but that a period in Berlin learning a musical trade of some kind would be an asset. When I was told that I should study with an experienced conductor called Viktor Zuckerkandl (if I tried to invent a more Viennese name than that, I couldn't) I had visions of being allowed to stand in front of an orchestra and wave a stick. I did nothing of the sort during the whole six months I spent in Berlin.

I hated Berlin almost from the first moment I arrived in the city at the beginning of January, 1928. I could never adjust myself to the idea that because they spoke German the Berliners should not therefore be as *sympathisch* as the Viennese. I was shocked to find a city full of people lacking in charm, patience and good manners and was petulantly intolerant of their refusal to understand the normal Viennese words and phrases which I naturally used when speaking German.

I loathed the restaurant food, the self-conscious "modernity" of the place with its aggressive inferiority-complex and pathetic desire to ape what it imagined was the American way of living. I could not have had a worse introduction to Berlin food, anyway; within a few hours of my arrival I found myself at a rather Bohemian kind of party, full of Communists and assorted left-wing intelligentsia, to which I was taken by another friend from Cambridge, Geoffrey Gorer.

I unwisely mixed vodka, whisky and vermouth and was very sick for four days afterwards. I did my best to eat a little food, but as everything tasted like blotting paper *au bleu* which had failed to absorb the sauce around it, none of it ever stayed down very long. When I eventually recovered, I found it was only the sauce that tasted of anything, not the blotting paper.

These experiments in public eating were inevitable, for the rent I paid for a room and bath just off the Kurfürsten-damm included no meals except breakfast. My landlady, who had been Miss Chadwick's landlady in Berlin some years before, was pleasant enough but was one of those people who really floor me by possessing not an atom of charm of any kind. Frau Norpert and her rather half-witted grown-up son were tolerant of my piano-playing but a little illogical in their attitude towards some aspects of my sex-life. Thus, Junior was sent in one day to ask me please not to bring any young ladies home to my room at night. I was a little puzzled by this; my room in the Schlüterstrasse could hardly have been branded as a brothel at any time; all I could think was that perhaps I had disturbed the Norpert's rest in the small hours, so I apologised. No, it wasn't that; it was just that there was a danger of my catching something which I would pass on to the Norperts who drank from the same cups as I did. Accordingly, would I please make Away

Fixtures with my *amours* and thus avoid the risk of passing on any infection I might acquire. I didn't quite believe that the risk of such infection was inevitably lessened by a change of venue, but henceforward I slept alone and my lessors made no more complaints.

I found Berlin extremely expensive to live in, and there were many times during the six months I was there when I had to eat on tick at a little *Bierstube* next door until my allowance arrived from my step-father in Egypt. The snacks in this cabmen's pull-up provided almost the only palatable food I ever found in Berlin, though I eventually discovered that I could eat tolerably if I sought out Russian and Italian restaurants, of which there were several in the neighbourhood.

Barbara always denies that Berlin food was as beastly as I make out. It is true that she lived there at the same time as I did, but then she lived at home and I know from experience that her mother, Lady McFadycan, has a genius for household management. Barbara's father, Sir Andrew, was at this time Commissioner of Controlled German Revenues in Berlin, and the family lived in a flat not very far away from the Schlüterstrasse, curiously enough in the only building in the whole street left standing by the R.A.F. One of Barbara's escapades as a child of eleven brought her as far as the steps of the municipal railway station two doors away from my lodgings. Offended one winter's evening by something her parents had said to her, she had collected her most precious belongings in a pillow-case, together with her savings and her mother's bridge winnings which she had found lying around, and set out to run away from home. She got as far as the station when she felt that perhaps her parents would be getting anxious by now and would certainly be prepared to right the wrong they had done to her. She returned home to find that her parents had not even

L*

missed her, and when she told the maid of her experience was assured that the whole story was nonsense. " You know perfectly well," said the maid, " that you're not allowed out after dark, and it's now six o'clock." To this day, of course, nobody in the McFadyean family believes Barbara tried to run away. But then Childhood is always full of frustrations like that.

In all fairness I must admit that the artistic life of Berlin more than made up for the unpleasantness I found in having to live there. My own work with Viktor Zuckerkandl was unspectacular but interesting ; it consisted largely of his sitting himself at my piano (he had just moved to Berlin and his own piano had not yet arrived from the provinces) while I conducted as he sang through an opera. These lessons, which usually occurred while I was still in my dressing gown, were designed to teach me the habits of the average opera singer—the tenor who decided to hang on to his top notes, the soprano who decided without warning that she had had enough of her high C and wanted to get on with the plot, the baritone who missed out a couple of bars of recitative and the bass who was in a hurry to get home.

At our very first lesson of all, Viktor took out a pocketknife and hacked the large wooden knob off the baton I had brought with me from London. " If you can't keep hold of a baton without that great thing to hang on to," he said, " then you'll never make a conductor." Looking around me today I can see he was right ; for though conducting with a knobless stick is no guarantee of success, it is surprising how nearly all thoroughly bad conductors affect unwieldy contraptions with huge cork handles to them.

I took to Dr. Zuckerkandl from the first ; he was extremely patient with me, especially with my unbelievable lack of dexterity as a pianist, and when he learned that none of the teachers he had recommended would bother to take such a backward pupil, he taught me a lot of tricks to cover up my failings. As an accompanist, therefore, to Viktor's hoarse renderings of operatic arias I was not distinguished for my accuracy ; on the other hand, I managed to give an impression of what the accompaniment was about, played more or less the correct harmonies and usually finished up on the right note at the right time in the right place.

My two " set books " during my time in Berlin were *La Traviata* and *Carmen*. I spent three months trying to conduct the ensembles from *Traviata* and another three months learning how to cope with the recitatives (and only the recitatives) from *Carmen*. I enjoyed my work because I found it interesting, but I made no great progress in it ; I had no real ambition to be a Kapellmeister and spend years playing the piano for singers in some provincial opera house.

Meanwhile, I began to find my creative activities somewhat divided. I started a second and more convincing version of *Orpheus*, completing about half the opening scene on some very elegant score-paper and in a quite pretty musical calligraphy. I had schemes, too, for another ballet based on a Hans Andersen story. The plot of this had been evolved one evening with Geoffrey Gorer, but no sooner had we committed it to paper than we read that another ballet on exactly the same subject had just been performed at Mainz. However, the idea was not entirely wasted, for I have since told the Andersen story with many of our refinements in the Children's Hour and used it as the basis of a radio play called *Nikki Makes News*.

Mainz, oddly enough, might well have proved the scene of the performance of my first ballet, *The Secret of the Goddess*, now retitled *Phantasmagoria*. I had a long correspondence with the Generalmusikdirektor of the

opera house there and his last letter stated that while he
could not arrange a performance for the moment, he had
liked the work very much, would keep the score and let
me know when he could add it to his repertoire. For all
I know, the Herr Generalmusikdirektor of Mainz still
has the score, for I have never set eyes on it since. I can't
truthfully say I miss it very much.

My second musical preoccupation was partly the
development of a spare-time interest in jazz, and partly
an optimistic means of getting rich quick. In our very
regular weekly correspondence Dan and I planned many
ambitious schemes for forming a band which was to
consist of ourselves and some enthusiasts from Oxford.
Dan was to play the guitar and occasionally that exotic
percussion instrument, the domestic washboard, while
I was to compose and arrange our repertoire and play
the piano. We were to cruise in P. & O. boats in the
summer, play at hunt balls, visit Cambridge for May Week,
Oxford for Commem., and finally land ourselves with a
world-beating engagement at the Savoy Hotel.

I had some startling ideas for novel instrumentation
including a scheme for using the harpsichord in place of
a piano (this was done in America about ten years later),
and for introducing the bass oboe and a Hungarian instrument known as the *tárogató*, which makes a noise like a
mixture of clarinet and cor anglais. Dan for his part
contributed plans for a gadget to be attached to a Wurlitzer organ which would enable the player to slide up to
a note instead of hitting it dead in the centre. I protested
quietly that while Dan's invention for adding a *portamento*
to the already versatile cinema organ might fill a long
felt want at the Plaza and elsewhere, it would not serve
much purpose in our dance band. We did not include
a cinema organist among our personnel, and even if we
did find the right player it was unlikely that we would

find an instrument for him on board a P. & O. boat or
in the marquee at the First and Third Trinity May Week
Ball.

Notwithstanding my carefully expressed lack of enthusiasm for his invention, Dan perfected his idea and depo-
sited the blue prints at the Patent Office.

Our band had to have a name, of course, so we picked
on " Paul C. Hartz and his Blue River Washboards."
We thought the name Paul C. Hartz, which was based on
my own initials, would give the combination the right
Jewish air of authority necessary for success in the world
of up-to-date " hot " music. I had a rubber stamp of
the name made in Berlin so that when we had built up
a library we could stamp all our music with it. I also
had personal visiting cards printed to wave in the faces
of publishers and send up to hotel managers. These were
inscribed, "Paul C. Hartz—Blues Composer and Pianist
—The Blue River Washboards—London, Berlin, Vienna."
I was very careful about the qualifying adjective before
" composer and pianist " because my technique on the
piano precluded my being able to play anything faster
than the slowest of blues tempo ; all fast solo passages
were to be played by a second, more accomplished
pianist from Oxford.

The make-believe world of our famous band provided
endless matter for discussion in the correspondence which
passed between Dan and me. But as far as I was concerned jazz was not all a question of theory ; I managed
to find a band in Berlin on which I could try out my
experiments and from which I could learn some of the
secrets of a form of music by no means so simple and
straightforward as many people think.

I found this band at the Eden Hotel, an establishment
I had first entered in my usual bar-fly search for a bit of
High Life. While the habit of visiting the Eden and

sitting up at the bar there for hours on end did not exactly help me in my eternal battle with the Cost of Living, I nevertheless succeeded in passing the time on the cheap—partly by making one drink last a long time, and partly by playing poker-dice successfully with the barman for a drink when I wanted another.

The bar at the Eden was not unrewarding ; it was a favourite rendezvous for many of the U.F.A. film actors and late at night conversation became general and quite amusing.   One of the most remarkable " regulars " was a middle-aged man who kept a delicatessen store in the north of Berlin somewhere, but who was said to have been Crown witness in card-sharping cases at the Old Bailey before the 1914 war.   He used to be called, it was said, to prove that what the defence declared was impossible could in fact be done if you knew how ; and certainly he was uncannily handy with a pack of cards, for no matter how one cut or shuffled the pack he invariably dealt himself a " natural " at Vingt-et-Un and a lot more besides.   His interest in his gifts, however, was purely that of a craftsman ; he never played cards for money and indeed hated playing cards at all.

I made friends with the several British members of the band, and with one of them—a Scot called Macpherson— in particular.   Mac was the trumpet player and greatly admired the playing of Red Nichols ; he also took me to the races at Grunewald and Ruhleben and to his flat where his wife would feed me with kippers imported from England by the Eden's head waiter.   Oskar, the head waiter, had been head waiter at the Randolph in Oxford until war broke out in 1914 when, he said, he had been " interred " in the Isle of Man.   His wife was English and it was her sister at home who sent a case of kippers every month.

When the time for the Oxford and Cambridge Boat

Race arrived, Oskar bet me 20 marks that Oxford would win. Oxford lost for the fifth consecutive year and Oskar had to pay up. He did so with good grace, remarking a little sadly that obviously Oxford was no longer the place it had been in his day. " It's all those under-graduettes." he said, " That causes fornication—too much fornication. But mind you," he added, brightening, " there's a great future for fornication ! " Oskar was quite a philosopher in his way.

The Eden Hotel and its bar was by no means the limit of my social activities in Berlin ; once having made friends with the leader of the band it became more a kind of workshop where I tried out new pieces in the jazz idiom with varying degrees of success. One of my tunes attracted the attention of the leader of the Eden's tango orchestra, a Portuguese violinist who assured me he had the best possible contacts with the best possible music publishers in Paris. If I would write tangos for him, he said, then we would go fifty-fifty in the proceeds of publication ; with yet another vision of untold wealth before me I made an agreement with him that he should have the sole rights in all my " popular " compositions for (as far as I remember) my life-time. I suppose I should be ashamed to confess that I have never kept to that agreement in the smallest detail ; on the other hand, I can quite truthfully say I have never written a popular composition.

Among people who lived in Berlin, as distinct from " visitors " like Walter, Christian and Geoffrey Gorer, I came to know the Zuckerkandls well. I found as time went by in Berlin that the only people with any charm or good manners were either Jews or Viennese ; the Zucker-kandls were both and I felt singularly at ease in their home. Viktor's wife was a writer and a well-known translator of French books ; their flat was extremely comfortable and with its pictures, books and piano and general air of quiet cultured elegance reminded me very much of Egon Wellesz's villa outside Vienna.

Another Berlin family whose flat I frequently visited was the Schnabel family. I first met Artur Schnabel through Harriet Cohen, who had come to Berlin to play and had persuaded me to sit up on the platform beside her to turn over her music. The Schnabels, I discovered, lived only a block away from my lodgings, and while Harriet was in Berlin I was invited over to lunch one Sunday. Thereafter, I made regular visits on Sunday mornings when Schnabel would talk and play the piano until lunch time and I eventually went off to my *Bierstube*.

I will admit, however, that these visits became a little less regular after what I hope everybody will agree was a pretty rough experience. One Sunday, just as I was on my way out of the door, Schnabel called me back and said he wanted to play me something. We had been talking about my cello sonata and the subject of solo sonatas had reminded him that he, too, had written one—for the violin.

Whereon Schnabel took down some music from a shelf and began to play it. It was a sonata for violin solo he had composed for Carl Flesch, and it was a whole hour before I was able to get away. The music lasted fifty-three minutes and the composer's explanations took up the rest of the time. It may have been all right played on the violin, but fifty-three minutes of it on the piano, with only occasional harmonies to relieve the austerity of the solo line, was more than a little trying. (I learned afterwards that Schnabel had also written a solo sonata for cello ; I can only think that the composer's appetite must have got the better of him on that gloomy Sunday, otherwise I cannot explain how I came to miss hearing that work as well.)

If, as I feel, Schnabel the Composer is known only to me, Schnabel the Pianist is a familiar enough figure in our concert halls. There is, however, a third Schnabel— Schnabel who sits at the piano and plays the accompaniments of Schubert's songs for his wife. During my time in Berlin, Artur and Therese Schnabel gave eight concerts by way of a private Schubert Festival in commemoration of the 100th anniversary of the composer's death. In the course of these concerts, Frau Schnabel sang no fewer than 83 Schubert songs, while Artur went to town with all the Schubert piano music he could lay hands on. It has always seemed to me a great pity that Frau Schnabel should never have been heard in this country, for she was one of the world's greatest Schubert singers. I asked Schnabel why his wife had not sung in England, and he explained that it was all right for her to sing in Berlin, where she was already well-known, but that not enough of her voice remained to risk a début elsewhere. I do not know what Therese Schnabel's voice had been like when she was younger, and certainly it was nothing to write home about when I heard her. But it was not her voice that made her Schubert ; it was her phrasing and a thousand subtleties of dynamics and of what one can only loosely describe as " interpretation."

There was never any question of comparing her with somebody like Lotte Lehmann, for instance ; Therese Schnabel's approach was one of unique intimacy ; she created an atmosphere that transformed a concert hall into something like a sitting room no bigger than the one which is the scene of the famous picture of Schubert playing to his friends in Vienna.

I do hope, however, that those of us who listened to Frau Schnabel had a more intelligent look on our faces than the figures in the picture. As I remember, Schubert's audience in that instance presented expressions of barmy

rapture such as can be conceived only by painters, who grow
more embarrassingly lyrical about music and musicians
than even Dr. Joad. (Cyril Joad recently distinguished
himself in a radio programme called " Desert Island
Discs " by announcing that a Mozart rondo reminded
him of little girls skipping and fauns winking at him from
behind rocks, while Bach presented him with a window
into heaven, or somewhere. But, as he was careful to say
at the beginning of his broadcast, Dr. Joad is an amateur
and plays the pianola in his carpet slippers every morning.
He is a " music-lover," not a musician.)

. The Schnabels and their Schubert, however, were not
much more than an incident in the artistic life of Berlin
at that time. I have heard the Berlin of 1928 described
as " decadent " ; maybe it was, if you believed that the
Jews should not be allowed to exploit their talent and
inventiveness in public. Certainly, on reflection, the
musical and theatrical vitality of the city was largely
based on a kind of artistic restlessness ; but then I think
that is bound to occur in a city which lacks tradition.
Vienna, for all the economic and political upheavals it
had experienced, gave an impression of being settled, even
if it was settled only in a rather nostalgic contemplation
of past glories. Berlin, on the other hand, had no past
glories to fall back on, so it had to put all its energies
into the creation of present ones. Thus, there were no
fewer than three opera houses in full swing, each trying
to outdo the other two in the lavishness and enterprise of
its productions.

The municipal opera in Charlottenburg was run by
Bruno Walter, the Kroll Opera House by Otto Klemperer
and the beautiful red-and-gold theatre Unter den Linden
by Erich Kleiber. Between them these three institutions
kept one pretty busy with first performances and much-
advertised revivals. Each opera house reflected the

personality of its director in a most curious way. Charlottenburg had more repose than the others, and there
was no question as to whose version of *Figaro* was the most
satisfying.

Bruno Walter's *Figaro* was incomparably more authentic
than Kleiber's. At Unter den Linden, Mozart's music
seemed to drag in surroundings that were too big for it ;
at Charlottenburg, Bruno Walter used a false proscenium
and so the whole production assumed the right proportions. I remarked to Viktor Zuckerkandl on the lack of
sparkle in Kleiber's version, and he said, significantly,
" You know why that is, don't you ? Walter is a much
better pianist than Kleiber " ; and from there Viktor
went on to explain the importance of being able to play
the piano at rehearsal. I understood well enough what
he was hinting at, and immediately changed the subject.

Klemperer's opera house was the most modern of the
three, and the repertoire included works by Hindemith
and an evening of Stravinsky—*Oedipus Rex*, *Mavra* and
Petroushka—at which the composer took his curtain call
dressed in a bright yellow mackintosh. The Stravinsky
triple-bill was rather a gloomy way to spend an evening,
for comedy was not the Kroll's strong point ; *Mavra* was
just a silly little opera and *Petroushka*, to those of us who
had ever seen the Russian Ballet, was sheer torture.
Klemperer's lack of a sense of humour in his productions
was particularly noticeable in the Kroll version of *Don
Giovanni*. The staging was incredibly elaborate and
ingenious, with a set consisting principally of two sweeping
staircases which were painted red and changed position
from scene to scene ; but there wasn't a smile in a carload.
Mozart called his opera a " dramma giocoso " ; with
Klemperer it was all " dramma " and no " giocoso."

At Charlottenburg, though the repertoire was more
conservative than at the Kroll, they had nothing to learn

about stage-craft when it came to the point. Their greatest *tour de force* was the production of *Jonny Spielt Auf*— a peculiarly boring opera which had a considerable success in Berlin by reason of its would-be " modernity." The hero was played by a black-face baritone, there was a tune which its composer thought was jazz, and the stage was littered with props like vacuum cleaners, radio sets, saxophones, telephones, motor cars and, as a grand finale, a railway engine which ran down stage and made the one in *Cavalcade* look like something from Woolworth's.

As entertainment, by operatic standards, *Jonny Spielt Auf* was daring and original ; but as I go to the opera largely to hear good music I was not greatly amused. It is a remarkable thing that an audience will be highly diverted by simple stage business in an opera house which would bore it to tears at a pantomime. I remember noticing during a performance of *Schwanda the Bagpiper* at Covent Garden, how the audience roared its head off when offered childish comedy that would have been " ham " at a school concert. I thought this was rather a silly opera, at any time, and the heavy-handed gagging during the scene in hell did nothing to convince me that the music was anything but muddy, over-orchestrated and over-rated. *Schwanda* struck me as being one of those operas likely to be remembered only by one excerpt, for the simple reason that the excerpt is the best thing ever likely to come out of it. The well-known polka from *Schwanda* is a fair synthesis : a simple tune, overloaded with chromatic mush and busy orchestral irrelevance. The music of *Schwanda* needs its hair cutting and a good wash behind the ears.

Berlin, in 1928, was in the throes of a great Verdi revival ; unfortunately, most of the unfamiliar operas were played before I had properly found my feet and all I managed to derive from the Verdi boom was one extremely efficient performance in the opera Unter den Linden of *La Forza del Destino*. The German enthusiasm for Verdi's music was a puzzling thing ; it was well-meaning, inasmuch as it represented a genuine effort on the part of a nation to find operatic freedom outside the concentration camp run by Wagner and his so-called "endless melody." But it was not, on the whole, entirely successful. The average German voice, trained to sing "endless melody"—which is a euphemistic term excusing the inability to finish a tune once you start it—tends to over-dramatise Verdi's vocal line, to add intensity of feeling and "significance" to music which is well able to look after itself.

One of the first results of this German way of singing is a loss of purity in the melody ; few German tenors or baritones are content to hit a Verdi note in the middle and let the tune "run" of its own accord. A German singer playing Rigoletto approaches the part as though it were melodrama, with words to be declaimed against an orchestral background ; one does not expect a German to be able to deliver *bel canto*, but one feels if he cannot do the *bel* he might at least have a stab at the *canto*. As it is, he produces neither. There is a great psychological treatise to be written on the Germans and their relationship to Italian art. As Nordics, they pine for the warmth of the south, but when they eventually get there they fail to understand the first thing about it. Ruth Draper's cruel little sketch of the German woman sight-seeing in a Florentine church and remarking "How beautiful Art is !" was more than a caricature. It was a profound observation, for with all their baroque architecture surely German culture has been less influenced by Italy than that of any other civilised European nation. The Italian influence on England, for instance, has been immensely strong ; it is found not only in the plays of Shakespeare, in our poetry, in our interest in the classics, in our domestic architecture, but also in such everyday things as the very form of our handwriting and the type used by our newspapers.

I have always hoped that the Italian campaign would result not only in the defeat of the Germans but also in the revival of our national interest in Italy and its traditions. Certainly the impact of Italy and the Italian way of life has been most extraordinary on the thousands of British troops stationed out there.

Barbara probably knows more of what is going on in Italy at present than I do, for her weekly Overseas broadcast, "Nights at the Opera," brings her into contact with all kinds of soldiers and airmen who have completely succumbed to the spell of Italy. Recently, for instance, she broadcast a serialised version of *Turandot*, justifying it on the grounds that this Puccini opera was not being performed in Italy just now. Not being performed? She was about half-way through the second act in fortnightly parts when she received a letter from Northern Italy saying that not only was *Turandot* being played, but that the R.E.'s had made a stage of Bailey bridges for the production and,—what's more,—no fewer than 65 sappers had actually appeared in the opera as supers.

The story of how the British military authorities put opera back on to the stages of the Italian theatres is a fascinating one, and unfortunately too long to tell here. But my admiration for the English mentality has never been greater than when I heard that the Scala in Milan, which was destroyed by the R.A.F., was to be rebuilt by the British—helped along by a gift of a million lire from Toscanini.

In addition to the activities of its three opera houses, Berlin also offered a very healthy choice of fun for the theatre-goer. Max Reinhardt was in full cry with a

super-colossal production of *The Mikado* at the Grosse
Schauspielhaus. I just failed to arrive in Berlin in time
to see this production, but from all accounts it was cheerfully irreverent and included more than the usual Reinhardt quota of kitchen-sinks. The success of *The Mikado*
was tremendous, and it was the memory of this success
which prompted me to an action during the 1939 war
involving me in a House of Commons question.

While I was working for the B.B.C'.s German Service at
Bush House, where I devised and produced a daily half-hour
programme of miscellaneous music on records, I celebrated Shakespeare's birthday with thirty minutes of
Arthur Young's jazz settings of The Bard's lyrics. An
infuriated Labour M.P. somehow came to hear of this
(I've never learned exactly how—I suspect a Fifth Column
in Aldwych) and asked the Minister of Information
whether it was true and if he considered, etc., etc. Mr.
Harold Nicolson, replying, stated that the report most
certainly was true and that, in answer to the second part
of the question, he did not consider it was good propaganda.

I suppose the question did some good ; nobody bothered
to reprimand me, and in any case I was no longer with
the B.B.C. when Shakespeare's birthday came around
again ; the United States had meanwhile come into the
war and " The Voice of America " pinched fifteen
minutes of my programme, leaving only a quarter-hour
period which was far too full of news and talks and
" actuality " recordings of tank factories to leave any time
for music. In my own conscience I know I was right to
play Arthur Young's tunes, for they were exactly the kind
of smartness and up-to-dateness which the Germans
understood and had not been allowed to hear since 1933.

My hunch about what the Germans liked to hear was
confirmed some months later. It was no good trying, as
Bush House was always so busy doing, to " project

English culture " to the German listener. If anybody had thought for a moment they'd have known that Vaughan Williams and Elgar bored the pants off the Germans years before Hitler arrived ; in the middle of a war it was not very likely that the Germans would risk arrest by the Gestapo for the sake of the Enigma Variations or an arrangement of " Greensleeves."

But the Germans did go for modern dance music in a big way and did their best to imitate it on their domestic radio. It was the realisation of this that made the British " black " station, Radio Atlantik, the most effective radio propaganda service of the whole war. It is odd to reflect, at this date, what silly elementary mistakes the Germans made in their radio propaganda to this country. It never once occurred to them to tell William Joyce, or whoever wrote his news bulletins, *not* to refer to the British as " the enemy." Time and again one heard the announcer state that " fifty enemy planes were shot down," and on each occasion the morale of the British listener rose. Naturally ; the phrase " the enemy " spoken in English could mean only the Nazis.

Radio Atlantik, with its non-stop dance music and its neatly interpolated spoken propaganda, made no such mistake ; its intelligence service was brilliant and its whole method of presentation was astonishingly convincing. It became my favourite station.

I will admit, however, that I spent many profitable hours listening to Germany. There was one particular short-wave programme directed to America which featured a band called " Charley and his Boys." Their technique was to put new, subversive lyrics to popular Tin Pan Alley tunes and between musical items to include dialogue in a very phoney American accent. The dialogue was spoken by a man and a woman who told jokes which have long been rubbed off the lavatory walls of most prep. schools. It was very entertaining, though hardly in the sense that was intended.

Dr. Goebbels' " Workers' Challenge Station " had quite a vogue at one time, but tended to bore the English listener once the novelty had worn off. This programme was another first-class example of German bungling. Somebody had obviously told the Reichspropaganda-minister that the British working classes swore a lot ; so with great industry all news items and talks were trans-lated into what the Germans thought was the British working class idiom.

Apart from the initial mistake of broadcasting bad language into a working class home (I can hear the indignant cries of " I won't have language like that in my bloody house ! "), the Germans were curiously ill-informed on the subject of colloquial English. I remember one attack on Mr. Bevin, which rose to a crescendo of obscenity and adjectival vituperation ; but as the climax approached and one wondered to what final heights of epithetic invention the announcer would rise, the tirade ended with the words : " Mr. Bevin—that—that jolly ass."

Meanwhile, I hope somebody will tell the full story of Radio Atlantik ; it can safely come off the secret list, for propaganda in the next war will be done by television—which really ought to be quite something.

Though Max Reinhardt was still the most important figure in the Berlin theatre, his position in the early months of 1928 was seriously challenged by Erwin Piscator's production of *The Good Soldier Schweik*. In Piscator's theatre the stage not only revolved but went sideways in both directions, so that Max Pallenberg, in the course of a superb performance of Schweik, appeared to walk miles on a kind of conveyor-belt while back-projected film created the illusion of the landscape he passed through.

Between scenes there was a commentary on the action in the form of cartoon films drawn by Georg Grosz at his bitterest and most violent. Just how satirical and viciously angry Grosz could be may be imagined from the fact that he didn't have to wait for the Nazis to burn his cartoons ; they were being banned by the authorities long before Hitler's time.

There was talk at one time of Charlie Chaplin making a film of *Schweik*, and it seems a pity he has never got round to it ; but he would never have been allowed to stress the physical horrors of warfare to the extent that Piscator and Grosz were able to show them. An up-to-date version of *Schweik* might well be put on at intervals in Germany, just to remind the population of things it may forget.

The emotional battering suffered at Piscator's theatre makes it difficult for me to remember at this date that there were other things to be seen on the Berlin stage. There was the usual batch of " realistic " plays on the problems of youth, Lesbians and drug-fiends ; there were several good revues, one of which produced an excellent tune by Mischa Spolianski called, " L'Heure Bleue " (now a jazz-classic known as " The Hour of Parting "), and also introduced a blonde girl in a minor part whose name was Marlene Dietrich. There were plays by Noel Coward, billed under unrecognisable titles ; and there was a production of *Twelfth Night* which provided me with my first experience of Shakespeare in German. I'm not surprised the Germans claim Shakespeare as a countryman, for the translation of the puns and the prose was astonishingly apt ; somehow, though, the poetry got lost in the wash.

While the opera houses and the theatres in Berlin flourished in a most lively fashion, the great days of the German silent film seemed to have passed. There were far too many pictures being made about Luther and Frederick the Great for my taste—dull, monstrous affairs guaranteed to cure sleeplessness without affecting the heart. But there were some early Hollywood pictures of Garbo with John Gilbert which more than made up for the epics of *Kultur* and the picaresque cavorting of little Fräulein Bergner dressed up as a Cinquecento street arab.

If the movies were dull, still pictures were not. There was a 400th anniversary offer of Dürer which positively could not be repeated, and a superb exhibition of Van Gogh which included some of the finest as well as some of the worst pictures he ever painted.

And as a final item in this catalogue of Berlin's attractions (a catalogue which I have set down mainly to show that I was still capable of appreciating the best side of a thoroughly loathsome city) there were several busy concert halls. The Berlin Philharmonic Orchestra had Furtwängler as its permanent conductor, a figure whose antics constantly fill me with alarm lest one day he should shake his head right off his shoulders in his efforts to obtain a *fortissimo* ; and there were regular guests such as Bruno Walter and Richard Strauss.

My greatest experience in Berlin, however, was supplied by four foreigners—Messrs. Brosa, Greenbaum, Rubens and Pini who traded under the name of the Brosa String Quartet. I use the adjective to describe my experience deliberately, for the visit of the Brosa Quartet first brought me into contact with a musician who became my dear friend and who, until he died in 1942, ha~ influence on my approach to music tl person in my life. His name was Hya

CHAPTER XX

HERE NEEDS NO MARBLE TOMB

Here needs no marble Tomb, since he is gone,
He, and about him, his, are turn'd to stone.
                                        —DONNE

I DEVELOPED an enormous affection for " Bumps "
Greenbaum from the very first moment, and if I can recall
any first impression it was one of an intensely human
being. The impression, I will confess, was unexpected,
for in my innocence I had always regarded executive
musicians (as distinct from composers) as serious and
aloof from the world. This air of seriousness and aloofness
was particularly apparent when the Brosa Quartet was
on the platform ; at the time I first heard them, they
were unmistakably the finest chamber music group in the
business. Each member of the quartet was a proven
master of his instrument ; Tony Brosa's technique was
prodigious, there were few finer viola players than
Leonard Rubens, and Anthony Pini (better known as
"Charlie," for some reason) could stand comparison
with the three best cellists in existence. But it was
Bumps who was the spiritual leader of the quartet ; it
was he, more than any, who set the style of the Brosa
performance and gave it what I can only describe as
" breeding."

Bumps was born in Brighton in 1901, the son of a
Polish Jewish tailor and a Scottish mother. He was the
eldest of four children ; his younger brother Bernard
promised to become a first-class painter until the war
interrupted his career and took him into the Royal
 ᵣtillery ; a still younger sister, Betty, has developed—as
  ᵣ Greenbaum—into a pianist who deliberately chooses

to make life difficult for herself by playing Liszt, Schönberg piano concertos, and late Beethoven with far less concern than most pianists more than twice her age. Miss Greenbaum is obviously Bumps' sister ; her taste is the faithful reflection of her brother's, whose wide experience and fantastic gifts of memory enabled him to understand and learn by heart any score from Monteverdi to Jerome Kern and Bartók.

As a child, Bumps' precocity had been unusual even among musical children. He was no more than seven when he made his first public appearance in his native town, dressed in a velvet suit with a lace collar and playing the Beethoven Violin Concerto. It was for this performance, I believe, that he was rewarded by the Mayor and Corporation with a free season ticket to the Aquarium—an honour which Bumps considered to be worth three Gold Medals from the Royal Philharmonic Society any time.

At one period Bumps saw himself as a composer, but I rather suspect he composed largely in order to gain experience as a conductor ; he became leader of the second violins in Sir Henry Wood's Queen's Hall Orchestra long before he was twenty, and when the Proms came round, Wood always encouraged young composers to conduct their own works. So Bumps naturally composed in order to be allowed to conduct. But Bumps' musical experience was by no means confined to playing in symphony orchestras and composing brilliantly scored occasional pieces of orchestral music. At one momen*~ *~ would be in the pit orchestra playing for *N*~ *~ at the next conducting a house or*~ *~ smaller gramophone companies—r*~ *~ Minor Symphony, Honegger's *Pasto*~ *~ English records of the waltzes from *Ros*~ *~ of which he approached with unprece*~ *~

and, above all, integrity. He spoke and understood the language of music better than anybody I have ever met, and he knew every dialect and every idiomatic subtlety of it.

If Bumps' heart was in conducting, he always remained *au fond* the chamber music player ; and that is almost the highest tribute that can be paid to him. Many years after I first met Bumps, I took Szigeti to hear him conduct a small orchestra at Wimborne House. As we stood in the doorway of the beautiful, candle-lit music room, Szigeti turned to me and whispered : " Your friend is a conductor. Anybody can see that from his back." And whenever Szigeti introduced Bumps to people after that, he always described him carefully as " Mr. Greenbaum—a fine chamber music player."

It is a curious thing among musicians, this respect for chamber music above all other forms. For virtuoso violinists like Szigeti and Heifetz to play informally in string quartets is not just a form of relaxation ; it is a desire to get under the very skin of music, by playing in the most perfect combination of musical sounds ever evolved by man. It is this hankering after chamber music, I believe, which is at the root of Toscanini's strange obsession with string-orchestra versions of movements from some of the Beethoven quartets. The effect on the listener is frankly appalling ; the only possible explanation of Toscanini's performance is the maestro's own, belated ambition to play chamber music. Toscanini, I feel, is a chamber music player *manqué*, and at seventy years of age or so he suddenly began to be aware of having missed something.

Bumps gave up playing string quartets about ten years fore he died, but the chamber music training was ething he never forgot and obviously never would forgotten. It was completely in his blood—the sensitive experiencing of music, the intimate feeling for detail and balance and, above all things for the *style* of the music he performed. There was an evening, some years before the war, when Bumps, Szigeti and four or five other string players came to my house and played Haydn, Debussy and Mozart until four o'clock the next morning. I had recently taken to scraping the violin again (Bumps gave me lessons for an hour every Saturday morning, after which we adjourned to the local to talk about something else) ; for weeks I practised the second violin part in a Haydn quartet until I could play it in time, if not in tune.

As host at this *soirée musicale* I was allowed to play just once ; I brought out my piece and muddled through the first movement, for I had Szigeti beside me to take over the fast passages I couldn't manage. It was the slow movement that was to be my Great Moment, however ; the Adagio was largely a solo for the second violin. Unfortunately, I was never allowed to play more than the first four bars ; Szigeti pushed me off my chair, refusing to allow me to play another note and completed the quartet in my place. It was better for Haydn that way, and I did the noble thing and became a listener for the rest of the evening.

Later on in the programme, Bumps picked up a violin and a quartet, led by Szigeti, with André Mangeot as violist and a cellist who had come along, played the Debussy Quartet. At least, Joseph Szigeti may have played the first violin part, but that quartet performance was not led by him. It was led by Bumps, and I know Szigeti well enough to believe that he realised how much of the experience and vitality of that informal, spontaneous performance came from the second violin desk.

My first glimpse of Bumps in Berlin was of a young man of 26, dark, serious and rather good looking with a fine head, demonstrating what a fine fiddler he was when he came to his solo in the variation movement of Haydn's Emperor Quartet. This movement displayed the Brosa Quartet in all its glory, for it gave each of the four players a chance to shine as soloist. Their performance of this quartet sent the Berlin Press into ecstasies ; at least, I think, reading between the adjectives, that the notices were excellent. It is always rather difficult to discover from German music criticism exactly how well any particular music is performed, and the Berlin fashion was to write in terms of anything but music. Thus the Brosas were compared to vintage champagne, Renaissance architecture and the majesty of Alpine scenery.

Once off the concert platform the character of the four Brosa quartet players underwent an astonishing change, and it was this change which so upset my preconceived ideas of how Serious Musicians should behave. Bumps, in particular, lost his grave platform air and became the most delightful and gay companion. It was the best part of four days after the Quartet's debut in Berlin before Bumps, Charlie Pini, Rubens, Christian Darnton or I went properly to bed. (We did keep Tony Brosa up for one whole night, but—for a Spaniard—he didn't last the pace very well.)

Our exploration of the night life of Berlin was quite an experience, for the city's after-dark attractions were then by far the most lurid in Europe. I acted as interpreter to the party, while the party—with the unerring instinct of foreigners in strange places—acted as guide to me. We found ourselves in most of the notoriously disreputable haunts, and in many which were merely disreputable without being notorious. One of the places we visited, of course, was El Dorado—a *Tanzlokal* where men and women could be distinguished from one another only by the fact that the men had fuller bosoms than the women

(I was a little shocked to read in a London gossip column some years later that Sir Austen Chamberlain had visited " all the smart places in Berlin—including El Dorado.")

There were other adventures, the details of which would be out of place in a respectable chronicle like this. The memory of one, however, caused me to disgrace myself the following day when the Quartet went to play at a private house. When they came to the famous slow movement of the Emperor Quartet, with its solo statements of the theme, I got the giggles and had to leave the room. The superb playing in turn of Bumps, Rubens and Charlie Pini suddenly seemed so wildly out of keeping with a particularly disreputable but comic experience of the previous night ; as each instrument was heard so I remembered what its player had been up to only a few hours before. The whole ludicrous vision became so vividly incongruous that I could no longer contain myself.

Christian also distinguished himself at this party when his host, whose name was Berliner, introduced himself in the German manner by clicking his heels and saying, " Berliner." Christian shook hands and laughed : " Yes, yes—of course—I'm a Londoner." However, the Quartet went down well.

Bumps meanwhile enjoyed himself hugely in Berlin, and by the end of his week's stay in the city had become fluent in German. Or so he thought. One of Bumps' most endearing characteristics was the conviction that if he spoke English with a foreign accent he was talking German. He employed the same method in France and Italy, and with the natural manners of a born host would drop into broken English whenever a foreigner struggled with our language in England. A conversation between Bumps and Szigeti (whose English is remarkably idiomatic

M

though not always perfectly pronounced) began to sound like Potash and Perlmutter after a while.

For all that he was a poor linguist, Bumps was never happier than when he was abroad. Paris was always his spiritual home (his English in France was almost incomprehensible) and I have rarely seen anybody's face light up so rapturously as when, a few months after we met in Berlin, Bumps looked on Florence for the first time.

There were many things which drew Bumps and me together but one of the strongest ties was our common love of the Mediterranean. Six months in Berlin and the long time I had spent at Cambridge had somehow succeeded in suppressing my natural leaning towards Italian music ; in those eighteen months or so I had absorbed germs in an infected area, and the germs were Teutonic. My own music, such as there was of it, lacked the clarity and directness of melody which I knew to be an essential part of my upbringing and my *Weltanschauung*.

Bumps brought all this back, sometimes by direct instruction, sometimes by subtle suggestion. For during the fifteen years I knew him—the first fifteen years of my adult life—my relationship with Bumps was very much that of pupil to master, not only where music was concerned but in many other ways. Bumps, with all his enthusiasms, his passions and violent opinions, was unusually well-read. He was so well-read, indeed, that it was a mystery to me how he had time to acquire the knowledge of literature and philosophy he possessed in the midst of a life devoted untiringly to music. It seemed almost as though he must have been born knowing more than most people.

When he died, one day after his 41st birthday, I realised what an enormous amount Bumps had meant in my life. There was scarcely a pub in London, a restaurant in Soho, an opera by Donizetti, a trick of orchestration that I had picked up which I had not originally discovered with Bumps. It was Bumps who first attracted me to the music of Sibelius, sitting on the floor of his flat with a portable gramophone and a pile of scores of the music of a composer which my education had somehow passed by. It was to Bumps that I instinctively turned for technical advice as William Walton and Constant Lambert and Alan Rawsthorne did. (A great deal of Willie Walton's film music was scored at great speed and with typical expertness by Bumps Greenbaum when the composer was pressed for time.)

I will not set down here my honest feelings on the way Bumps' peculiar genius was deliberately suppressed by the B.B.C. and others in a position to encourage his gift for conducting, for they are deep and bitter feelings. All I can do is echo what Cecil Gray wrote of him on his death : that orchestral musicians know a fine conductor when they see one and they respected Bumps as they respect only the very few.

If Bumps drank too much, he did so mainly to forget the miserable musical existence forced upon him by the war—exiled with a small orchestra in Bangor to provide "chords on" for radio comedians ; but even so I never once saw Bumps let a show down. If Bumps voiced his opinions loudly, and sometimes tactlessly, it was because he despised the mediocre and the pretentious. His detractors, those sanctimonious hypocrites whose tributes to Bumps after his death reminded Cecil Gray of " the lavish floral tributes paid by Chicago gangsters to the rivals whom they had successfully bumped off," may have thought that he threw his weight about. Maybe he did, but with it all Bumps had a touching and genuine humility. It was the sort of humility which led him, the world's first Television Music Director, to play the celeste in the orchestra at Covent Garden purely so that he should

have the experience of playing in *Turandot* under Marin-
uzzi, whom he considered a great conductor. That action
was so completely characteristic of a man who respected
only the best in music and had no time for compromise.

For my own part, I know only that the death of Hyam
Greenbaum left me feeling oddly, helplessly alone. I
do not know enough about music to be completely independent and self-supporting ; and even today, three and a
half years afterwards, I have found no possible substitute
to take Bumps' place.

For only with Bumps could I really talk music
and be understood, find answers to the thousands
of questions which confronted me in my everyday
life, encounter opinion, judgment and advice that I
could respect, and find inspiration in a few words
of encouragement.

CHAPTER XXI

IMPERFECT CADENCE

NOT even the delights of Berlin's spring climate caused
me to have the slightest regret at the idea of returning
to England in June of 1928. I left Berlin with pleasure
and relief to take up residence with Dan in a large
furnished house in Grosvenor Road. The rent was £250
a year and it had been leased to Dan and four other
medical students who considered they had a bargain.
The rent was low because the Thames had recently
jumped the Embankment just there and flooded every
basement in the street.

It was a very gay household, and though the rent

divided by six did not amount to very much, there was scarcely one of us who was not constantly in some financial scrape or other. The most common form of currency seemed to be pawn-tickets, and in spite of a reprehensible tendency for tenants to pawn their co-tenants' property, we lived in comparative harmony. After all, suppose a chap did go and pawn one's gramophone, at least he was honest enough to give one the ticket when he had done it.

The first month back in England brought an idyllic if rather topsy-turvy existence. I found myself living in one of the most pleasant parts of London ; there were parties which lasted until breakfast, when those who remained started a poker school. It was the era, too, of the bottle party ; as hosts we would supply a couple of dozen bottles of beer, and wait for our guests to arrive with bottles of spirits. If we asked enough people, there was usually sufficient gin and whisky left over in the morning to last us for three or four weeks, when we would give another party to replenish our stocks.

Away from home, Dan and I found our relaxation at the Diaghileff Ballet, where the orchestra was conducted by Eugène Goossens, Bumps' brother-in-law, and all four members of the Brosa Quartet led the respective string sections. This Russian Ballet orchestra, looking back, must have been one of the finest ever got together in London ; it included almost every orchestral principal of note and the rank-and-file consisted of first-class players.

One visit to the Ballet led to an experience which I have never yet understood. During the interval, Jack Cheatle and I went to a neighbouring pub and sat ourselves down at a table at which there were a man and his wife—a little man in a bowler hat, and his very buxom wife. Jack and I were discussing some technical aspect of the ballet, *La Chatte*, which we had just heard, when the little man leaned over and cried : " Do you mind repeating that remark ? " As neither of us could remember what we had just said we asked, politely, which remark he meant.

" You know perfectly well," he retorted, " that remark about my wife's chest."

Jack and I looked at each other, and at the little man's wife's chest, and managing somehow to keep a straight face went on with our conversation. At this the little man flew into a rage, crying that we had insulted a lady, and created such a din that the management came and asked us—Jack and me, that is—to leave. As we were more than faintly puzzled by the whole business we naturally sat where we were and remarked that there must have been some misunderstanding.

The little man (from his appearance a flourishing paranoic type) continued his shouting, and as we refused to move, a burly bouncer arrived on the scene, took us by the scruff of the neck and the seat of the pants and threw us out of the pub. From that day to this I have made it a rule never to sit at a table in a pub, and who can blame me ?

During this same summer I made one half-hearted attempt to get a job. Dan and I had been up to Cambridge for May Week and during the course of a visit to the Festival had met an actor whose main business in the theatre seemed to be that of sliding down a rope from the gallery in order to get to the stage and play a part in *The Birds*. (Terence Gray had not changed his habits since I had last been there.) The actor was Peter Creswell, and we suggested that as there would soon be a vacancy at Grosvenor Road he should come and lodge with us. Which he did ; but he let us down badly inasmuch as he was the first person we had ever known who actually went out after a job and got it. One day, on the strength of an introduction given him by Mrs. Greenbaum, who is Sidonie Goossens, Peter Creswell went off to the B.B.C. a gentleman and came back to Grosvenor Road a producer. This astonishing success at once inspired both Dan and me ; Dan had visions of being able to sell the B.B.C. his gadget for producing a *portamento* on an organ, while I saw myself signed up with a huge radio contract for the Blue River Washboards. Sidonie, being a wise woman and full of experience, talked us out of our schemes ; she recommended that Dan should continue to study medicine, and that if I wanted a job at the B.B.C. there were more likely ways than trying to sell the Corporation a non-existent band.

So it came about that I found myself being interviewed by Percy Pitt at Savoy Hill, a cheerful, spherical little man who was the B.B.C.'s first Director of Music and forever swivelling himself round in a revolving chair. Mr. Pitt did me what I consider the greatest service I have ever been rendered. He turned me down flat, saying I was far too young to be allowed to sit with a score and balance symphony concert broadcasts. If, on the other hand, I should care to apply in a couple of years' time . . . but by then I was far too busy. The real reason for my gratitude, for my relief at my narrow escape from joining the B.B.C.'s staff is a subject to be dealt with in another chapter in another book another time. I would never have been much good as a member of the Established Staff. I did, in fact, spend a year with the B.B.C. during the war and I wouldn't have missed it for worlds ; but by then I had developed a sense of humour and independence. At nineteen I shudder to think where the step would have led me.

As it was, my failure to get a job with the B.B.C. did not perturb me ; not because I was in any way aware of what I had avoided, but because I did not yet relish the idea of having to earn my own living before it was necessary. If I had to make money then it must be the easy way.

From the affairs of the Blue River Washboards, Dan and I turned our attention and energies to song-writing. We did not waste our time thinking up lyrics and tunes on the off-chance that they would be published and sung by anybody who happened to come across them. We wrote exclusively for one artist, Miss Sophie Tucker. Wherever Miss Tucker appeared there Dan and I could be found, and as soon as she had finished her act we were round in her accompanist's dressing room, talking the poor man's head off—for Ted Shapiro was a real live American and we were sure he could give us all kinds of low-downs on the Art of Hot Music. Together Dan and I wrote about half a dozen songs for Sophie Tucker ; but we made the mistake of writing them for a Sophie Tucker who no longer existed. *Our* Miss Tucker was the rather raucous-voiced singer of " After You've Gone " and other classics of an earlier period ; the Sophie Tucker then appearing in London had quietened down considerably and was now concentrating on " point " numbers. However, we never lost hope that she might revert to her earlier style, so in due course we thrust into Ted Shapiro's hands a master-piece entitled " Nobody Knows and Nobody Cares."

If we were optimistic we had every reason to be. Only a few months before, a song written for an O.U.D.S. Smoking Concert had been sung by Marie Burke at the Coliseum, and we were quite sure ours was better than that. It may have been, but Miss Tucker still did not think our best was good enough. She wrote from the Savoy Hotel : " I read your song over and regret so much I did a number called, ' Nobody Knows and Nobody Cares '—a very fine comedy number it was. Looking for new ideas. I'm sure you understand. Thanks so much—Sincerely—Sophie Tucker."

I still have that letter, and for no other reason than that Sophie Tucker took the trouble to write it herself; I treasure it as an example of really good manners on the part of a busy woman who, instead of dictating an impersonal note of rejection to a secretary, took up pen and ink and delighted two unsuccessful song-writers almost as much as if she had accepted our jejune effort.

Song-writing, however, was the merest pastime. Bumps lent me his car to play with, a lively little sports model Austin Seven in which driver and passenger sat on the floor; Dan, who was an expert mechanic, took it all to pieces and the machine became even more lively than before. Nowadays when I possess a car I drive in the most leisurely manner and in the maximum available comfort; but at nineteen I drove about for the sheer love of driving, making spontaneous excursions to Brighton and back at the first signs of daylight on a summer morning. I drove by myself, taking with me a packet of sandwiches and a flask of Chianti which I consumed sitting in the car on Brighton Front. They were usually uneventful journeys; in the fresh morning air the engine ran like a dream, the roads were deserted and there was enough light to see by without using headlights.

These excursions were easy enought to explain to myself; they were difficult to explain to the police. On one occasion, I was parked on the Front and sitting in the car quietly eating my midnight meal, when I felt the car moving. I put on the hand-brake to find two policemen had been trying to push me towards Hove police station. The car looked abandoned, they said. I had to answer a number of questions and had the greatest difficulty in convincing the police that I was up to no mischief. They presumed I was mad and left me. I thought they were mad, come to that, for pushing an abandoned car instead of getting in and driving it.

M*

I got married from Bumps' car. I drove Dan up to Oxford to see a young lady to whom he was very attracted and much to his annoyance fell in love with her myself. It wasn't so much that I stole Bobbie from Dan, as that he thought I was being greedy. I was very much in love at that time with a woman nine years older than myself and Dan thought the whole Rosenkavalier situation of my leaving a married woman for an unmarried one of my own age was carrying my enthusiasm for opera a bit too far. In the end Bobbie and I were married and Dan became our first daughter's godfather. I have been happily married ever since—to one woman or another.

Dan did not take things too much to heart, however. He had exchanged his monster bass saxophone for a few pounds and a French horn, and once, when occasion arose that I wanted to go to Oxford to see Bobbie, Dan pawned the French horn to raise money for my train fare. That, surely, was a gesture of true friendship, even though he could never get a note out of the horn anyway.

Meanwhile, though the course of True Love ran smoothly, it was interrupted. The Rosenkavalier Renunciation Scene proved far less of an ordeal that I had expected ; the Feldmarschallin behaved like the great lady she was and returned to her normal married life. Bobbie and I received her blessing, though she rather ruined the effect by telling Bobbie what I liked for breakfast.

The interruption was caused by an altogether delightful interlude in the form of a journey to the International Contemporary Music Festival at Siena. I joined up with the Brosa Quartet and Bumps' wife Sidonie, and together we embarked on what is known in the Navy as a " P.U. Ex."—which, mildly translated, is the equivalent of a jag, binge, or bender.

Unlike Salzburg, the musical side of the Siena Festival was almost as lively as the social side. There were a couple of satisfactory riots originated, not by the visiting foreigners, but by the Italians.

A morning performance of Willie Walton's *Façade* caused something of a stir at the local Teatro dei Rozzi which, since a *rozzone* is a "rough fellow," could hardly have been better named. *Façade* was performed in its original form, with a small orchestra behind a painted drop curtain and Constant Lambert reciting Edith Sitwell's poems through a megaphone.

The work, conducted by the composer, went along smoothly and successfully for some time. The "Popular Song" was a great hit with the audience, who cheered so wildly that the item was repeated three times and a shirt-sleeved conductor had to come from his back-stage hide-out and take a couple of calls.

Very shortly afterwards, however, came the Tarantella. The enthusiastic audience of a little time before now became the angry mob, infuriated by this irreverent parody of a national dance. There were shouts and cat-calls, hats and shoes thrown at the stage and the kind of uproar which only the Latins know how to create. It was a puzzling *volte face*.

The other musical riot was created by the performance of a string trio by Anton von Webern. Now one of the most familiar characteristics of the chamber music of Schönberg's pupils is its reticence ; the dynamics are so consistently on the *pppp* level that it is difficult to hear the music at all, let alone gather what it's all about.

On this occasion, however, an Italian in the audience happened to overhear a bar or two which disturbed him somewhat. He took a key out of his pocket, blew down it loudly and then stood up to protest in the name of " Il Popolo d'Italia." As usual, the Festival's President,

Edward Dent, had to bring all his diplomatic gifts to bear on the situation and by the time the protesting individual had been subdued the Trio had come to its almost inaudible conclusion.

What I have never understood about this particular demonstration was the true significance of the protest. Was the Italian protesting in the name of The People of Italy, or of Mussolini's newspaper, or both ? Nobody ever discovered which it was.

No International Festival was ever complete without a side-show of some kind. At Siena this was provided by a body known as Burian's Speech Choir, a group of performers in full evening dress who entertained us one Sunday morning.

The Choir came from Prague, but their repertoire was multi-lingual and consisted of prose and verse recited with a variety of dynamics and intonation under the careful direction of their conductor. As a music hall turn of prodigious virtuosity, the Burian Speech Choir could have filled the Palladium for months ; as it was they brought the house down with a number which sounded like this :

" Eh heff en unt in Yucatan
" Hoo bot eh py-sun from eh mun."

This was encored when closer scrutiny of the programme revealed the author of the words to be Hilaire Belloc. Following the performance with the score, as it were, we learned that Mr. Belloc's words ran :

" I have an aunt in Yucatan
" Who bought a python from a man. . . ."

The Sienese, true to custom, needed only the slightest excuse to put on a special Palio for their visitors. The Palio, in case you have never seen it, is a bare-back horse race run round the main square of the city ; each jockey is

dressed in a distinctive mediæval costume and represents
one of the many communes of Siena. Before the race
begins there are innumerable fanfares and flourishes, and
then, marching from a side-street on to the piazza comes
a long procession. About fifty people from each *comune*
enter the square and march round it, carrying banners
with the arms of their ward and wearing 14th century
clothes in their district colours. The spectators are
strictly partisan and the event has all the excitement and
atmosphere of a cup-tie.

Two Palios were arranged for our benefit. At the
first, the spectators, seated in specially erected stands
around the piazza, were in a state of unusually excited
anticipation ; it was likely to be a close race. The
trumpets blew. As the final flourish came to an end, there
appeared in the piazza not the procession, but the rather
unsteady figures of Messrs. Walton and Lambert, who,
feeling the heat, had stopped off at a little wine shop we
all knew where the wine was cheap and strong, and had
lost their way to their seats. Neither composer admits to
having received such an ovation since.

The second Palio was rained off, for it can rain harder
in Siena than in Manchester. But the weather did not
affect the optimism of two figures long familiar at these
Festivals. As one passed by the empty piazza in the
teeming rain there could be seen, sitting huddled together
under a large umbrella, the touching spectacle of Edwin
Evans and his secretary Miss Lacey, patiently waiting for
the horse race that was never run and the fanfares that
were never blown.

Siena brought only one major disappointment. The
visitors to the Festival, who had already been lavishly
entertained by the ruling Prince Chigi and the Mayor,
were invited *en masse* to dine with Sir George and Lady
Sitwell at their castle some thirty or forty miles away.

When I say castle, I mean castle ; Montegufoni was built to withstand a siege of 200 people for six months. This being the case, the invasion of the place by three bus-loads of cosmopolitan musicians and critics must have passed almost unnoticed by Sir George's staff.

Our invitation promised a gay evening. Constant and Willie were both staying at Montegufoni ; so, too, were Edith, Osbert and Sacheverell Sitwell—three charming members of a family possessed of the best manners I have ever encountered—and a pretty girl called Zita, to whom I sat next at dinner. Unfortunately, owing to a series of misdirections given to our bus drivers, we arrived from Siena nearly four hours late, having seen every vineyard and mountain in the whole of Tuscany on the way. With our timetable ruined like this, there was only time to have dinner and revive a Central European composer who passed out, before we all had to climb into our coaches and set off again. It was a sad excursion and I was most reluctant to leave ; my flirtation with Zita had been getting along fine.

I have seen Zita since then, but the surroundings have never been quite so romantic. For, heaven knows, Montegufoni fairly dripped with romance and it never surprised me to hear that this castle, in which Dante and Petrarch had stayed, should have been the scene of one of the most romantic incidents of the war in Italy.

During the advance of our armies on Florence, Montegufoni was occupied by British and Indian troops. The castle seems to have struck Other Ranks as a pretty dull place ; there appeared to be nothing to loot but a lot of books on gardens written by Sir George Sitwell and stacks of invitation cards on which was printed " Lady Ida Sitwell requests the pleasure. . . ."

Among the occupants of the castle, however, was Wynford Vaughan Thomas, the B.B.C. war correspondent, who arrived to find all the large rooms filled with pictures which had presumably been taken down from the walls and stacked in disorderly piles against the sides and in the corners of the rooms. The rooms were in semi-darkness, for the shutters were closed, and Wynford was unable to discern the details of the pictures ; all he could see in the great hall, for instance—the same great hall in which we had dined in 1928—was that an entire Italian family had chosen this part of the castle as a dormitory and had placed palliasses close to the pictures.

As Wynford entered the hall he was greeted excitedly by a group of Italians, who, crying " Capolavoro ! Capolavoro ! " went to the shutters and with a dramatic gesture opened them, to let the sunlight stream in and reveal, leaning drunkenly against a wall, the Primavera of Botticelli.

At first Wynford was inclined to regard the picture as a full-scale copy ; but he reasoned that, since the taste of the Sitwells obviously ran to original pictures, it was unlikely that their collection would include a copy of the Primavera. Besides, the sunlight enabled him to see that, in addition to the Botticelli, the room contained the famous Madonna by Cimabue and a lot more besides.

While Wynford was working all this out, the Italians went off and returned with a little man who was introduced as Dr. Fasola, assistant curator of the Uffizi. Dr. Fasola had been put in charge of the pictures on their evacuation from Florence. He was delighted to discover that Wynford had recognized the Primavera and, seeing a British uniform, began to beg him to have the war moved away from Montegufoni.

It seemed that poor Dr. Fasola had been through the hell of a time. Fearing for the safety of his treasures as the battle approached the castle, he had decided to try and make peace between the warring parties himself and had set off in the direction of the Nazi lines. He had reached the lines by running along a ridge which had exposed him to the view—and machine-gun fire—of both sides. The Germans had been sympathetic, but said they could do nothing to divert the action from the neighbourhood of the Botticelli unless the British agreed. Whereon Dr. Fasola, still heavily silhouetted against the skyline, had set off to talk to the British.

He had reached a British machine-gun post and explained his mission only to be greeted by the tough Yorkshireman in charge with "Stop firing? I should bloody think so!"

In despair Dr. Fasola had returned to Montegufoni, convinced that human nature was not what it should be. His meeting with Wynford Vaughan Thomas revived his faith. By the time he had heard the little doctor's story Wynford was beginning to get as anxious about the Botticelli as Fasola himself; he went off to report on the situation to the Colonel in charge of the Indian troops. The Colonel couldn't say he knew much about Botticelli himself, though his wife was very fond of art and that sort of thing. Nevertheless, while he was in no position to move the battle away from Montegufoni, he would detail a squad of Indians to stand guard over the picture to see that it came to no harm; which he did.

In the end Wynford contrived to get the whole affair to the ears of Field Marshal Alexander and the war was moved away from the castle and its priceless treasure. "Alex" himself came over to see the Primavera, posed in front of it with Wynford for a photograph and muttered quietly, while the picture was being taken, —" Personally, I prefer the Impressionists, you know."

The news of the discovery of the Botticelli in the Sitwells' castle eventually reached England, and Miss Edith Sitwell was understandably indignant to hear the age-old pile described as " a ramshackle farm." But the description was deliberately disparaging, for security reasons ; the Botticelli was officially discovered (according to Wynford's story as it left Italy) in " a small country house." All references to its being found in a castle were avoided, lest the Germans—then in a most spiteful and destructive mood—should have gone out of their way to destroy every castle in Tuscany on the off-chance that it contained, among other pictures evacuated from Florence, the Primavera of Botticelli.

Back in London, life suddenly began to be real and earnest. One by one the original tenants of the house in Grosvenor Road had drifted away to various jobs, until at last Bobbie and I were left alone at the top of the house with an expensive lease on our hands. I still had an allowance from my step-father and we managed to lure one or two friends into sharing the house with us from time to time, but the total income from these sources didn't help much towards raising the annual rent of £250 payable quarterly. To say that my finances became a little involved would be a wild understatement.

We didn't starve, but there were occasions when we were glad to receive 12s. 6d. for a concert notice in *The Musical Times*, for it meant then that we could afford a bottle of beer or a blow-out at Lyons' Popular Café in Piccadilly.

These little essays in music criticism proved useful in the end, and I found myself deputising for the critic of *The Daily Mail*. I had met Richard Capell in Siena, and on my return to England he had sent me with an introduction to the News Editor of *The Evening News*. Once again I was considered too young for the job, so Capell fed me with odd assignments and commissions for articles in a monthly he edited. I also collaborated with

Peter Creswell in supplying a provincial musical magazine with a couple of pages of radio notes. We wrote as " Richard Wolf " and as neither of us possessed a radio set our copy was based on what we read in *The Radio Times*. This journal, we learned, was not always such a reliable guide to broadcasting programmes as it was cracked up to be.

In the course of my semi-professional duties I was brought into contact again with my father whom I had not seen for some years. Herbert seemed unusually friendly, if surprised, the first time he discovered me sitting in the *Mail's* seat next to him at the Albert Hall, and there was every promise of a reasonable relationship developing between us. He disapproved strongly of my marriage but solely, it appeared, because he disliked Bobbie's name. I told him he really couldn't expect me to call her either Margery or Lilian, which were her real names, so the subject was dropped.

Relations were occasionally strained even so, and it was only when I was invited to his studio parties and he got a bit tiddly that the tension between Herbert and me was ever really relaxed. My father sometimes put on a heavy-father act, when he would tell me that if I wanted to be a journalist I should start in the provinces, or if I wanted to be a musician then I should follow Gustav Holst's example and play the trombone in a theatre orchestra.

I don't think he ever forgave me for falling on my feet slap into a job on a national daily, or for earning £10 a week when I first played in a dance band.

Apart from his rather austere recommendations that I should work on the *Northern Whig* in Belfast and play the trombone (which I couldn't play anyway) at the Newbiggin Hippodrome, Herbert did give me one sound piece of advice. I took it and it was hardly my father's fault that nothing came of it. He suggested that I should think about composing background music for the talkies which were just beginning.

By exercising a certain amount of bluff I contrived to see a Big Boss at Elstree. I put forward my father's suggestion, which was listened to politely, and awaited the reaction.

"Yes, very interesting," said the Big Boss, "but the talking pictures won't last, you know."

The man who said that was the most important figure in the British film industry.

In the end, when I was a little over twenty, it was Dan who was indirectly responsible for my getting my first serious job. Having discarded his Big Guitar and the Big Bass Saxophone, Dan was suddenly struck with the idea of a Big Double Bass ; so off he went and bought one, giving in part exchange a trumpet and a number of obsolete printed dance band orchestrations. It should be explained that the string bass was in those days a comparatively rare instrument in the dance band, and Dan naturally foresaw great wealth and fame in becoming its first and most famous British exponent.

In due course the instrument found its way to Grosvenor Road, where Dan plucked at its strings from time to time without disturbing the neighbours too much. (There was one strong complaint which was greatly resented by our Mrs. Mopp and caused her to say indignantly : "Fancy complaining like that ! No wonder people b—— off to France ! ")

The day came in the end, however, when Dan tired of the string bass and went off to work with Anthony Asquith in the film studios at Welwyn. The instrument languished in a corner of the drawing-room, until I decided that I, too, could learn to play the double bass—at least well enough to produce the two-notes-per-bar needed in a dance band. And the end of it all was that I got a job and went to play with a band in France. Exactly how is a long story and irrelevant at the moment.

I will tell you *why* I learned to play it, though. It was too big to go under the stairs, it was too conspicuous to lose, and it wasn't mine to sell.

What else could I do with it?

THE END

London, 1945-46.

INDEX

373